SECRECY AT WORK

SECRECY AT WORK

THE HIDDEN ARCHITECTURE OF ORGANIZATIONAL LIFE

Jana Costas and Christopher Grey

STANFORD BUSINESS BOOKS

An Imprint of Stanford University Press

Stanford, California

Stanford University Press
Stanford, California

Special discounts for bulk quantities of Stanford Business Books are available
to corporations, professional associations, and other organizations. For details
and discount information, contact the special sales department of Stanford
University Press. Tel: (650) 736-1782, Fax: (650) 725-3457.

Printed in the United States of America on acid-free, archival-quality paper

Library of Congress Cataloging-in-Publication Data

Costas, Jana, author.
Secrecy at work : the hidden architecture of organizational life / Jana Costas
and Christopher Grey.
pages cm
Includes bibliographical references and index.
ISBN 978-0-8047-8901-1 (cloth : alk. paper) —
ISBN 978-0-8047-9814-3 (pbk. : alk. paper) —
ISBN 978-0-8047-9816-7 (electronic)
1. Organizational behavior. 2. Secrecy—Social aspects. I. Grey, Christopher,
1964- author. II. Title.
HM791.C67 2016
302.3'5—dc23

Typeset by Bruce Lundquist in 10/15 Sabon

At the most obvious, functional level, the laboratory's colored badges, locked trash cans, exclusion areas, and conversational restrictions are part of a system that, however erratic, exists to ensure that foreign governments do not gain access to American military secrets. Looking at the laboratory's system of secrecy with a less literal eye, however, I argue that these regulations also have a role to play in the construction of a particular social order within the laboratory and a particular relationship between laboratory scientists and the outside world.

HUGH GUSTERSON, *Nuclear Rites*

Contents

Acknowledgments   ix

Introduction: The Plan   1

1   Laying the Theoretical Foundations   19

2   Bricks and Mortar:
From Organizing Secrecy to Secrecy as Organizing   45

3   Walls and Corridors: Organizing Formal Secrecy   69

4   Open and Closed Doors:
Organizing Informal and Public Secrecy   91

5   The Hidden Architecture of Organizational Life   115

Conclusion: Finishing Touches   141

Notes   157

Works Cited   175

Index   193

Acknowledgments

THE ORIGINS OF THIS BOOK lie in a conversation between us in the gardens of Wolfson College, University of Cambridge, England, in 2009 when we realized that from different directions and for different reasons we had a shared interest in secrecy. From that and many subsequent conversations this book has grown. Thus our first acknowledgment is to our many friends and former colleagues at the University of Cambridge, including Sandra Dawson, Philip Stiles, Juliane Reinecke (now at Warwick University, UK), John Roberts (now at Sydney University, Australia) and Hugh Willmott (now at City University, UK).

As the work on this book developed, we presented parts of it in many forums, including at the 2010 EGOS Colloquium at the University of Lisbon, Portugal; Copenhagen Business School, Denmark; Université Paris-Dauphine, France; Hautes Études Commerciales (HEC), Paris, France; Leicester University, UK; Open University, UK; Freie Universität Berlin, Germany; Wharton Business School, United States; New York University, United States; Hanken School of Economics, Finland. We particularly thank Christina Garsten (Copenhagen Business School and Stockholm University, Sweden), Dan Kärreman (Copenhagen Business School), Gideon Kunda (Tel Aviv University, Israel), François-Xavier de Vaujaney and Stèphanie Dameron (both Université Paris-Dauphine) for their encouragement, and Anouk Mukerjee (Université Paris-Dauphine) and Basak Sarac-LaSevre (École des Mines, France) for some specific suggestions. Some provisional ideas that have informed the book were published in Costas, J. & Grey, C. (2014) "Bringing Secrecy into the Open: Towards a Theorization of the Social Processes of Organizational Secrecy," *Organization Studies*, 35 (10): 1423–47.

Some examples referred to in the book come from a study by Christopher Grey of the organization of the Bletchley Park codebreaking centre; we thank Andrew Sturdy (Bristol University, UK) for his work on the initial phases of that project, and the Nuffield Foundation and Lever-hulme Foundation for funding parts of it. Other examples come from studies of professional services firms, some of which were funded by the Institute of Chartered Accountants in England and Wales (ICAEW) and conducted with Keith Robson (HEC, France) and Fiona Anderson-Gough (Warwick University, UK).

The preparation of this book was also supported by the European Union Marie Curie Fellowship held by Jana Costas and hosted at Copenhagen Business School by Dan Kärreman.

Finally, we are grateful to Margo Beth Fleming at Stanford University Press for commissioning this book and giving feedback on some draft material, to Paul du Gay, Kerstin Sahlin, and Craig Scott for acting as SUP's reviewers on the draft manuscript, to James Holt for providing administrative support, and to Gigi Mark for managing the production process.

Jana Costas and Christopher Grey
Berlin and London, 2016

SECRECY AT WORK

Introduction

The Plan

THE CENTRAL CONTENTION OF THIS BOOK is that secrecy is endemic within work organizations. It is not an anomaly nor is it only found in unusual or special organizations, but rather it is woven into the fabric of all organizations in a multitude of ways. It has an obvious functionality in, for example, protecting knowledge and information[1] from competitors. It is present when information about clients and employees is restricted, and in everyday interactions, for example, when people share confidential gossip. Secrecy is a part of work, and the keeping of secrets is a form of work. But apart from being omnipresent, secrecy creates a social order, for example, by establishing boundaries between insiders and outsiders. How secrecy organizes social relations and thus brings about what we call "the hidden architecture of organizational life" is the focus of this book.

This broadly conceived understanding of organizational secrecy perhaps accounts for the paradoxical nature of attempting to study it. The paradox is that there is both a little and a lot in the way of relevant existing research: on the one hand, there is no single literature on organizational secrecy; on the other, there are multiple mentions of it scattered across many different literatures and disciplines. This presents us with a considerable challenge because our aim in this book is an ambitious one, namely to bring into focus the many ways that secrecy occurs within organizations so as to recognize both their diversity but also their unity: that which makes them all understandable as secrecy. This then leads to an even more ambitious aim, which is to suggest that, as a discipline, organization studies should incorporate secrecy as a central concept within its analytical repertoire.[2]

Within the scholarly literature on organizations remarkably little attention is given to secrecy, which is surprising and unsatisfactory given its ubiquity.[3] This may reflect at least in part the way that the different meanings of secrecy are treated as separate topics: thus the literature on, for example, trade secrecy is rarely, if ever, considered alongside that on organizational networks. That said, it is possible to find various more or less well-developed discussions of secrecy embedded within writings on organizations that have some other primary focus—for example, Edgar Schein's work on organizational culture or Robert Jackall's study of corporate morality.[4] Yet it could not be said that these constitute a literature on organizational secrecy. It is rather that secrecy lurks in the margins of the organization studies literature, almost as if it were itself a secret. One task of this book is to, as it were, coax secrecy out of hiding. But we also look beyond the organization studies literature. Secrecy has been the subject of considerable investigation in other disciplines, and we make use of a number of classic social scientific theorizations of secrecy, such as Georg Simmel's sociology, Erving Goffman's social psychology, and Michael Taussig's anthropology, even where these are not explicitly concerned with work organizations.

In considering secrecy we can find a number of adjacent concepts, all of which relate to or intersect with secrecy and each of which is the subject of a large literature. These are of two sorts. First, there are concepts such as privacy, silence, anonymity, and taboo that overlap in some way with secrecy. Second, there are concepts such as knowledge, identity, power, control, trust, transparency, and many others which come into play whenever secrecy is discussed. These latter are manifestly not the same as nor do they necessarily intersect with secrecy, but they are highly relevant to understanding how it works.

We have recourse to a wide range of literatures within and beyond organization studies, none of which we can do full justice to if we are to retain our central focus. We therefore apologize in advance if this leads us to deal some violence to these literatures. However, there have been a string of vociferous complaints that organization studies has become too fragmented and overspecialized.[5] If we want to avoid that—and, emphatically, we do—we need to work within the broad contours of the discipline and closely related disciplines and not be too concerned with the niceties of each and every subtopic. We hope that our discussion of secrecy can speak to a variety of research topics and debates within the field of organization studies and beyond.

In pursuit of the central analytic objectives, we deploy examples taken from academic research and from public, media, and fictional sources. These range from novels by Franz Kafka and Fyodor Dostoyevsky to studies of factory workers, a secret nuclear weapons laboratory, aircraft development plants, homosexuality in corporations, and WikiLeaks, to take just a few examples.[6] Apart from these, we draw especially on two empirical sources. These are studies we have ourselves conducted that exemplify the diverse ways in which secrecy features in organizational settings, namely a state intelligence agency and several professional services firms. These are not presented as case studies of secrecy but as a source of illustrative examples to leaven what might otherwise be an overly abstract analysis. Indeed, we want at all times to emphasize how rich in meaning secrecy is for organizational life, and how deep are its emotional and cultural resonances.

DEFINING SECRECY

Let us now turn to the basic question of what we mean by "secrecy." In her extensive and authoritative discussion of the topic, the philosopher Sissela Bok provides a first orienting definition: secrecy constitutes "the methods used to conceal . . . and the practices of concealment."[7] For concealment to denote secrecy Bok says it needs to be intentional, because people must be to some degree aware of the ways they differentiate between those with whom they share and those from whom they conceal information. It is important to stress that the term *intentional* does not mean that secrecy necessarily results from some kind of consciously crafted or discussed plan (although on many occasions that may be so). However, it is equally important to recognize that accidentally forgetting to mention something would not be secrecy, nor would be the omission of irrelevant information in a particular interaction.

Following this initial definition of secrecy, we can see how it overlaps with and differs from privacy. This is an important distinction to draw, especially because many contemporary public discussions of both secrecy and privacy the two are interrelated. Bok points out that this, in fact, has long been the case, because privacy entails seeking to control access to things that are taken to be in the personal domain, and so "privacy and secrecy overlap whenever the efforts at such control rely on hiding. But privacy need not hide; and secrecy hides far more than what is private. A private garden need not be a secret garden . . . conversely secret diplomacy rarely concerns what is private."[8]

What we have then are intersecting but nonidentical concepts. We might think of the way that, in many although not all societies, certain bodily functions are considered to be private, yet they are by no means secret. Imagine that a hidden camera were installed in our houses that recorded these functions. Then, our privacy would have certainly have been violated, but no secrets would necessarily have been revealed. But of course other things that are private may also be secret—for example, our true feelings about other people—and if these were discovered, say because our diary was read, then not only would our privacy have been violated but also our secrets exposed. Organizationally (and politically), in this intersection the limits to the personal domain can be highly contested. For example, to what extent can an organization legitimately test employees for drug use outside of work?[9] And, of course, where organizations do seek to intrude extensively into the personal domain it may well be that individuals seek to keep secret some facts about themselves, such as recreational use of illegal drugs.

A more specific case of such hiding of personal information concerns anonymity. Anonymity is about keeping one's name and thus identity secret.[10] This can take various forms, from being a nameless member in a group such as Alcoholics Anonymous that physically meets or participating in anonymous surveys, through to engaging in anonymous virtual interactions on the Internet, such as in chat forums or hacker groups.[11] Anonymity overlaps with secrecy to the extent that individuals engage in secrecy to become anonymous. Yet such secrecy is of a particular kind in that it is solely concerned with information concerning the individual identity. Moreover, anonymity involves both keeping and revealing secrets. Participation in, say, anonymous groups or surveys involves that everyone keeps their identities secret. Thus, having a secret as opposed to sharing is common to all participants. At the same time, such anonymity allows people to reveal and share information about themselves that, if the source were identified, could potentially harm them, as with the Experience Project,[12] which is devoted to anonymously sharing experience and at the time of writing contains more than 36 million entries. In this sense, anonymity may entail not secrecy but a very substantial sharing of secrets.

A further intersection exists between secrecy and taboo. Taboos, defined as "a social prohibition against a particular act, object, word, or subject," cannot themselves be secret because to operate as taboos they must be widely, perhaps universally, known.[13] However, there are complicated cases of open, or what we later term "public," secrecy where secrets are both known and not known. Such open secrecy can serve to uphold social prohibitions and existing norms through taboos and tact. And, of course, violations of taboos may well entail secrecy because they are likely to be concealed. Organizationally this is significant when some things are regarded as taboo subjects that should not be spoken of, for example, as one study has shown, gender conflict,[14] and thus secrecy is involved as a consequence. Certain uncomfortable or controversial issues may also be the subject of organizational silence.[15] This silence may well be one of the ways in which secrecy is enacted. Nevertheless, secrecy is not itself just silence, both because it can involve other methods of concealment and because it also involves communication, in terms of the sharing of secrets among particular groups. Conversely, not all silence betokens secrecy—there may be all sorts of reason why we do not speak of certain topics.

APPROACHING SECRECY

In this book we are concerned with, in principle, any and every way in which nonaccidental concealment occurs within work organizations. We add a caveat, though. We do not directly deal with secret organizations, in the sense of, for example, criminal and underworld gangs,[16] even though some concepts relevant to these are drawn upon. This is because our primary concern is to show how secrecy is pertinent to organizations in general rather than just to those particular and unusual cases where the organization itself exists in secret.[17]

This relates to another specific and possibly controversial feature of our analysis, namely that we approach secrecy as being, so to speak, "beyond good and evil." We began this introduction by saying that secrecy is endemic in organizational life. Following this, we do not regard secrecy as being *a priori* ethically wrong. This is contentious in that, especially in debates of public accountability and transparency, secrecy is often regarded as being so. Yet as the earliest and most elaborate sociological theorization of secrecy, that of Georg Simmel, emphasizes, there is a need to approach secrecy not simply from the standpoint of ethics: "We must not allow ourselves to be deceived by the manifold ethical negativeness of secrecy. *Secrecy is a universal sociological form*, which, as such, has nothing to do with the moral valuations of its contents."[18] Similarly, Bok argues that "if we regard secrecy as inherently deceptive or as concealing primarily what is discreditable then we shall be using loaded concepts before we even look at the practices that require us to make a choice."[19]

Organizationally, that is easy to see. It is not unethical for a health care organization to keep patient medical records secret: indeed we would normally regard it as unethical were they not to do so. At the same time, if that organization conceals medical malpractice, then we would normally regard that as being unethical. In short, although some secrets may be ethically dubious, secrecy itself is not inherently ethically problematic. We would certainly not want to align ourselves with the increasingly vociferous "information libertarians" of both left and right: not all forms of secrecy (including those practiced by states and corporations) are illegitimate and unethical. That is not to deny that secrets and secrecy occur within an ethical terrain—but so, too, do all human activities, and secrecy is not special in this respect. Similarly, we do not regard transparency as a self-evident or unqualified good. Later we seek to go further than this by arguing that secrecy and transparency are mutually intertwined and are not binary opposites.

There is another aspect of what we have just said about secrecy and ethics, though, that may also be contentious. In aligning ourselves with Simmel we are also aligning with his claim about secrecy as a "universal sociological form." This may be taken to imply an essentialist understanding of secrecy as being, somehow, inherent to human society. We think that this is so, but in a very particular sense. It is certainly the case that the things that are kept secret are highly socially, culturally, and historically variable. That is so whether we think about people in organizations concealing particular kinds of stigmatized sexuality or state organizations concealing particular military secrets. The ways in which those secrets are kept may also vary considerably. But that human beings and human organizations typically engage in secrecy about some things (whatever they may be) in some ways (whatever they may be) is, we think, universally true: at least, we know of no counterexamples.

Secrets and Secrecy

Embedded within the previous claims is an important distinction, which is that between secrets and secrecy. This may be understood as a difference between content and process, so that a secret is the thing that is concealed—typically some piece of knowledge or information—whereas secrecy is the act of concealment, the keeping of a secret. But this act is typically not a single event in that secrecy is usually an ongoing series of acts and, as such, may be understood to be a process. Clearly, secrets and secrecy are intimately interwoven in numerous ways. At the most basic level, it is impossible to speak meaningfully of a secret if there is not a way in which that secret is held.[20] However, there is a wide variety of ways in which secrets are kept: the process through which a state military secret is kept is likely to be quite different than that relating to confidential organizational gossip. Thus secrets and secrecy are different but interrelated in general and the manner in which they are interrelated takes a variety of different forms in practice.

The focus of this book is primarily on secrecy—the processes through which secrets are kept. This means that we are interested in secrecy as an ongoing accomplishment of social interactions in organizations. On the one hand, to keep a secret requires certain social conditions (e.g., the existence of regulative mechanisms), while, on the other hand, it has certain social consequences (e.g., the production of particular kinds of group identity among the holders of secrets). This is not a linear process in which conditions lead to secrecy lead to consequences: the consequences of secrecy may become the conditions of further secrecy. It is this iterative sense of the conditions and consequences of secrecy that we explore. This is also what is intended by the title of the book: *Secrecy at Work*. That title denotes the ongoing social accomplishment of secrecy as well as the fact that our focus is upon secrecy in work organizations.

Because we approach secrecy in this way, we are concerned with what can broadly be called both formal and informal secrecy. Indeed we use this distinction to structure our detailed examination of organizational secrecy in chapters 3 and 4. One could hardly give an adequate account of organizational life that did not attend to both the formal and the informal, that is, its official and unofficial aspects. Drawing on this long-standing distinction, by *formal secrecy* we mean cases, such as trade secrecy, that are officially sanctioned and organized through prescriptive rules or laws. The secret search algorithm of Google is a prominent example of such formal secrecy. By *informal secrecy* we mean cases such as confidential gossip, which operate unofficially and are organized through social norms. An example of informal secrecy is the gossip about the illness of Apple's former CEO Steve Jobs prior to it being officially announced.[21] As a variant of informal secrecy, we also refer to public secrecy to denote cases in which something is informally known by those involved and yet not openly spoken about. An example of public secrecy is the ways in which homosexuality in the military often remains an undiscussed yet known issue.[22] It is manifestly the case that formal and informal organization are interrelated —and the same is true for formal and informal secrecy. Nevertheless, it is a heuristic distinction that helps to clarify the breadth of what we want to consider as contained under the umbrella term of *secrecy*. Moreover, it is consonant with our ambition to show how secrecy is embedded within the fundamental axes of organization studies and throughout organizations themselves.

Beyond Information

Although secrets and secrecy are interrelated, our focus on secrecy means that we are not as much interested in secrets themselves. Thus the content of what is kept secret is not in itself very important for our analysis. This does not mean that for all kinds of other purposes it is unimportant to consider what is kept secret. Indeed, this may well be a matter of pressing political, economic, or social concern—for example, what data governments and corporations may secretly gather about citizens, employees, and consumers. But our contention is that whether or not the secret has an importance in these ways does not affect the fact that there will be some kind of process of secrecy. It is upon this that we focus.

This is not a matter of pragmatic convenience to limit the scope of our analysis. The dominant way in which secrets and secrecy have been considered in the organizational literature has been through what we call an informational approach. That approach is based on the assumption that "the foundation of all secrets, whether related to government or business, is to protect an *informational* asset perceived to be of high value—whether tactical or strategic."[23] Here secrecy—the process of keeping secret—is understood to flow from the secrets themselves. Some informational asset has or is seen to have a high value and *therefore* it is kept secret. But we repeatedly argue that secrecy does not just come from the value of the secret held. It is also the case that things may, and often do, acquire a value precisely because they are kept secret; that they are kept secret and *therefore* they have a high value. That does not mean that secrets are valuable only because they are kept secret, it just means that they are not only kept secret because they are valuable. This, then, is the analytical reason why secrets are not themselves important for us: we cannot understand secrecy if we take it as given that the secrets thereby kept are valuable. This becomes organizationally significant when, for example, organizations with ingrained cultures of secrecy keep secret more than they need to for functional reasons. In such cases secrecy itself is valorized, and we miss that if we begin by valorizing the secrets these organizations keep.

The Richness of Secrecy

Some of these issues may come into sharper focus if we consider the etymology of the terms *secrecy* and *secret*, which derive from the Latin noun *secretus* ("separate, set apart") and the verb *secernere* (*se-* "apart" and *cernere* "sift"). In this meaning, secrecy is to exclude, segregate, and distinguish—that is, to create a boundary between the known and the unknown. But this reflects only the first of what have been called the three related logics of *secretus*, *arcanum*, and *mysterium*.[24] The term *arcanum* "emphasizes withdrawal from communication and knowledge by locking something away."[25] The logic of *mysterium* refers to secrets and secrecy in terms of the "supernatural . . . the religious or cultic,"[26] so that secrecy holds an aura of mystery that can "elicit awe."[27]

From these combined senses of the secret, the arcane, and the mysterious we can begin to see some of the complexity and richness of secrecy.
It is about the drawing of boundaries—boundaries around knowledge,
yes, but also boundaries between knowers. That secrets are held by some
people and not others implies that secrecy is both about *concealment* from
some and *sharing* with others. Secrecy is about the realm of the hidden
and the arcane, but this realm can exist only if a boundary is drawn: to
lock something away it is necessary to have a key. And secrecy is mysterious, a word that shares its root with mysticism and is ultimately derived
from the Greek word μυστικό. This has as one of its meanings an initiated person, so, again, a social process (initiation) that draws boundaries
between those who are in the know and those who are not. Moreover,
these initiations sometimes involve the taking of oaths and a conception
of sacred duty.

The resonance of some of these words serves to remind us of something
that is at the heart of the claims we make in this book and our reasons for
writing it. Secrecy speaks of and to something very deep within our lives.
Deep within our personal but also cultural lives: the labyrinth, the hidden
room and the creaking stair; the dark and the light; the things we hold innermost to ourselves and the trust we place when confiding these to others; the unspoken shames within our families and the secret laboratories of
our scientists; the thick curtain and what lies behind it; initiates, cults, and
priests; whispers, promises, confessions, and betrayals. Secrecy is both seductive and exciting, dismaying and frightening—something that is both a
part of our everyday lives and yet also somehow extraordinary.

If this is so, then it could hardly be the case that secrecy is anything
other than important in organizational life, which, after all, is not some
realm separate from the rest of human experience. It also means that even
if we talk about secrecy in the dry language of social science, and even if
we refer to the apparently mundane practices of organizational life, we
are dealing with something that has a potentially very high emotional and
political charge. One has only to consider the searing pain that can come
when someone betrays a friend's secrets or the extraordinarily savage punishments that many societies visit upon traitors to recognize this. At the
same time, the thrill of knowing a secret can be immense, as can be the

guilty burden of doing so, as can be the desire to know what lies behind the locked door of secrecy. And beyond this there can be a seductiveness in betraying a secret, or hinting at our possession of it, perhaps to demonstrate our importance to others or to unburden ourselves to them.

The stakes here are therefore potentially high. It is this that explains why secrecy can have such potency in organizations. All this remains hidden if the focus is on valuable information and the content of secrets rather upon the always also present process of secrecy.

A Hidden Architecture

Secrecy does not just occur within organizations, but in some important ways it can *make* organizations. The subtitle of this book—*The Hidden Architecture of Organizational Life*—is intended to capture something of this claim. It suggests that secrecy erects a series of more or less thick walls as well as a series of channels of communication between organizational members and therefore serves to organize social relations. Hiding information from some while sharing it with others creates particular communication grids with different channels and networks; these grids and channels are "constitutive" of organizations, as several communication scholars have argued.[28]

Secrecy entails, on the one hand, keeping knowledge from people—those outside an organization, perhaps, or from particular groups within an organization—and, on the other hand, sharing knowledge within an organization or among particular groups therein. Thus we can think of organization itself as having a kind of "epistemic" architecture in which boundaries between the inside and outside of an organization, or subsections of an organization, are constructed.[29] We can envisage this as epistemic compartmentalization, metaphorically constructing external or internal walls—and not always necessarily metaphorically because, in some cases, the possession of secrets may itself be marked by a physical architecture (e.g., access to laboratories).

At the same time we can think of organizations as having an epistemic cabling, rather like the wiring of a building, through which secret knowledge flows, when people for various reasons and in various ways share secrets. Again one can think of this literally—for example, in terms of differential access to, say, networked databases of confidential information—as well as metaphorically, as when informal networks to share confidential organizational gossip are constituted. Thus we are not talking here about knowledge-sharing in the normal and generic sense of the word, but about the sharing of, specifically, secret knowledge.

These senses of a hidden architecture are intended to suggest that although organizations are in all kinds of way *creators of* secrets—generating, for example, trade secrets or utilizing confidential discussions as part of politicking—they are also in some way *created by* secrecy. Without secrecy in its various forms there would still be boundaries within and between organizations, but they would be different sorts of boundaries. Thus, although certainly not the only way in which social relations are organized, secrecy is an important and largely ignored way in which this takes place. Moreover, the way in which the hidden architecture of organizational life works is by creating boundaries that can cut across both the hierarchies and networks that we normally think of as constituting organizational relations. Instead, we might think of the epistemic compartments and cabling of secrecy as a social glue that binds organizations together. For example, and in particular, secrecy can initiate "concentric circles,"[30] or even a series of cross-cutting concentric circles, with multiple centers and boundaries associated with them. But it is important always to understand that these boundaries are inherently vulnerable, because secrecy always creates the possibility of accidental or deliberate disclosures or revelations. In this sense, again, secrecy is to be regarded as an ongoing process through which organizations can be made, remade, or, potentially, unmade.

EMPIRICAL SOURCES

In order to illustrate our theoretical arguments as well as do justice to the richness of secrecy we have recourse to a variety of sources: from academic research to media to fiction. The academic examples come from a multiplicity of studies, but we return frequently to studies that we ourselves have undertaken, both together and separately. They encompass different kinds of organizations and work and speak to the diversity of issues that we are bringing together under the rubric of secrecy. In this section we briefly outline each of these sources that we mine for illustrations, so that they will make sense when they are given. In the outlines we draw particular attention to the issues of secrecy the studies give rise to, but we do not present these as case studies of secrecy (and they were not conducted as such) but simply as sources of running examples of it.[31]

Codebreaking at Bletchley Park in the 1940s

This was an historical study of a state intelligence agency.[32] Its historical status is significant because one of the problems of studying secrecy is precisely that it is difficult to gain access to it. But an historical study, in which once secret information is now publicly available, avoids this problem. The study was primarily archive based, with some limited interview material and a larger amount of secondary source material.

Bletchley Park (BP)[33] was the site where, in Britain during the Second World War, signals intelligence was centered. It is most famous now for the breaking of the various Enigma ciphers used by the German military forces, although other codes were also dealt with. The codebreaking organization, called the Government Code and Cypher [sic] School (GC & CS), between 1939 and 1945 grew from about 200 to almost 10,000 employees who were engaged in a very wide array of activities, not just codebreaking (or cryptanalysis). There were a large number of people involved in clerical and machine operating work in support of cryptanalysis as well as intelligence analysis and distribution work.

The key thing for the purposes of this book is that all of these operations were conducted in conditions of the most stringent secrecy; were there to be any hint that Enigma was successfully being read it would lead to its modification or abandonment by German forces. Moreover, the various operations were highly compartmentalized, so that as well as maintaining secrecy from the outside world there was an elaborate system of internal secrecy. This secrecy was maintained until some partial revelations were made in 1974, and since then most of the documents relating to it have been declassified by the British government.

Every person working at BP was told upon joining, and repeatedly thereafter, that they must say nothing whatsoever about their work to anyone in the outside world, including families, friends, and spouses; nor must they talk about their work to people at BP beyond those they actually worked with, and not to them when outside their working area at BP. Although they were not necessarily aware of it, everyone who worked at BP had security checks made upon them. These checks would relate to general issues of trustworthiness as well as to vulnerabilities to blackmail and political sympathies. Alongside a culture of "not telling," the other element of secrecy was "not asking" about the work of others. This meant that the majority of those who worked at BP did not know the reality of what they were working on (some did not even know they were part of a codebreaking organization). Thus the secrecy at BP was not just secrecy from the outside world but also an internal secrecy. Many who worked at BP died without knowing what work they had been involved in. Despite the remarkable strength of the secrecy culture at BP, there were throughout the war a string of minor security breaches. Nevertheless, the most striking feature is the way that the secret persisted for so long after the war, which is remarkable considering the number of people who worked there.

So, in summary, secrecy at BP had three elements: ignorance—not knowing what was going on beyond one's immediate work; silence—not speaking to anyone about any aspect of one's work; surveillance—vetting checks and ongoing monitoring of behavior.

Professional Services Work in the 1990s and Early 2000s

Here we refer to a string of studies of accounting, consulting, and allied professional services firms we conducted separately, together, or with others.[34] The studies were primarily interview based, with some participant and nonparticipant observation, and conducted between 1992 and 2009. The firms in question, which are not identified, were a variety of major, global organizations, although the sites studied were all in the United Kingdom. The professional service firms (PSFs), as we collectively refer to them, were very similarly organized, and it is not necessary for the purposes of this book to differentiate between them.

The PSFs are major, high-status employers of graduates who are recruited from leading universities and then undergo training, in some cases leading to a professional qualification in accounting. There is in all cases some form of "up or out" hierarchy, so that the large intake of junior staff is progressively whittled down as those remaining ascend to managerial levels, potentially culminating in partnership. One consequence of this structure is an intense degree of competition and insecurity, even though salaries are high. It is relevant to this book that this competition and insecurity is a fertile ground for confidential and semi-confidential discussions of pay, prospects, and reputations.

Work is team and project based, and junior staff typically undertake very routine tasks.[35] Long working hours and high levels of stress characterize working lives, with many staff preoccupied by dreams of an escape into more fulfilling and more autonomous work.[36] These dreams, however, are not publicly revealed because they would betoken a lack of commitment that would violate key organizational norms. The firms are replete with examples of tensions between the experiences of staff and what can be openly spoken of within the context of organizational norms.

These organizational norms are primarily centered around the idea of professional behavior[37] within which an ideal of client service is central.[38] Professional behavior is particularly envisaged in terms of outward appearance, clothing, and grooming. Hidden from view are the ways that this is taught, regulated, and enforced. Within client service and professional conduct, one aspect is the need to maintain client confidentiality in terms of both data protection and informal conversation. The presentation of a professional self is itself important in signaling trustworthiness to the client.

There is an ongoing trade or exchange of knowledge between staff about how to deliver services to clients. Some of this is codified and accessible to staff via organizational knowledge management systems that are strictly confidential to the firms because they contain commercially valuable material and client-specific data. In addition, a large amount of knowledge is shared through informal networks, and this is of two types. First, specific technical knowledge is shared informally shared between friends and networks because it is often too cumbersome to use organizational knowledge systems. Second, because of the way that work is structured, there is a great deal of informal knowledge-sharing about upcoming projects and worthwhile or prestigious assignments as staff try to navigate the career structures of the firms.[39] The informal nature of these networks means that access to them is differential, with some people included and others excluded from knowledge.[40]

In summary, a variety of kinds of secrecy can be found in these PSFs, ranging from client confidentiality to the unspoken tensions regarding organizational norms and the knowledge sharing and hiding in informal networks.

In the remainder of this book, we explore in detail these various themes of secrecy. The analysis is structured so as to start with general theoretical concepts, then to explain how these apply to organizations, then to develop a detailed analysis of these organizational issues, and finally to pull together the different strands of the argument to articulate why secrecy is so crucial to understanding organization itself.

In chapter 1, we trace how secrecy appears in theoretical writings in the social sciences and particularly in the works of Max Weber, Georg Simmel, Erving Goffman, Elias Canetti, Michael Taussig, and others. This allows us to develop a theoretical and conceptual vocabulary that we bring together as seven "foundations" to guide the subsequent analysis. In chapter 2, we deploy these concepts to explain that secrecy is not just something that organizations habitually engage in but can also be seen as a way of organizing. To do this, we draw upon fragmented discussions of secrecy within classic (if now sometimes forgotten or neglected) texts within organization studies by, among others, Edgar Schein, Melville Dalton, Robert Jackall, Chris Argyris, Michel Crozier, and Wilbert Moore. We call this the "bricks and mortar" of the analysis because it provides us with so many of the ideas that we later deploy.

Having established the key social scientific and organizational terms of debate, we then move to a detailed examination of how secrecy works in organizations, orchestrated by the heuristic separation of formal and informal secrecy. Chapter 3 tackles formal secrecy, showing how rational-legal processes of law, regulation, and surveillance construct organizational boundaries around secret knowledge as well as rules for sharing this knowledge within organizations. We take "walls and corridors" as the principal metaphor to connote how formal boundaries both make barriers and define paths of communication for secrets. But we also explain how these processes have an irrational and paradoxical nature, so that formal organizational secrecy does not occur on the basis of clear principles or by reason of functional necessity. Chapter 4 considers informal and public secrecy. Here the processes involved are based on trust and norms rather than law, and have ramifications for many organizational phenomena including groups, cliques, decision making, politicking, and leadership. The case of public secrecy poses particular complexities because it relates to the paradoxical situation in which secrets are both known and not known. In this chapter we again stress secrecy as both concealing and sharing knowledge; we denote this through the metaphor of "open and closed doors."

Chapter 5 brings together the main lines of analysis to explicate the metaphor of secrecy as a hidden architecture of organizational life, that is, how secrecy can construct the social order of organizations. The focus is on how secrecy can create and be created by organizations, in the epistemic compartmentalization and cabling it involves, and also how it brings to life particular organizational experiences. What we are trying to express here is how secrecy enacts a joining together of what might normally be thought of as different domains: the inside and outside; the structural and the experiential.

In the conclusion we put forward as "finishing touches" a series of claims as to why the arguments we have developed are important for the study of organizations. We aim to show how this is not just a matter of studying secrecy *per se* but is necessary for studying organizations, and we present this not as a new approach but as a reconnection with a classic vein of organizational analysis. We also address the methodological issues of empirically researching organizational secrecy and invite others to pursue further the themes we have advanced in this exploratory study.

CHAPTER I

Laying the Theoretical Foundations

IN HIS 1925 NOVEL *THE TRIAL*, Franz Kafka describes how after his unexpected arrest for an unspecified offence, Josef K. enters the secret world of the court system with its own laws, proceedings, and dynamics—a world that is unknown and nonsensical to him, yet at the same time increasingly absorbing. As Josef K. seeks to gather information and confront the court, he faces only closed doors: documents related to cases remain locked in the advocate's drawer because "official secrets were involved."[1] The entire proceedings are "kept secret not only from the public but from the defendant too,"[2] placing him in a continual state of worry, uncertainty, and distrust. Even within the "endless" hierarchical structure of the court, "beyond comprehension even of the initiated, court proceedings were in general kept secret from minor officials and only those higher up the hierarchy followed them."[3] Despite his various efforts, until the end this organizational world full of secrecy remains an absurd "theatre"[4] to Josef K. that, however, takes complete control over him.

Kafka's novel parallels the observations of the German sociologist Max Weber, who, writing at around the same time as Kafka, points to the prevalence of "official secrets" in bureaucracies. One can also read in Kafka's novel the fear of the existence of a secret powerful elite working behind the scenes—such a link between secrecy and power underlies the writings of Elias Canetti. *The Trial* provides a powerful description of how, as theorized by Georg Simmel, another German sociologist and Kafka contemporary, a separate reality can be created through secrecy with boundaries between the initiated and outsiders. This entails the creation of a dramaturgical reality, as described in the writings of the American social psychologist Erving Goffman on social interactional practices.

So *The Trial* not only constitutes one example of how secrecy is deeply ingrained in our social and cultural imaginations; it also points to different aspects of its various theorizations in social science. These theorizations of secrecy are the focus of this chapter. We trace secrecy in the works of in particular, Max Weber, Elias Canetti, Georg Simmel, Erving Goffman, Michael Taussig, and Eviator Zerubavel. Although secrecy is not central in all these writings, together they provide complementary insights on the diverse nature of secrecy as well as its varied social dynamics, conditions, and consequences. We do not give a detailed discussion of the work of these authors but rather draw out the key insights from what they write about secrecy and also introduce some of the conceptual terminology we use. From this, we develop seven "foundations" that guide our subsequent analysis of organizational secrecy.

SECRETS AND POWER: BEYOND FUNCTIONALITY

Let us begin by turning to one of the foundational thinkers of the field of organization studies: Max Weber. In the seminal work *Economy and Society* he points briefly to the prevalence of secrecy in bureaucracy— one that cannot only be explained through secrecy's immediate function of concealing information. As knowledge becomes the base of domination of bureaucratic organizations, Weber argues that there is a tendency among office holders to withhold knowledge from others. In a bureaucracy, knowledge is codified and stored in the form of documents that only organizational members have access to and thus can hide, leading to the rise of the "office secret":

The concept of the "office secret" is the specific invention of bureaucracy, and few things it defends so fanatically as this attitude which . . . cannot be justified with purely functional arguments.[5]

According to "purely functional arguments," a bureaucracy engages in secrecy to conceal valuable knowledge for strategic reasons. This is the case when there are external threats, such as war, foreign politics, or competition. Yet Weber also emphasizes that organizational actors' motivation to hide knowledge often results from "pure power interests"; this goes "far beyond these areas of functionally motivated secrecy."[6]

Following Weber, we can see that there is a connection between the formal documentation of knowledge and the invention of the "official secret." The locking away of knowledge (the logic of *arcanum*) requires the possibility of documenting and codifying knowledge, as in the advocate's drawer, described by Kafka, where all the secret documents remain hidden, or, more prosaically, government archives. This in turn can explain why, in the public eye, state bureaucracies, associated with the hoarding of documents, papers, and files, are often portrayed as epitomizing sites of secrecy—though Weber notes that secrecy can be equally ubiquitous in commercial organizations to which the public has even less access.[7] Secrecy can also constitute a habituated response to outsiders. In situations of competition, conflict, and public encounters, it can assume strategic importance for organizations. Most important for our purposes is Weber's insight that organizations are prone to keep secrets for the previous reasons and beyond the intrinsic functionality of doing so. This opens up a new and highly significant terrain of investigation. For if the interest in secrecy is not simply about concealing valuable knowledge for strategic purposes, what else is at stake?

Secrecy, Power, and the Powerful

One answer that Weber provides to this question concerns the striving for power, but he does so only in passing and we must look elsewhere for its elaboration. In fact, the connections between among secrecy, power, and the powerful goes back a long way. The Roman historian Tacitus drew attention to it through his notion of the *arcana imperii*. This carries a number of meanings ranging from the secret practices of the state and its rulers, the means of protecting a government, the sacred character of political knowledge to a mysterious and cultic aura of kingship and some kind of deceptive and manipulative Machiavellian conduct of the state.[8] The principle that the ruler, the king, or the state can successfully function only under the veil of secrecy has greatly shaped the mode of governing throughout Western history. Although the revolutions in England and France and the subsequent rise of the democratic state have sought to counter this principle, secrecy still constitutes a widespread mode of governing today.[9]

Although not explicitly concerned with the arcana imperii, in *Crowds and Power* the Bulgarian-born polymath Elias Canetti also argues that "secrecy lies at the very core of power."[10] This is epitomized in the system of secrecy that typically surrounds dictatorships. Here we might think of the notoriously secretive nature of totalitarian regimes, with their networks of secret police and informers, their secret archives on citizens, control of information, and their proclivity for night-time arrests and the disappearing of opponents. More specifically, Canetti describes how rulers mobilize secrecy to shape their relation to subordinates as well as the relations between subordinates. They reveal certain secrets to others and observe the information flows so as to see whether those entrusted with secrets are reliable and loyal. The ways in which rulers use a system of secrecy to test loyalty, break and create ties with others is particularly well described by Canetti's example of the last Persian king, Chosroes II:

> If he [the king] knew that two of his courtiers were close friends and stood against all comers he closeted himself with one of them, told him as a secret that he had decided to have the other executed and forbade him under threat of punishment to reveal this to him. From then on he watched the behavior of the threatened man as he came and went in the palace, the colour of his face and his demeanor as he stood before him. If he saw that his behavior was in no way changed he knew that the first man had not betrayed the secret and he then took him even more into his confidence. . . . But if he saw that the threatened man was afraid and kept apart, or turned his face away, then he knew that his secret had been betrayed and thrust the offender from his favour.[11]

Through developing a system of secrets, rulers stand out as the only people with an overview of the situation and are thus uniquely in the position to make decisions. Canetti also describes how rulers try to remain opaque by refraining from sharing their opinions and intentions with others yet seeking to see through those others. In this way, the hierarchy between the rulers and the others is reinforced and produced. Here the workings of the logic of *mysterium*, that is, the creation of a certain awe and magic, can be in play too. In saying little and remaining silent, Canetti argues that outsiders attribute to the rulers that rulers conceal and hence know something that the outsiders do not know. If the taciturn ruler then says something, outsiders attach to this special importance. Thus by presenting themselves "a closed book," the rulers' words carry particular weight and in this way they are placed and place themselves above ordinary people.[12]

Although Canetti develops his insights in the context of dictatorships,[13] Weber's student Robert Michels and the American sociologist C. Wright Mills show how the interaction of power and secrecy also shape modern democracy. In his writing on *Political Parties* Michels notes that despite the democratic rule of the political party system, there is a small group of leaders in power over the masses. In a similar vein to Canetti, Michels describes how the leaders' power is sustained through their ability to evoke an aura of mysteriousness and be "masters of the situation: [they] . . . are adepts in the art of employing digressions, periphrases, and terminological subtleties, by means of which they surround the simplest matter with a maze of obscurity to which they alone have the clue."[14] Under the veil of secrecy, Michels notes that the powerful group makes decisions without engaging with the public.

Such decision-making processes behind closed doors are also central in C. Wright Mills's classic study *The Power Elite*. Mills shows that although this power elite greatly shapes the US government and its political decisions, such as those related to the atomic bomb, their influence remains largely hidden. Here we have a different intersection between power and secrecy: although in the dictatorial setting Canetti analyzes it is known who are the powerful and that they rule through a system of secrecy, in the democratic setting secrecy serves to hide the powerful people and their influence from public sight:

Many higher events that would reveal the working of the power elite can be withheld from public knowledge under the guise of secrecy. With the wide secrecy covering their operations and decision, the power elite can mask their intentions, operations, and further consolidation. Any secrecy that is imposed upon those in positions to observe high decision-makers clearly works for and not against the operations of the power elite.[15]

Rather than constituting a tool for exercising power, here secrecy provides a separate space, outside the public's eye, for operating, maneuvering, and making decisions. In this way, power itself becomes disguised: "So long as power is not nakedly displayed, it must not be power. And of course you do not consider the difficulties posed for you as an observer by the fact of secrecy, official and otherwise."[16]

Summary of Key Insights

The discussion of the *arcana imperii* and Canetti, Michels, and Mills provide explanations for Weber's observation concerning secrecy's significance beyond its immediate functionality of concealing information. They elaborate the link between secrecy and power, namely that power or more precisely positions of power are bolstered by, if not based on, secrecy. It is through the mysteriousness created by secrecy that rulers, kings, and statesmen can surround themselves with a certain sacredness that is otherwise reserved for the divine men, the priests and, of course, God. That secrecy can constitute a form of governing is apparent in the medieval notion of the secretary, namely the official person entrusted with secrets. Though it may no longer evoke any mystery, it is still prevalent in governments today, as exemplified in the US Secretary of State, or the job title of the most senior British civil servants, Permanent Secretary. Apart from the creation of a sacred and therefore somewhat untouchable position of those in power, secrecy can be used to test, manipulate, and keep others in check as well as to operate and make decisions without having to involve outsiders. As with Kafka's descriptions of the secret court system, Canetti shows that those in power can seek to control and survey information flows (i.e., not allowing others to hide anything from them), while a system of secrecy surrounds them. But this is hardly the preserve of dictatorships. The same kind of information surveillance accompanied by secrecy has led to the current heated debates about governmental organizations such as the National Security Agency in the United States.

That secrecy provides a separate space to maneuver, make, and potentially manipulate decisions outside the gaze of the public explains the ethical concerns often raised by transparency advocates against secrecy.[17] This separate space can bring about what Carl Schmitt terms the "state of exception," wherein the actions of those in power are exempt from the rule of law, thus potentially entailing violence, corruption, and forms of oppression.[18] The ongoing existence of such dark secret spaces of power— examples range from the Guantanamo Bay detention camp to the often-hidden influence of lobbying groups on politics—seems undeniable. However, equating power necessarily with secrecy, and vice versa, can evoke a paranoid outlook—one that we often find in conspiracy theories with their "conviction that a secret, omnipotent individual or group covertly controls the political and social order."[19] Although secrecy and power intersect, it is important not to approach secrecy as inherently serving the powerful in an unethical or undemocratic manner. Secrecy has many facets; its intersection with power is only one, and, for instance, it can be important for resistance. Indeed, in the discussions of power we can see how secrecy shapes relations and brings about social differentiations—something that is centrally developed in Georg Simmel's foundational theorization of secrecy, to which we now turn.

SECRECY AS A UNIVERSAL SOCIOLOGICAL FORM

In his landmark 1906 study *The Sociology of Secrecy and Secret Societies* Simmel provides one of the most comprehensive, and certainly the foundational, sociological treatments of secrecy. It is evident to Simmel that individuals often engage in secrecy for purposes relating to the need to conceal valuable knowledge in order to attain a favorable position in the social environment. Yet, like Weber, Simmel stresses that this functional, informational view is too limited. In a key sentence he argues that

not so evident are the charms and the values which it [secrecy] possesses over and above its significance as means, the peculiar attention of the relation which is mysterious in form, regardless of its accidental content.[20]

So secrecy does not necessarily derive its importance from the specific knowledge that is kept hidden. Instead Simmel argues that it is the social process of secrecy that is important: through the very process of concealment a boundary between the individuals in the know and not in the know, between insiders and outsiders, is created, leading to social differentiation.[21] Regardless of the content, secrecy, as the logic of *secretus* highlights, allows a distinguishing of oneself from others. This argument is central to Simmel's work, and to this book, and we elaborate it at some length.

Group Formation, Social Distinctions, and Mysteriousness

Simmel draws attention to how secrecy organizes social life[22]—an insight that places secrecy right at the heart of organizational analysis. For Simmel, secrecy constitutes "a universal sociological form," because without secrecy it would be impossible to draw boundaries between individuals.[23] It is our ability to hold secrets that allows us to define ourselves as singular human beings:

Secrecy . . . is one of the greatest accomplishments of humanity. In contrast with the juvenile condition in which every mental picture is at once revealed, every undertaking is open to everyone's view, secrecy procures enormous extension of life. . . . Secrecy secures, so to speak, the possibility of a second world alongside of the obvious world, and the latter is most strenuously affected by the former.[24]

Think about what it means to grow up and develop an individual self-understanding: this requires that one can differentiate oneself from another, especially from one's parents. Being able to hold secrets from others is one important way in which this differentiation takes places—something that might explain why children often form secret groups and find stories about such groups highly appealing.

For Simmel, relationships between individuals or groups are shaped by the "ratio of secrecy" entailed. They create distinctions between those in the know and those who do not know. These can in turn make insiders feel special.[25] By excluding others, which is inherent to the process of intentional concealment, insiders are elevated to an exceptional position. The social differentiation produced by secrecy accompanies some kind of valuation and ordering. Although the sense of exclusivity is amplified in the case of valuable knowledge, the reverse relation might also be true; the value of knowledge may increase precisely because it is held secret: "That which is withheld from the many appears to have a special value. . . . subjective possessions of the most various sorts acquire a decisive accentuation of value through the form of secrecy."[26] Secrecy can indicate that one, in contrast to others, has access to hidden and, by this very fact, valuable knowledge. Rather than knowledge being kept secret because it is valuable (the logic of *arcanum*), there can also be the inverse logic: because knowledge is kept secret, it is valuable (the logic of *mysterium*).

Secrecy may thus interrelate with the desire of creating a mysterious aura and acquiring superior status, as Simmel highlights in this passage:

> The separation [resulting from secrecy] has the force of an expression of value. There is separation from others because there is unwillingness to give oneself a character common with that of others. . . . Everywhere this motive leads to the formation of groups. . . . That exclusiveness and formation of groups are thus bound together by the aristocracy-building motive [that] gives . . . in many cases from the outset the stamp of the "special" in the sense of value. We may observe, even in school classes, how small, closely attached groups of comrades, though the mere formal fact that they form a special group, come to consider themselves an elite. . . . Secrecy and the pretense of secrecy are means of building higher the wall of separation, and therein a reinforcement of the aristocratic nature of the group.[27]

Regardless of the content, secrecy, or just the appearance of secrecy, can make one be seen as special because of the distinction it creates. This can be important for the formation of groups, particularly those of "aristocratic nature"—something that may explain the prevalence of secret codes, rituals, and various other practices among elite groups, such as the "Skull and Bones" Society[28] at Yale University, to which George W. Bush, among many others, is said to have belonged.

There can be a further inverse relation between secrecy and social distinction. Secrecy, in the form of mysteriousness, is often ascribed to individuals who are socially distinct from others. This is the case because their superiority cannot be made sense of in any other way but through the idea that they have access to some hidden knowledge that others do not have.[29] As a prime example of this connection, we may think of how religious belief is based on the idea that God has magical powers and mysterious wisdom, unattainable to humans on earth although somewhat accessible to and represented by mystics and priests. Although individuals may engage in secrecy to acquire a special status, a mysterious aura is also often attributed to people of higher status: the two interact and reinforce each other.

Simmel notes how secrecy interrelates with social cohesion in groups.[30] Such cohesion comes about to the extent that the group's life is separate from the public and its influences. The veil of secrecy can also make individuals feel "safer" by keeping their face in front of outsiders: "An English statesman has attempted to discover the source of the strength of the English cabinet in the secrecy which surrounds it. Everyone who has been active in public life knows that a small collection of people may be brought to agreement much more easily if their transactions are secret."[31] This observation explains why diplomatic negotiations, collective bargaining processes, and situations of contentious decision making often take place behind closed doors. Even when not formally secret, it is common for discussions, especially involving policymakers, to take place under what in the United Kingdom and some other countries is called the "Chatham House Rule," placing limits on what may be said about them to outsiders so as to encourage frank debate.[32]

The Play of Concealment and Revelation, Rituals, and Socialization Processes

Simmel also explains that secrecy involves socialization processes, rituals, and requires certain emotional bonds and trust. Sharing a secret means that one can trust that the other will protect the secret by keeping silent in front of outsiders. Here emotional bonding is both necessary as well as reinforced; secrecy implies the creation of a common situation unknown and separate to outsiders and in which the different members rely on each other. Secrecy can spur excitement and heightened emotionality, not least because it inherently involves the vulnerability of revelation. Simmel speaks here of the tension, temptation, and possibility of revelation that is only released when the secret is revealed.[33] But what can make secrecy vulnerable to revelation?

Low differentiation in a social setting can make it difficult for actors to maintain the boundary to outsiders. Although secrecy brings about differentiation, it also *requires* a certain degree of differentiation because otherwise the "seductive temptation to break through barriers by gossip or confession" are too great.[34] The seductiveness of revelation can also relate to the sense of superiority involved in secrecy, which is particularly experienced when outsiders become aware of the insider's secret:

[There can be] the inability to endure longer the tension of reticence, and by the superiority which is latent, so to speak, in secrecy, but which is actualized for the feelings only at the moment of revelation, and often also, on the other hand, by the joy of confession.[35]

To be perceived as distinct, individuals holding a secret can be prone to hint at its existence to outsiders. This hinting of superiority based on being in the know is important in relation to the logic of *mysterium* because a secret that was completely locked away (*arcanum*) would not provoke awe because outsiders would be completely unaware of it. This implies that a secret that is latent, as Simmel puts it, takes on a different quality, because it involves different social dynamics and implications than one that is manifest as outsiders know about its existence.[36]

Secrecy always involves the awareness that "it might be exploited, and therefore confers power to modify fortunes, to produce surprises, joys, and calamities."[37] Given this, groups constructed around secrecy, such as the secret society of the Freemasons, pay great attention to rituals, socialization processes, and disciplinary measures that make individuals morally accountable—something that can further explain their social cohesion. Membership is controlled in that it does not grow organically, but through careful selection of incomers. For example, at an annual "Tap Day" the Yale Skull and Bones Society selects fifteen new students a year considered to be suitable to join.

Secret groups socialize their members in ways to overcome the sense of isolation that can accompany secrecy given the barrier to outsiders involved. There can be a number of initiation practices to socialize novices and teach them how to maintain the secret in front of outsiders. This can entail oaths and being made aware of possible penalties following any breach of secrecy. There can also be a system of signs that function as credentials for membership. This is exemplified in Stanley Kubrick's film *Eyes Wide Shut*, in which the main character needs not only to wear certain clothes and a mask but also know passwords for being allowed to enter the secret group's ceremony. In addition, Simmel argues that rituals can mark group life, which serve to counterbalance the group's separateness from the societal norms outside it. Secret groups can create their own norms, values, and hierarchy that are often highly centralized. Following Simmel, another distinct feature of secret groups is their heightened awareness of themselves, because with the risk of revelation membership, practices and procedures need to be (re)produced in intentional ways.

Summary of Key Insights

Simmel's theorization provides a rich resource for studying secrecy. Like Weber, Simmel stresses the need to approach secrecy above and beyond its immediate function of hiding knowledge. Instead—or additionally— secrecy serves to create important boundaries upon which social life is based (the logic of *secretus*). These boundaries are never fixed, though, given the inherent possibility of revelation. Following Simmel, secrecy can bring about social distinctions, a sense of exclusivity and superior status. By virtue of hiding something (regardless of its content), individuals (and the knowledge they hide) are perceived to be special. This observation counters the "logically fallacious, but typical error, that everything secret is something essential and significant."[38] At the same time, those who have a superior status are often perceived as mysterious. Thus, there can be a reinforcing relationship between secrecy, social differentiation, and superiority—an insight that can contribute to understanding the dynamics of distinction and elite groups.[39] In addition, secrecy can serve to save face—for example, in front of the public—by providing a separate space for handling conflicts and thus create and/or maintain a certain image in front of outsiders. Simmel illuminates how groups constructed around secrecy are particularly cohesive because group members rely on each other and share a secret world. Secrecy can be an immensely powerful emotional phenomenon, tying individuals together yet also potentially involving treason and the painful feeling of betrayal. It can affect individuals' behavior and the groups created around secrecy in various ways, particularly given its disciplinary influence as well as the socialization processes, rituals, and other practices involved. As a result, and as Kafka describes in the case of the secret court system, group life can take place in a world markedly different from the outside world, entailing its own rules, proceedings, and norms.

The Simmelian insights have been taken up in the classic work of Erving Goffman and, in particular, his theorization of the social interactions in impression management. He draws attention to secrecy as one way in which actors seek to manage interactions and engage in expression games in everyday life. In addition, Goffman sheds further light on the social significance of secrecy for groups by introducing the distinction of strategic, dark, and inside secrets.

Impression Management, Stigma, and Total Institutions

In reading Goffman's work through the lens of secrecy, a variety of reasons for actors' engagement in the concealment of information[40] can be detected. Famously, in *The Presentation of Self in Everyday Life* Goffman shows how actors seek to give a favorable impression that is in line with prevalent societal values. This impression is based on the information the actors present in front of others, namely what they say and how they intentionally or unintentionally conduct and express themselves. As in the theater, there is a frontstage performance whereby the performer attempts to give a good impression by emphasizing certain aspects of self and hiding others that remain backstage.[41] Although impression management entails information concealment, this does not mean that secrecy is an inherent part of it. For instance, an impression might be created simply through accentuating certain aspects and thus not intentionally concealing others.[42] Moreover, actors may take on established roles in a social setting. These roles may have already ascribed to them understandings of how they are to be performed so that the hiding and accentuation of information may take place in unintentional ways.[43]

Although not always part of impression management, secrecy can overlap with it. Performers can seek to hide aspects of self, unofficial intentions, interests and views, errors and mistakes, and anything that could be seen as socially degrading and thus is not in line with the idealized impression they seek to give to outsiders.[44] Avoiding social stigmatization through secrecy is central in another of Goffman's classic works, *Stigma*. Concerned with people who are stigmatized by a certain differentness relating to the body, character, or social group to which they belong, Goffman studies how they seek to engage in "information control" in front of nonstigmatized others. Individuals with an invisible stigma face the dilemmas of "to display or not to display; to tell or not to tell; to let on or not to let on; to lie or not to lie; and in each case, to whom, how, when and where."[45] By engaging in secrecy, individuals can conceal their stigma, overcome the sense of shame accompanying it, and "pass" as "normal." Interestingly, we can see here how secrecy can also serve to facilitate being accepted as part of the public rather than seeking to separate from it in the way described by Simmel.

Although such a case of impression management through secrecy entails the creation of a discrepancy between appearance and "reality," Goffman also stresses that "there is often no reason for claiming that facts discrepant with the fostered impression are any more the real reality than is the fostered reality they embarrass."[46] Impression management and thus secrecy do not derive their sociological significance from the content, that is, the question of what is real and what is not, but rather from the very process of creating a boundary. Indeed, in a vein similar to Simmel, Goffman notes that the audience may sometimes attribute secretiveness to the performer without there being anything secret.[47]

Understanding secrecy as a social interaction can also explain its meaning in total institutions. In *Asylums* Goffman is interested in the interactions between the inmates of such institutions, such as patients in psychiatric clinics, and staff. A total institution represents an extreme social situation because the staff seeks to know and document all sorts of information about the inmates that the latter would ordinarily seek to conceal. For this reason, finding a way to engage in secrecy carries great symbolic and emotional weight for the inmates. This can take the form of cliques that conduct "concerted activity" or of individual "undercover practices":

Some illicit activities are pursued with a measure of spite, malice, glee, and triumph, and at a personal cost, that cannot be account for by the intrinsic pleasure of consuming the product [e.g. of an alcohol beverage] . . . [but instead] the sense one gets of a practice being employed *merely* because it is forbidden.[48]

This underlines yet again that what is hidden (the secret) can be much less significant than the very act of hiding (secrecy). The enjoyment of the forbidden can make actors seek to test the "limits of safe concealment" by signaling to outsiders the very fact that they are engaging in forbidden practices.[49] Goffman describes how one alcoholic inmate purposely drank the smuggled alcohol in front of staff. In exposing his secrecy, he signaled his autonomy. Indeed, in the total institution the social significance of secrecy lies in providing individuals with a sense of self and personal autonomy outside the institution.[50] Precisely because total institutions aim to strip individuals of their autonomy through total information control, actors may engage in resistance through secrecy, because this allows them to maintain and regain autonomy—something that is heightened at the moment of revelation toward the outsiders.

Secrecy in Interaction: Expression Games

Goffman provides insights on the dynamic social interactions between insiders and outsiders of secrecy. In *Strategic Interaction* he points to actors' use of "covering," namely the intentional concealment of information to engage in impression management. However, such covering can be suspected by the observer. Sensing that the information presented may be manipulated, obfuscated, and based on misrepresentation, the observer can make an "uncovering move" by engaging in interrogations, inquisitions, and examinations. The performer may then in turn respond with "counter-uncovering moves." Goffman illustrates this in relation to the John F. Kennedy administration:

To forestall suspicion among the Press that a crisis had occurred in regard to offensive missiles in Cuba, the members of the National Security Council, coming together or a crucial meeting in the Oval Room of the White House, arrived at different times and entered through different gates. During the same tense period, Kennedy apparently maintained his normal schedule of appointments to avoid arousing suspicions.[51]

These moves highlight the interactional and dynamic nature of secrecy and how it can greatly influence the performer's behavior, his or her physical and emotional expressions. Secrecy requires "emotional self-control"—

something that actors often struggle with. Their expressive behavior can easily reveal the secret (e.g., when blushing or avoiding eye contact), and they can have difficulties in not giving away the secret though inadvertent slips.[52] Moral norms about sincerity, honesty, and integrity as well as the sense of guilt can pose further limits to secrecy.[53] Moreover, the keeping up of secrets may be undermined by outside pressures, in the form of black-mailing and bribery. Secrecy therefore constitutes a complex, interactive, ongoing yet highly elusive accomplishment that can easily collapse like a house of cards.

Secrecy in Teams

Goffman also introduces a useful distinction of secrecy among groups (which he terms "teams" and which are akin to Simmel's secret societies), namely *dark*, *strategic*, and *inside* secrets.[54] We draw repeatedly on this vocabulary. *Dark secrets* concern the attempt to hide information that would place the image of the team and its members in a negative light. Such secrets are "double secrets"; their very existence needs to be kept secret (like latent secrets in Simmel). An example of dark secrecy from recent history is the practice of "extraordinary rendition" in the so-called War on Terror, where the US government, with the help of a number of other Western countries (e.g., Germany), sent people who allegedly had ties to al-Qaeda to Syrian prisons for torture.[55] Not only does the notion of "extraordinary rendition" serve to hide what this practice of transfer-ring entails, but also governments have sought to keep the very fact that such a practice takes place hidden.

Strategic secrets "pertain to intentions and capacities of a team which it conceals from its audience in order to prevent them from adapting effec-tively to the state of affairs the team is planning to bring about."[56] These secrets are important in situations of competition because they provide the team with strategic advantages and so are more akin to the functional and informational motivations for secrecy. Such secrecy is exemplified in Virgil's *Aeneid* by the tale of the Greeks winning the Trojan War by hiding inside the Trojan horse to carry out a surprise attack. In a more contemporary way, product development groups conceal new innovations until they are ready to be unleashed on competitors. In contrast to dark secrets, intended to remain concealed forever, strategic secrets may eventually be revealed by the group when, for instance, the strategic actions are put into place.

Inside secrets "are ones whose possession marks an individual as being a member of a group and helps the group feel separate and different from those individuals who are not 'in the know.'"[57] This kind of secrecy parallels the Simmelian insight that secrets may be held not because information needs to be concealed but to create a demarcation between insiders and outsiders for group formation. Although inside secrets may be neither (or either) strategic nor dark, they can overlap with these: "Secrets that are strategic and/or dark serve extremely well as inside secrets and we find, in fact, that the strategic and dark character of secrets is often exaggerated for this reason."[58]

Goffman also points out that teams constructed around secrecy are characterized by relations of mutual dependency because each member needs to behave in accordance with the requirements of secrecy. This can bring about social cohesion, as Simmel had noted. But Goffman elaborates that keeping a secret in a team requires dramaturgical loyalty, discipline, and circumspection. *Dramaturgical loyalty* means that team members are committed to certain performances in front of outsiders and refrain from "becoming so sympathetically attached to the audience that the performers disclose to them" the secret.[59] For counteracting disloyalty, high solidarity among the team members is necessary. *Dramaturgical discipline* refers to the team members' ability to engage in self-control and discretion, whereas *dramaturgical circumspection* denotes actors' ability to prepare for the performance by foreseeing what the audience already knows and can easily find out. Thus secrecy for Goffman entails more than a simple and abstract binary of belonging or not belonging to an in-group: there are complex social dynamics in place through which both secrecy and group membership are maintained.

Summary of Key Insights

Goffman's substantial *oeuvre* provides extensive insights into secrecy, particularly regarding the social interactions among and between insiders and outsiders. It illuminates a variety of reasons why an individual or a group keeps secrets: from the attempt to give a favorable impression to outsiders, reducing shame, hiding dark information, gaining a sense of autonomy, and evoking awe through to gaining a strategic advantage and forming a group. Goffman is mostly concerned with what we term "informal secrecy," namely secrecy that takes places in everyday social interactions rather than being governed by law and formal rules. The social interactions entailed in informal secrecy can be dynamic, involving covering, uncovering, and counter-uncovering moves. Keeping a secret is conceptualized as enacting a certain frontstage performance that requires self-discipline in communication, expressions, emotions, and behaviors. However, the performance can easily be disrupted because of intentional or unintentional disclosure; the performer may give out inadvertent expressions contradicting the intended image, or be overcome by a sense of guilt and start to identify with the audience instead of the in-group. Sharing secrets in groups can be particularly vulnerable given the mutual dependency involved. For this reason, solidarity, loyalty, and discipline are important. Goffman also shows that actors may intentionally reveal the secret in situations of loss of control and autonomy. In these cases, secrecy provides a space for resistance—something that is important to keep in mind because it contradicts the all-too-common equation of secrecy and the powerful.

PUBLIC SECRECY: KNOWING WHAT NOT TO KNOW

So far we have referred to formal (or official) and informal secrecy, both of which imply that insiders know and discuss secrets that outsiders do not know the existence and/or content of. However, often secrets are known and shared yet remain unarticulated, with the insider and outsider distinction being much less clear cut or even absent. Here we have a kind of "open" or "public" secrecy found, for example, in families or between couples when unspoken truths often abound. The sociologist Eviator Zerubavel illustrates such secrecy through Hans Christian Andersen's fairy tale of the *Emperor's New Clothes,* in which everybody[60] pretends that the emperor is wearing clothes when he is in fact wearing nothing at all—something that cannot be articulated because one would then be perceived negatively and even sanctioned. Such situations, which are commonly described as the "Elephant in the Room"—an expression that Zerubavel uses as the title of his book—involve open secrets. These are characterized by a "conspiracy of silence whereby a group of people tacitly agree to outwardly ignore something of which they are personally aware."[61] The anthropologist Michael Taussig is similarly concerned with what he calls "public secrecy," defined "as that which is generally known but cannot be articulated."[62]

The Tension between Concealment and Revelation

Such public secrecy entails a "fundamental tension between knowledge and acknowledgement, personal awareness and public discourse"[63]: actors seek to conceal what they know and that they engage in such concealment, thus public secrecy is meant to remain latent and involves a meta-secrecy. Yet at the same time public secrecy requires a shared effort of keeping up such concealment in that everybody needs to know *not* to bring up the very issue that has to remain hidden. Thus, every participant in the social situation needs to be aware of the existence of public secrecy yet not openly show his or her awareness. There can be subtle social pressures on the participants to engage in public secrecy—something that outsiders can fail to pick up and therefore easily upset the social situation.[64]

Paradoxically, in situations of public secrecy, that which is supposed to be hidden yet everybody is aware of can become all the more present because of its concealment. Precisely because people aim to ignore certain issues or "talk around" them, these issues shape the social situation even more; returning to the earlier example, the elephant becomes the more present as those involved try to keep it absent. This can create a tension around the public secret.[65] Given this tension, the secret can take on a "fetish" character, whereby "instead of disappearing as its realness is solidified, and instead of being out-maneuvered and trapped, the secret has assumed command over persons and sets the rules of the game."[66] Although such a fetish character can also surround other kinds of secrets, it is magnified in the case of public secrecy. Here all the members of the social situation need to be involved, and the nature of revelation, that is, the explosive force released after revelation, differs: "It is precisely this explosive force which . . . separates the secret from the public secret. For with the latter, *the explosion never comes*, and remains instead as tensed possibility."[67]

There is a lack of "explosion" because public secrecy does not involve the "two-realities model of world, surface and depth, appearance and a hidden essence"[68] because what is hidden is simultaneously present. But if everybody knows the secret, why is it kept secret?

Power, Taboo, and Tact

Public secrecy serves to deny those very things that could upset the current order.[69] It carries the norms concerning what is acceptable to publically speak about, say, and hear and what needs to remain unspoken. In delineating the limits of acceptable discourse, public secrecy involves the workings of power:

What we notice and what we discuss with others is socially delineated not only by normative pressures to suppress certain information from our awareness or at least refrain from acknowledging its presence, but also by political constraints. Power, after all, involves the ability to control the scope of the information others can access as well as what they pass on and thus promotes various forms of forced blindness, deafness, and muteness.[70]

The intersection of power and public secrecy differs from that described in the previous section; rather than one party seeking to influence another by keeping that person in the dark, public secrecy is about keeping the issue in front of ourselves so as to maintain power. We referred earlier to the Yale Skull and Bones Society; the role of public secrecy in this is well described in Edward Wilson's espionage novel *The Envoy*, where he discusses how Skull and Bones operates:

The initiation rituals of the society are supposed to be secret—and so are the names of the members, but everyone knows who they are. Total anonymity would be pointless and counterproductive. The essence of their power is that members are known by rumour rather than by published list. The sham secrecy is intended to create an aura of mystery and awe.[71]

This quotation is notable for implicitly locating secrecy in the logic of *mysterium*[72] and, in particular, illustrating how public secrecy—the secret that "everyone knows"—can foster this in a way that complete secrecy, or "total anonymity," could never achieve. Total anonymity, if successful, could not have the aura of mystery: for *mysterium* to operate some degree of permeability in the boundary between those who hold the secret and those who do not is needed if awe is to be provoked. Wilson is wrong, though, to call this "sham" secrecy. Rather, it is a particular form of secrecy. Public secrecy overlaps with taboos and tact (the latter being a "softer" version of the former). The dance around knowing and not knowing allows us to sustain the social prohibition created by the taboo.[73] This intersection is apparent in the taboo around homosexuality in the US military, which between 1994 and 2011 was upheld through the "Don't ask don't tell" policy, namely the need to actively disregard and hide the existence of homosexuality.[74] A further example of the handling of taboos through public secrecy can be found in Michel Foucault's famous discussion of sexuality in modernity. Here, notwithstanding the "repressive hypothesis," he argues that sex was in fact continually and ever more prolifically spoken about in a variety of coded ways[75] and institutionally inscribed in a wide variety of practices.[76] In this way it became, as Taussig puts it, the "secret we are henceforth doomed to always speak about precisely because it is secret."[77]

This kind of public secrecy in which taboo subjects are simultaneously recognized and denied calls for some elaborate social maneuvers. A nice illustration of this can be found in Olivia Manning's novel *The Great Fortune*,[78] set in 1940s Romania, where respectable women are supposed not to understand references to sex. Thus, when hearing a sexual joke made in mixed company the men laugh while the women assume stony expressions. Yet the very fact of those expressions—rather than ones of bafflement—indicates that they do, in fact, understand the reference: they know but they do not know. Goffman describes the operation of tact in similar ways:

Tact in regard to face-work often relies for its operation on a tacit agreement to do business through the language of hint—the language of innuendo, ambiguities, well-placed pauses, carefully worded jokes, and so on. . . . Hinted communication, then, is deniable communication; it need not be faced up to.[79]

This is not just a matter of upholding social conventions or avoiding personal embarrassment. It is a potent way of keeping secrets, precisely because it allows deniability. This in fact is how cover-ups are often achieved: the hinter can deny having given some information or instruction although the person taking the hint is in no doubt that this has (implicitly) happened.

Summary of Key Insights

Public secrecy adds further dimensions to the phenomenon of secrecy by drawing attention to the ways in which people may both know and not know, be aware of and simultaneously ignore, certain issues. It therefore disturbs the neat distinction between hidden truth and appearance that might otherwise be thought to underlie secrecy. Public secrecy, moreover, shows how the sharing of secrets is at the heart of secrecy itself (and not just within secret groups); secrets are often known and in this sense part of public knowledge. As such, they may require particularly elaborate social games, somewhere on the boundary of what is spoken and unspoken and interacting with power, taboo, and tact. Public secrecy creates a boundary between what is acceptable to talk about and what needs to remain ignored. This serves to cope with social prohibitions, avoid potential embarrassments, yet also to uphold the existing social order. Despite being elusive and almost oxymoronic, public secrecy is instantly recognizable as part of the texture of everyday life.

CONCLUSION: FOUNDATIONAL CONCEPTS
FOR THEORIZING SECRECY

Secrecy is a multifaceted phenomenon that deeply shapes our lives. In everyday social interactions, relations of power, elite groups, situations of competition, diplomacy, totalitarian dictatorships, and liberal democracies secrecy is present in some form or other. This variety highlights not just secrecy's pervasiveness but also that it is neither inherently good nor bad. Indeed Simmel's assertion of secrecy as a universal sociological form underscores the redundancy of making *a priori* ethical judgments about it: it is present as a basic category of social experience. In appreciating the wide-ranging ways in which secrecy is intimately linked to the fundamental "stuff" that makes up social life we can begin to glimpse its importance for specifically, organizational life. Thus, although the theorizations discussed in this chapter serve to explore the richness of secrecy, they also allow us to develop the analytical coordinates that underlie and provide a foundational conceptual vocabulary for our study of organizational secrecy.

The first foundation is the insight, derived from Weber's remarks about bureaucratic organizations: that secrets are not just kept for the obvious, functional reason of concealing knowledge of value. That is emphatically not to say that secrets are *not* kept for this reason, but that they are not *only* kept for this reason. Instead, drawing in particular on Canetti, Michels, and Mills we showed how secrecy is imbricated with the exercise of power and especially political and administrative power. By decoupling secrecy from value, we can see not only that secrets may be kept for reasons other than their value but also that value may be an actual or perceived effect of secrecy. This is the second foundation of this book: the idea, articulated by Simmel, that things that are kept secret take on a value simply by virtue of the fact that they are kept secret.

Even conceived of in terms of the concealment of valuable knowledge, there are different modalities of secrecy. From Goffman we took the term "dark secrecy" to denote cases in which the value of concealment lies in hiding shameful or damaging knowledge, as opposed to what he calls "strategic secrecy," in which the value lies in hiding useful knowledge. But in any case Goffman's third form of secrecy—inside secrecy—points us toward the ways that secrecy can organize social relations. This insight, which also derives from Simmel's work, is the third foundation of this book. Secrecy serves to create boundaries between people on the basis of which relations are formed. As secrecy brings about the webs of social relations that make up our social life, it shapes these in important ways: creating distinctions and a sense of exclusivity, exercising power, evoking mysteriousness, promoting group cohesion, providing spaces of autonomy and resistance, giving an impression, or saving contradictory situations from potential embarrassment and disrupting the social order. The social relations we are concerned with can be between insiders and outsiders as well as within a group of insiders.

Although Simmel explained the way that secrecy organizes social relations, it is in Goffman's work that we find the most elaborate exploration of the everyday ways in which this occurs. An attention to these is the fourth foundation of the analysis in this book. Keeping secrets requires actors to manage the social interactions with outsiders by being careful about the information they present. This underlines why secrecy needs to be understood as intentional; it requires self-discipline regarding what one says, but also how one looks and behaves in front of others. At the core of secrecy as intentional concealment lie various practices, such as silence and/or covering. Silence refers to refraining from communicating about the secret, that is, not speaking about, ignoring it, and making it seem one is not aware of it in front of outsiders. Although silence involves the lack of speech, covering means actively blocking access to that information supposed to be kept secret by providing other (often contrary) information, for example, through disguising, fabricating, feigning (that is, misrepresenting information), or disinforming outsiders. Engaging in these practices, however, does not suffice; secrecy requires that there is consistency in the entire performance, in the actor's face, bodily posture, and general expressions. The social interactions with outsiders are dynamic, potentially entailing covering, uncovering, and counter-covering moves.

The keeping of secrets therefore represents an ongoing accomplishment that is inherently accompanied by the possibility of revelation, as identified by Sissela Bok among others. To make a secret is, at the very same moment of doing so, to make the possibility of its being revealed; this inherent vulnerability in secrecy is the sixth foundation of this book. Revelation might occur in unintentional ways, but as Simmel argues, individuals might also have the urge to reveal secrets because they feel isolated, overridden with guilt, or because they seek to create a certain connection with others. Indeed, secrecy can be a powerful emotional phenomenon, involving strong bonds, feelings of guilt, shame, and betrayal. Keeping secrets is a question of disciplining oneself, one's emotions and expressions, along with matters of identification, loyalty, moral norms, and the fear of punishment (either for keeping or disclosing secrets). Yet revelation can be seductive; the sense of superiority or autonomy is the greatest at the moment outsiders are made aware of the insider's secret. For that matter, just as secrets may be kept for their dark or strategic value, so too may they deliberate revelation be similarly motivated. Whistleblowers may leak dark secrets for reasons of conscience; spies may leak strategic secrets for reasons of ideology, principle, or financial gain.

Even when secrets are concealed, they are for their possessors a shared phenomenon. Indeed, this makes it possible for secrecy to form the basis of in-groups and group identification. This idea of secrecy as something shared *as well as* something concealed is the seventh foundation of our analysis. But the manner in which secrets are shared varies. Formal secrecy relates to knowledge that is codified and documented and shared by official access. Following Weber, such secrecy has particularly emerged with the rise of bureaucracy. Informal secrecy, by contrast, concerns information that is not officially codified and documented and is shared through everyday social interactions. A particular variant of this is open or public secrecy, which points us toward the grey area where secrets are both known and not-known and the dynamics of this. Secrecy thereby emerges not as a binary between knowledge and ignorance, or silence and speech, but as a spectrum of more-or-less shared and more-or-less concealed knowledge.

Throughout this book, we return to these core foundations derived from the theorists of secrecy whose work we have discussed in this chapter. But those theorists were for the most part concerned with secrecy in general, whereas our focus is the more specific one of organizational secrecy. Kafka's hapless protagonist, Josef K., with whom we began this chapter, encounters what, mystifying as it may be to him, appears to be an organizational world of rules, systems, and functionaries. It is to this organizational world that we turn our attention in the next chapter.

CHAPTER 2

Bricks and Mortar
From Organizing Secrecy to Secrecy as Organizing

EVERYDAY LANGUAGE reveals that secrecy is an integral part of organizational life. Participants in meetings may attribute to others a "hidden
agenda" that keeps some people "in the dark." Organizational members
often believe that important organizational decisions occur "behind closed
doors" and are kept "off the record." A "closed-door policy" can even
characterize organizations at large, so that their members are admonished
not to discuss in-house matters with outsiders. Apart from the language of
hiding, secrecy features in the language of sharing, namely in the context
of social interactions between organizational actors. This is apparent in the
notions of "keeping it within these four walls" or "just between us," which
are first moves in the joint construction of a secret, to which the response
is typically something like "My lips are sealed" or "It will go no further."

Considering practices of hiding and sharing brings to light how secrecy
can constitute a central way in which people make sense of, experience,
and practice organizational life. However, this is easy to overlook if we
think about it only in terms of strategic or dark secrets held or possessed
by organizations. Although both these kinds of secrets are undoubtedly
significant to both public and private organizations, and can carry various
implications for society at large, they neglect the significance of secrecy
more broadly by focusing on scenarios in which secrecy is required to meet
a particular aim. Specifically, these approaches provide only limited insight
into how secrecy can organize social relationships, bring about groups,
networks, and hierarchies, and thereby contribute to the construction of
the organization itself. These things constitute, so to speak, the bricks and
mortar of organizational life.

In this chapter we begin to draw attention to the ways in which secrecy
pervades many kinds of organizational phenomena: the construction of
boundaries and definition of membership, dyadic and intergroup relations,
hierarchies, power, and decision-making processes. First, we outline more

conventional ways of approaching strategic and dark secrecy. This is what we mean by "organizing secrecy": some of the ways in which, and the reasons why, organizations engage in secrecy. Then, we turn to some classic (if in some cases neglected) works in organization studies that have given attention to secrecy. From these, we derive an understanding of "secrecy as organizing," which is to say the ways in which secrecy can be understood not just as something that organizations do, but something that is constitutive of organizations themselves.

STRATEGIC AND DARK SECRECY
IN ORGANIZATIONS

To begin, let us consider the ways that secrecy has been traditionally conceived of within organization studies. Here the focus is mainly on strategic secrecy, which is about the protection of valuable organizational assets through concealment, and dark secrecy, which concerns the keeping of shameful or "dirty" secrets. Although strategic secrecy is mostly formal in character, dark secrecy can be both formal and informal. But in both cases secrecy is mostly concerned with informational issues and the implications of secrecy for the organization as a whole vis-à-vis its external environment.[1]

Strategic Secrecy

It is easy to see why organizations have a strategic interest in secrecy; it allows them to protect their new inventions and incremental product innovations, client lists, customer data, or military and company strategies. In concealing information by engaging in trade, financial, or military secrecy, organizations hope to gain a competitive advantage. The risk of imitation by competitors is reduced; organizations can enjoy a first-mover advantage and they can engage in surprise attacks against their competitors.[2] Prominent examples of such competitive advantage are the secret search algorithm on which Google's dominance is based or the Swiss tradition of bank secrecy from which its financial sector derived a competitive edge—at least until recently. How secrecy can be of strategic importance for competition is especially apparent in innovation races and during war time. Skunk Works, the US Lockheed aircraft secret development plant that thrived during the Cold War, offers a perfect example of this. As Ben R. Rich, who worked there as a head engineer, explains:

Time and again, our marching orders from Washington were to produce airplanes or weapon systems that were so advanced that the Soviet bloc would be impotent to stop their missions. Which was why most of the airplanes we built remained shrouded in the deepest operational secrecy. If the other side didn't know these aircraft existed until we introduced them in action, they would be that much farther behind in building defenses to bring them down. So inside the Skunk Works we operated on a tight-lipped need-to-know basis.[3]

Sometimes protection and keeping of strategic secrets is a literal or metaphorical arms race with opponents, but other times it is embedded in collaborative relationships, including military alliances. For instance, entrepreneurial firms may risk the misappropriation of their valuable resources by a partner firm if they share something too early in a corporate relationship.[4] More generally, the risk of theft or leaking of trade secrets is often discussed in the context of partnerships between US and overseas firms. The partnership between the manufacturers of medical equipment, Boston Scientific, and Medinol, an Israeli stent developer, exemplifies a case in which trade secrets were nabbed; Medinol sued Boston Scientific for secretly and independently developing and selling stents that were based on Medinol's proprietary design. Medinol won the protracted case and was awarded damages.[5]

In cases of strategic secrecy, management needs to ensure that the employees protect the secrets through internal rules, something that can be a problem if employees leave the firm and join competitors.[6] The danger of organizational members leaking or taking confidential information with them as they leave the firm partly explains why, in many cases, employees who are laid off are prevented from copying any files and taking them outside of the office. In many organizations as soon as the decision to lay them off has been made, employees are no longer allowed to return to their desks unless accompanied by a security guard and their email accounts and other IT facilities are immediately frozen. The same issue explains employment contracts that prevent workers who leave from establishing ties with clients or competitors of the company for fixed periods of time.

Common examples of strategic secrecy—including trade secrecy, intellectual property rights, and legal and professional duties of confidentiality—are understandable in terms of the processes of formal secrecy that we discuss extensively in chapter 3. But to give some idea of how strategic secrecy may be woven into everyday organizational life, consider the case of pay secrecy. It is common practice in many organizations to prohibit the open disclosure of the pay levels of employees. This pay secrecy can be legally enforced so that if employees discuss their pay with colleagues they may risk being dismissed. Such secrecy provides organizations with control in avoiding conflicts, protecting individual's privacy, and decreasing labor mobility[7]: "By keeping pay secret, one can never be sure about the hierarchical differentials, and thus, one is less likely to argue about their fairness. Because of the secrecy, these differentials are not as likely to be obvious, and therefore important, to organizational participants."[8] If pay is kept secret, questions of its fairness, legitimacy, or equity are suppressed. Even without legal sanctions, pay secrecy can be so strongly embedded in some social, cultural, and organizational contexts that it would be considered extremely rude to ask someone what they are paid or to volunteer such information. However, it can also bring with it certain costs, such as lower employee perceptions of fairness, trust, and motivation, as well as a less efficient internal labor market.[9] In recent years there have been calls to abolish the prevalent code of pay secrecy because it may be used simply to hide pay discrimination against women and minority group members.[10] In these cases, pay secrecy turns from strategic into dark secrecy.

Dark Secrecy

That secrecy is typically perceived as ethically dubious in large part results from the ways in which it can serve to hide various forms of misconduct in public and private organizations.[11] Indeed, secrecy's "bad name" might not be a surprise given the long list of corporate and political scandals: from Enron's fraudulent accounting practices[12] to German industrial giant Siemens's large-scale and systematic bribery activities in Greece[13] to the George W. Bush administration's presentation of, arguably, exaggerated evidence concerning weapons of mass destruction[14] through to the Indian sweatshops hidden in Primark's production line[15]—and any number of other cases. Such forms of organizational misconduct might be so prevalent in some companies, and so dangerous to the organizations engaging in them, that the "cover-up" is deeply ingrained in the organizational fabric (as seems allegedly to have been the case at Siemens[16]). But it might also be the case that only certain organizational members are responsible for the misconduct, for example, the case of Nick Leeson's unauthorized speculative financial trades in Singapore, resulting in the collapse of Barings, the world's oldest investment bank.[17] Or it may be the case that dark secrets come into play in extraordinary circumstances,[18] such as those following accidents (e.g., the 2010 British Petroleum *Deepwater Horizon* oil spill in the Gulf of Mexico[19]). In these cases, actors may seek to hide under the veil of secrecy or shield themselves from internal consequences and public criticism, but also to reap the benefits of their transgressive behavior. Yet the cases mentioned, and more precisely the public knowledge of them, highlight how dark secrecy produces vulnerabilities for the organization as a whole, because their revelation can lead to distrust, reputational damage, and legal sanctions that may include substantial fines and imprisonment of executives.[20]

Although ingrained organizational misconduct, such as corruption, deception, and general ethical wrongdoing, can involve secrecy, this is not necessarily the case. For instance, in her analysis of the *Challenger* space shuttle disaster, Diane Vaughan describes how deviant behaviors may become "normalized" in an organization and members may not necessarily attempt to conceal them. In such circumstances, organizational misconduct may be a matter of "organizational blindness" rather than intentionality.[21] Such normalization may occur across whole societies, as with the widespread practice of *fakelaki* bribery in Greece—whereby a patient gives a doctor in a little envelope of cash (the *fakelaki*) to receive better and faster treatment—which was (if not still is) a common and by no means hidden practice. The extent of the use of secrecy in cases of organizational misconduct—whether people attempt to hide their conduct or not—may therefore be a question of ethical awareness but also of the specific cultural, social, and legal contexts.

Although secrecy is not necessarily involved in each and every case of organizational misconduct, it can play an important role and is therefore implicitly or explicitly mentioned in the vast literatures on corruption, deviance, deception, whistleblowing, and, more generally, business ethics.[22] Although discussing these literatures in any depth is clearly beyond the scope of this chapter, noting the individual and organizational factors that drive misconduct and thus potentially secrecy[23] allows us to move closer to exploring secrecy in relation to the inner workings of organizations—the focus of our analysis. The idea, for example, that organizational structure can influence the extent to which concealment takes place is underlined by Vaughan's notion of "structural secrecy," namely the "the way that patterns of information, organizational structure, processes, and transactions, and the structure of regulatory relations systematically undermine the attempt to know and interpret situations in all organizations."[24]

Whereas Vaughan shows that such structural secrecy is not necessarily related to *intentional* concealment (and thus her use of the notion of secrecy differs from ours), her study draws attention to the ways in which particular organizational structures, such as complex ones, can foster secrecy. At the same time, we can think of examples in which actors intentionally create organizational structures that provide spaces for concealment.[25] Consider how dark secrecy related to tax evasion, money laundering, and other misconduct can be found in complex, global, and largely invisible corporate ownership structures.[26] An example in this regard is the case of UK Bank Northern Rock that employed off-shore accounts registered under the ownership of a charity to hide its losses.[27]

Studies of organizational misconduct also reveal the significance of social dynamics for secrecy in terms of conformity, group pressures, and social sanctions. This is particularly apparent in discussions of whistleblowing.[28] Whether an individual discloses dark secrets can be related to various situational factors, such as organizational culture and climate, but also, and more important, to his or her identification with the group or organization and its moral outlook.[29] Perhaps the most famous incident of whistleblowing is Daniel Ellsberg's leaking of the Pentagon Papers related to the Vietnam War (something that later on led to the Watergate Scandal and the resignation of President Nixon). Ellsberg was a military analyst at the Pentagon who had access to top-secret information and the behind-the-scenes decision-making processes regarding the Vietnam War:

I realized something crucial: that the president's ability to escalate, his entire strategy throughout the war, had depended on secrecy and lying and thus on his ability to deter unauthorized disclosures—truth telling—by officials. That did not mean with certainty that he could not have carried out his plans openly or that he still could not do so. The fact was, however, that he had never chosen to test that possibility.[30]

The US military strategy in Vietnam was based on a "system of secrecy and lying" to Congress and the public at large.[31] Becoming increasingly aware of the need to end the Vietnam War, and the high number of casualties and failed military strategy, Ellsberg decided to copy and leak top secret files to the *New York Times* and other newspapers. In *Secrets: A Memoir of Vietnam and the Pentagon Papers* he describes various incidents that influenced his decision to leak the papers, among them his attendance of antiwar campaigns and also the antiwar attitudes of his partner and the social group surrounding him.

That such an individual act of whistleblowing can have a huge impact is epitomized by the case of the former US intelligence analyst, Chelsea Manning, who leaked more than 250,000 classified files, 500,000 Army reports, and videos to WikiLeaks, and also by the case of Edward Snowden, who made public top-secret National Security Agency (NSA) documents. These examples show that whether someone engages in or discloses secrecy, it is significantly related to her or his social (and moral) identity and therefore sense of loyalty, commitment, and identification toward her or his organization and/or outsiders, such as the general public. In other words, keeping a secret may be a moral act, but so too may disclosing a secret, if it is animated by, for example, a sense of civic duty. For this reason, whistleblowing can spark strong yet polarized reactions, from seeing whistleblowers as heroes putting moral concerns above legal ones at potentially high risk to themselves, to regarding them as traitors to their organizations or even the country at large. Indeed, Manning and Snowden have garnered both these reactions. The Manning and Snowden examples also underline how the preservation of secrecy is a highly vulnerable phenomenon, particularly in the current information age where a single CD (onto which Manning copied all the secret material) was able to capture the attention of the entire world and shape the fate of entire regions (e.g., the 2011 Arab Spring uprisings and their consequences). But how can organizations be prevented from holding dark secrets in the first place?

Transparency, which means "come in sight," is invariably discussed as the central way to counter secrecy and therefore organizational wrongdoings.[32] During the past decades various global civil society movements, political parties, and international nongovernmental organizations (NGOs) have emerged to take up the cause of transparency both in political institutions and corporations. Among other things, these seek to challenge the principle of *arcanii imperium* discussed in the previous chapter. The workings of secrecy are seen to be prevalent in today's governments, particularly when the presumed pretext of (national) security provides the basis for dark secrecy, for example, during the War on Terror.[33] As transparency studies from many different disciplines—such as political science, law, sociology, cultural studies, and organization studies—note, access to information, having the right to know, and being able to see has become a political demand. Supposedly, only in this way can democratic, fair, and efficient decision-making processes with the involvement of different stakeholders take place.[34] However, such demands often fail to account for the ways in which transparency itself is not neutral; it can go hand in hand with the rise of auditing regimes, undermine trust, and bring about various power effects.[35] Regarding the latter, we may think of the link, very widely explored in recent organization studies, between surveillance and transparency, especially as theorized in the Foucauldian notion of disciplinary power and the Panopticon:[36] transparency may be a tool of control as much as route to liberation.

Nevertheless, in the light of the possibilities of rapid information dissemination and global networking provided by the Internet, "the age of transparency" has been proclaimed:

Old institutions and incumbent powers are inexorably coming to terms with this new reality. The "Age of Transparency" is here: not because one transnational online network dedicated to open information and whistle-blowing named WikiLeaks exists, but because the knowledge of how to build and maintain such networks is now widespread. It both helps and hurts that we are living in a time of radical uncertainty about the "official" version of truth. All kinds of "authoritative" claims made by leading public figures in recent years have turned out to be little more than thin air.[37]

Keeping secrets in public and private organizations has therefore become increasingly difficult: "Secrecy and the hoarding of information are ending; openness and the sharing of information are coming."[38] It indeed seems to be the case that information leakage has become easier and perhaps more prevalent in the current information age. Yet this does not mean that we are witnessing the "end of secrecy."[39] Secrecy in its formal, informal, and public variants is a central part of organizations, and complete transparency is not only undesirable but also impossible.[40] As we claimed in the previous chapter about total institutions, even in such extreme settings of transparency and surveillance actors find spaces for secrecy. Furthermore, the increasingly complex structures of organizations and new forms of organizing, such as networks, may promote secrecy to the extent that they promote informal, unrecorded knowledge-sharing. More important, such claims imply that secrecy is the antonym of transparency.[41] This conception is problematic; it fails to see that transparency initiatives can always only disclose certain information whereby other information may remain or be made opaque and invisible.[42] Information is also not something neutral, simply visible, and objectively available but is of a social and political nature: the issue is what things are secret and what things are transparent, to whom, how, and when. Indeed, one can even see how increased transparency entails increased secrecy, because the very proliferation of information makes it easy to hide secrets that get overlooked in the overwhelming torrent of disclosure. For example, consider the ubiquitous "terms and conditions" to which one agrees when using Web-based services. These are so detailed and complex that few of us bother to read them, and fewer still understand them. So we just check the box indicating agreement. If subsequently this causes problems the provider can legitimately say that nothing was kept secret and, indeed, that there had been the fullest transparency possible. Yet it is a transparency that obscures rather than reveals. The relationship between secrecy and transparency is therefore more intricate than commonly assumed; we return to this issue in the concluding chapter.

Beyond Strategic and Dark Secrecy: Inside Organizations

Discussions of strategic and dark secrecy typically follow what we have termed an "informational" approach, namely one that focuses on the knowledge concealed and is neglectful of the various ways in which secrecy organizes social relations by creating boundaries, membership, and control—all of which are central to the inner workings of organizations. In order to get at these facets of secrecy, it is crucial to move beyond a conception of secrecy as good or at least justifiable (strategic) or evil and unjustifiable (dark), and to view it rather as inevitably imbricated within organizational life. It is perhaps now clearer why we laid such stress upon this in the previous chapter, because the concepts we developed there help to move us beyond conventional understandings of strategic and dark secrecy.

For example, discussions of strategic and dark secrecy do not account for the ways in which actors may simultaneously know, without publicly acknowledging, the existence of certain secrets; this is what, following Taussig, we have termed "public secrecy." Yet, such public secrecy can surround both formal and informal secrecy. For instance, in negotiations between social movement activists and corporate firms over contentious issues, change activists may signal to the organizational members their awareness of some of the organization's dark secrets without openly articulating them.[43] Moreover, strategic and dark secrecy provide only what Weber terms "functional arguments" for secrecy.[44] They therefore do not allow us to see the "charms and values which it possesses over and above its significance as means" that Simmel identified.[45] It is important to focus on the process of secrecy, rather than content of secrets, in order to explore its significance beyond its immediate function. Indeed, the information that is hidden may be of little or in fact no value at all, as underlined by Goffman's notion of inside secrets.

Secrecy is about more than organizations concealing things, for whatever reason, from the outside world. We need to move beyond approaching it through a lens driven by external issues; it can organize, bring about, and shape the social webs of organizations or relations of hierarchy, thus placing secrecy at the core of enterprises. It is to the inside of this "black box" of organization and also the internal small black boxes within the black box that we now turn.

INSIDE SECRECY

There exist some "classic" works on organizations that provide some indication of how secrecy can shape organizational life above and beyond its immediate function of concealing information. In some cases these works are almost forgotten or have been relegated to the prehistory of organization studies; others are textbook staples. Together, they allow us to see how secrecy can be central to the inner workings of organizations.

Secrecy: Group Boundaries, Identity, and Mysteriousness

In his foundational work on *Organizational Culture and Leadership*, the organizational psychologist Edgar Schein draws attention to secrecy's prevalence in organizations. He notes that "what is at the heart of a culture will not be revealed in the rules of behavior taught to newcomers. It will only be revealed by members as they gain permanent status and are allowed into the inner circles of the group where group secrets then are shared."[46] In a similar vein to Simmel's account of secret societies, Schein argues that secrecy fundamentally defines organizational groups by erecting a boundary between who is in and who is out:

As people move farther "in," they become privy to some of the more secret assumptions of the group. They learn the special meanings attached to certain words and the special rituals that define membership—such as the secret fraternity handshake—and they discover that one of the most important bases for status in the group is to be entrusted with group secrets. Such secrets involved historical accounts of how and why some of the things in the past really happened, who is really part of the dominant coalition or insider group, and what some of the latent functions of the organization are.[47]

Secrecy, in the form of such ritualistic "handshakes" and more generally the use of "a set of communication rules" involving certain "acronyms and special jargon," has the performative function of differentiating in-groups from others.[48] This is exemplified by Schein with reference to the Swiss chemical company Ciba-Geigy, where the senior management is made up of the "Basel aristocracy" and its secret rules and norms. Referring to the Christmas party there, he observes that "the secrecy surrounding what would be done each year heightened the emotionality associated with the event and made the ritual comparable to a group of children anticipating what their Christmas gifts would be."[49] Here, in line with the logic of *mysterium*, organizational secrecy serves to stimulate a certain excitement and aura.

Secrecy and Cliques:
Bridging the Informal and Formal Organization

In another classic text in organization studies, Melville Dalton's *Men Who Manage* (which has a strong claim to be regarded as the first ethnographic study of managers), the significance of secrecy for groups and the organization at large is highlighted. Secrecy is regarded as so fundamental to organizations that "one may well ask *what organization is without secrets* held by some members?"[50] Fascinated by the relation between the formal and informal organization, Dalton observes that "cliques and secrets . . . [are] inseparable and essential for group life."[51] Although, like secrecy, the notion of cliques carries negative overtones, Dalton suggests that, irrespective of their moral or immoral ends, they provide the social fabric that knits together organizations.[52] This, indeed, is also our point with respect to secrecy in general. Dalton shows that cliques formed around secrecy structure organizational relations and—instead of official rules and structure—govern organizational life; they constitute one aspect of what in this book we term the "hidden architecture" of organizational life. In these cliques, organizational members can build "closer ties to conceal current departmental actions and alternatives from outsiders" and foster "obedience" among its members.[53] This illustrates the insights of Simmel and Goffman that groups formed around secrecy display a particular level of bonding as well as forms of disciplinary control. In Dalton's industrial plants, the cliques pursue various ends:

To increase the status and reward of one or all members; to get more support in job activities; to find social satisfactions; to hide facts or conditions that would be frowned on by superiors; to escape unpleasant situations or annoyances; to get more privileges, especially those peculiar higher-ups; and to share the limelight with superiors.[54]

This shows the link between the sharing of secrets in groups, status and social differentiation, and also, as pointed out by Goffman, that such groups may provide members with a supportive backstage.

The nature, functions, and ends of cliques and thus the shared secrecy upon which they are based may differ. There can be "vertical symbiotic cliques" formed between superiors and subordinates. Here secrecy comes into play because the superior may treat the subordinate like a protégé by concealing his or her mistakes in front of outsiders, whereas the subordinate shares with the superior confidential gossip that may be potentially threatening. Such "a symbiotic clique is essential for a given department to compete on a par with other departments for favors from higher-ups and to set up workable arrangements with other departments."⁵⁵ In addition, organizations may involve horizontal cliques. In circumstances of reorganization, crisis, and change, members across departments may secretively coordinate their actions and share information in a clique as to resist organizational initiatives. There may also be "random cliques" between individuals of various ranks and departments, exchanging confidential gossip and other activities.

Part and parcel of the cliques is the sharing and potentially the revealing of secrets between organizational members; secrecy serves to create or break bonds. These bonds in turn constitute the powerful factions in organizations that can greatly shape decision-making processes and organizational actions. In both Schein's and Dalton's discussions of secrecy we can detect not just its organizational significance beyond the immediate function of concealing knowledge but also its informal nature. Clearly in these accounts we are a long way from issues of, say, trade secrets enforced by law. Secrecy here does not refer to a discrete "thing"—some specific piece of information being protected—but something woven into the workaday fabric of organizational life.

From Formal to Informal Secrecy in Managerial Circles

Robert Jackall, who like Dalton drew on sociology and anthropology to understand the world of corporate managers, also touched on secrecy in his classic study *Moral Mazes*.⁵⁶ Indeed, he regards "secrecy [as] . . . a pervasive corporate phenomenon." In a more critical tone than Dalton, Jackall links secrecy to managerial misconduct. He observes that "bureaucracy breaks work into pieces and, in the process, the knowledge required and conferred by each piece of work."[57] The resulting compartmentalization not only provides spaces for secrecy but in fact requires managers with access to knowledge to publicly conceal it:

When such knowledge is possessed, and known to be possessed, organizational protocol usually demands that is be concealed behind public faces of discreet unconcern. Such a demand for secrecy or at least its appearance separates managers emotionally, except for shared confidences between trusted friends or allies, but it actually provides an important stimulus to link them socially.[58]

Jackall is mainly concerned with the way that secrecy serves to produce and maintain a favorable impression in front of outsiders within the organization or the public at large. "Behind the public faces"— what Goffman terms the "frontstage"—various organizational issues, problems, and mistakes can be hidden. The formal, bureaucratic compartmentalization of knowledge and the concomitant secrecy provides managers with "wholly acceptable rationales for not knowing about problems or for not trying to find out,"[59] providing the basis for organizational misconduct but also a basis for viable organization because management would become an impossible task without some rationales of this sort.

Although secrecy creates segmentation, the informal sharing of secrets can bring about and reinforce social bonds. Like Schein and Dalton, Jackall underlines secrecy's role in group formation processes as managers "experience the peculiar bonds with one's fellow produced by shared secrecy."[60] Becoming connected by such bonds entails a powerful "social psychological lure of entrance into such select group."[61] This "lure" can be explained by the way in which, as theorized by Simmel, secrecy creates social distinctions and a sense of exclusivity. To enter the secret managerial circles, individuals need to prove themselves as trustworthy members. In the world of managers

secrecy [is] at the core of managerial circles not as a suppression of dissent but an integral component of a compartmentalized world where one establishes faith with others precisely by proving that one can tolerate the ambiguities that expedient action and stone-faced silence impose.[62]

The notion of "stone-faced silence" highlights how secrecy requires the behavioral control described by Goffman, namely a disciplined presentation of self. Moreover, perhaps the "moral mazes" that Jackall finds in the bureaucratic set-up might be juxtaposed with the "moral accountability among men [sic]" that Simmel attaches to secret groups.[63] Rather than a general absence of morality, we might conjecture that members may have established a separate form of morality, loyalty, and trust in their secret managerial circles. This again serves to undermine any assumption that secrecy is necessarily amoral or immoral.

Informal Secrecy among Employees: Alignment and Resistance
Secrecy can also shape the relation between managers and employees. In *Personality and Organization* the organizational psychologist Chris Argyris discusses the dynamics of the relations between employees and management and managerial efforts to influence these dynamics. Corporate culture programs emphasizing harmony and loyalty bring about a "tendency for secrecy" among employees who "in the presence of leaders . . . are careful to communicate only that which they know is approved by the leader."[64] Such a "barrier of secrecy serves an important function for the employees because it prevents their informal behavior from being discovered, and decreases the possible embarrassment and conflict with management."[65] As employees engage in impression management in front of the leaders, they hide their actual attitudes and feelings. Following Argyris, such secrecy creates a central "barrier . . . between formal and informal aspects of organization" and in this way a realm unmanageable beyond formal organizational control.[66]

Although in Argyris informal secrecy is driven by employees' desire to integrate themselves into the organization, in Michel Crozier's *The Bureaucratic Phenomenon* workers engage in it to signal their independence and gain control. Aiming to keep control over their work areas, maintenance workers keep their skills, know-how, and activities secret.[67] Moreover, production workers frequently engage in "making out," that is, producing more than the given work quota but concealing this from supervisors.[68] This allows them to gain "greater freedom to action to cover up any personal activities in which they want to engage"—something that carries "symbolic" weight "since its affective side—showing off one's in-dependence—is very important."[69] Such making out remains secret not only because of the other kinds of activities it enables but also because if disclosed it would imply a further increase in output quotas. Here we can see how secrecy, particularly of the informal kind, can provide a space outside of management control and thus for resistance. Indeed, following Marx, the world of labor is a "hidden abode."[70] That secrecy can play a role in the labor process; industrial struggles are apparent in labor strikes. Although illegal in some countries, the tactic of the "wildcat strike" was analyzed in yet another classic work, this time in industrial sociology, Alvin Gouldner's book of that name.[71] Wildcat strikes, in a way very similar to the secret production of new weapons or products to unleash on rivals, are highly effective because of the element of surprise. This involves not just keeping plans hidden from managers but also, often, from official trade unions. Indeed, it is their potency derived from secrecy that explains why they are often illegal.

Secrecy and Power

These works point toward the idea that secrecy is in various ways linked to power in organizations (e.g., the power of managers and the power relations between managers and employees). This is apparent in Dalton's observation that rather than employing a democratic management style of sharing information about future plans, managers need to engage in se-crecy so that subordinates cannot use the information for their purposes.[72] This is reminiscent of Canetti's authoritarian ruler who "alone keeps the key" to information held secret from outsiders, because in this way his or her position of power is secured.

Jackall points out[73] that where knowledge is power, this power is rein-forced by secrecy. This is made explicit in Wilbert Moore's now perhaps largely neglected work *The Conduct of the Corporation*: "If knowledge is power, then differential knowledge is likely to enhance the position of its possessors."[74] There is therefore a "temptation to maintain power by restricting knowledge, that is to keep potentially common knowledge uncommon."[75] Distinguishing between secrecy where knowledge is inac-cessible except to experts (e.g., professionals) and that where "readily understandable information . . . is kept from common currency by deliberate blocks to communicate," Moore notes: "The second kind of secrecy may be used to fake the first [as] the aura of mystery . . . may give occult power to those whose privileged position could not withstand full disclosure."[76] This connects to the definitional point about mystery and secrecy: what is kept secret may not be valuable as such but may acquire "symbolic value" through the process of secrecy:

Access to secrets may come to have symbolic value, both because it indicates that one can be trusted and practically no one is immune to the heady sense of importance in being able to say, or preferably to think and not to say, "I know something you don't know."[77]

To understand secrecy's relation to power, social differentiation, and the creation of a mysterious aura, the social and political nature of knowledge needs to be brought into light. One way in which secrecy, knowledge, and power interrelate is highlighted in the aphorism attributed to the philosopher Francis Bacon's that "knowledge is power."[78] Here knowledge is conceived of as a resource that bestows power. In organization studies this is reflected in the classic formulation that expertise and information are key bases of power.[79] Although it can take many forms, one obvious way that knowledge translates into power is by reducing uncertainty, which is necessary for making rational decisions—rational in the sense that these decisions serve the interests of the agent and lead to the best possible outcome given the resources and constraints available. Through knowledge, we have a move from fate (where actors' future is externally given and outside of their control) to fortune (where they have control over the environment and through their rational decisions can determine their path). The significance of secrecy in this relation concerns the ways in which it involves differential levels of knowledge distribution among people; through concealment one person possesses more knowledge than another so that the former has strategic advantages in terms of making better decisions vis-à-vis the latter. Furthermore, those who keep knowledge secret from outsiders can have the power to influence the latters' decisions by reducing the stock of knowledge available to them. This form of power relates to the first "dimension of power" of the sociologist

Steven Lukes's framework,[80] namely that of influencing the outcomes and behaviors of actors involved in decision making. The assumption underpinning this relationship between secrecy, knowledge, and power is that the knowledge involved is of value (because otherwise actors would not derive strategic advantages from possessing it) and is a finite possession (so that if someone has more another must have less). Such a functional understanding is relevant in competitive situations and, for this reason, it underlies discussions of strategic secrecy.

However, in moving away from the assumption that knowledge is necessarily of strategic value, a more dynamic interrelation can be detected. The classic works illustrate the point that secrets may be kept for their own sake—for their "symbolic value," as Moore puts is—rather than for their intrinsic value. Observing how organizational actors continually seek to gather more and more information beyond what it is functionally useful and necessary for making decisions while simultaneously complaining about a lack of information, organizations theorists such as Martha Feldman and James March have noted that there can be a "weak link" between information and decisions.[81] Instead of improving decision making, Feldman and March argue, the significance of possessing information can lie in signaling and symbolizing intelligent choice and competence. In societies that greatly value reason, rationality, and intelligence, a *well-informed* decision might well be considered synonymous with a *good* decision. In possessing information, actors are perceived by outsiders, and perceive themselves, as intelligent, competent, and in a better position to make rational decisions. This in turn implies that their legitimacy is enhanced and their decisions, judgments, and, more generally, words are granted greater authoritative force. If we believe that better knowledge leads to better decisions, and believe that decision makers have more knowledge than us, then we are likely to believe that they make good decisions and to obey them.

Secrecy reinforces this relation between decisions and information in that it creates and builds upon the (attribution of) differential stocks of knowledge. Those who are believed to hold secrets and have access to information concealed from others—for example, the CEO of an organization or high-level political decision makers like the president of the United States—may be seen by others as more knowledgeable than others. As a result, their judgments are granted more weight and they have power to influence others. This is also the case for experts: by the very fact of their position as expert it is assumed that they know more than others and as a result are particularly able to influence others. Here secrecy, for instance, in the use of acronyms and language inaccessible to others, can serve to demonstrate the expert status. Thus, being perceived as having access to otherwise concealed information provides people with power and reinforces their positions of power.[82] This can explain why secrecy can make insiders feel special; in knowing something others do not know they can perceive themselves as more competent, intelligent, and for this very reason powerful.

There is a further way in which knowledge, power, and secrecy may interrelate. Taking a social constructivist view, knowledge forms the basis to socially construct the reality of everyday life. In their groundbreaking sociological work, Peter Berger and Thomas Luckmann express it as follows: "Knowledge . . . is thus a realization in the double sense of the word, in the sense of apprehending the objectivated social reality, and in the sense of ongoingly producing this reality."[83] From every day, routine-based know-how to highly complex and esoteric expertise, knowledge produces and shapes meaning—how we make sense of the world—and this in turn guides conduct. Secrecy involves a differential stock of knowledge between different actors, bringing about "sub-universes of meaning."[84] Depending on the knowledge available, individuals construct and therefore enact reality in different ways. In this way, secrecy may be seen as having a role in the operation of Lukes's second and third "dimensions of power," in which nondecisional agenda control and the control of meaning are central.[85] The conception of knowledge is different here from that of a conventional "Baconian" account because knowledge does not exist independently of, and as a resource for, the exercise of power. Rather knowledge is itself an outcome as well as a medium of power. This is most evident in Foucauldian theorizations of power-knowledge that have been widely influential within organization studies and social science more generally.[86] Foucault approaches power as a relational and productive rather than a negative and repressive phenomenon executed in a top-down manner. Yet the gap between this and the more conventional linkage of knowledge and power may not, for present purposes, be so great. One of the key themes in Foucault's work is how bodies of knowledge create new forms of expertise—for example, in medicine, criminology, or economics —with their own vocabularies, conceptual categories, methods, and measures that serve to structure and discipline various practices—such as sexuality, prisons, and economies.

Within organization studies, an obvious example is the way that the development of scientific management created a new class of expert manager, versed in the complex techniques of time and motion studies.[87] For both workers and for traditional managers, these techniques had the character of an arcane mystery from which they were excluded and yet to which they were subject. Similarly, both within the workplace and much more widely, psychoanalytic knowledge and its accompanying techniques created a new form of 'therapeutic authority.'[88] Human experience thus became redescribed in a language that only experts could understand. So, in this general sense, access to the secret mysteries of new ways of knowing may create new elites, hierarchies, and power relations in similar ways to those of more conventional accounts.

In Foucauldian analysis, power-knowledge regimes are productive of subject positions and secrecy has a particular role, in at least two ways. First, Foucault's work emphasizes how power-knowledge creates an imperative to confession, but within special, delineated places where secrets may be spoken of: the priest's confession box or the psychologist's couch. Thus secrecy initiates not just a metaphorical architecture but a literal one in which certain rooms are devoted to the sharing of secrets and, within these rooms, certain norms of conduct (complete honesty, total confidentiality) are in play. Second, from a Foucauldian perspective secrecy might itself be seen as a kind of discourse that constructs, in disciplinary fashion, bearers of secrets who must comport themselves in a particular way, regulating and monitoring their behavior so as to keep the secret. This would be consistent with our discussion of Goffman in the previous chapter and the ways that secrecy links to the presentation of self. From this perspective we can see secrecy as organizing particular spaces, behaviors, and subjectivities.

Whether secrecy, power, and knowledge are linked via constructivist rather than realist approaches to knowledge, relational rather than possessive approaches to power, or poststructuralist rather than symbolic interactionist approaches to subjectivity and identity will inflect the issue of secrecy differently. From our point of view the important point is that no matter which approach one takes in some form or other secrecy is relevant: whenever we consider knowledge and its ramifications in organizations we must also consider that special sort of knowledge, that which is secret.

CONCLUSION: SECRECY AS ORGANIZING

From this reading of some classic works we can begin to see glimpses of how secrecy can assume significance in organization above and beyond those aspects that are commonly discussed under the informational approach concerned with strategic and dark secrecy. Secrecy is not a singular organizational phenomenon simply relevant for the organization in its relation vis-à-vis the environment, but is instead central to the inner workings of organizations and thereby shapes organizational life and experiences in various ways. Indeed, we suggest that secrecy is constitutive of the very making of organizations: creating, maintaining, and sometimes destroying groups, cliques, and managerial circles, so that, as Dalton has it, we can hardly envisage organization without envisaging secrecy. Secrecy is or may be present in everything from employee–management relations to decision making to corporate image. It is involved with power, control, resistance, and expertise. It can take place both within the formal and informal realms, and it allows bridging those two realms (e.g., as in Jackall's work, through informal secrecy the official organizational image is upheld) or can make them irreconcilable (e.g., as in Argyris's work, when informal secrecy cannot be eliminated or fully controlled through formal organization).

Secrecy can bring about, alter, and potentially break the social webs on the basis of which, and through which, organizational actions and decisions take place. The organizing of social formations through secrecy can occur vertically or horizontally, within or across functions and departments, and can do so in a designed or unplanned manner. The social formations can be in line with, alongside, or a replacement to the formal structures of the organization. Apart from creating a boundary between insiders and outsiders that is foundational to any social formation, secrecy can enhance and bring about a particular level of emotional engagement and excitement around the bonds it produces.[89] It can have a powerful lure and allure; not only does sharing secrets create dependencies among insiders, vulnerabilities, and possible exhilarations of revelation, but secrecy engenders a degree of mysteriousness around peoples, activities, and events. Not knowing something, yet being aware of its existence, can greatly capture people's attention and imagination.[90] A desire to "figure things out" can arise, which finds its release only when the puzzle is solved, and, if not solved, a perpetual tension remains in play.

Part and parcel of secrecy's role in shaping social formations and creating a mysterious aura is the construction of some kind of hierarchical differentiation. Secrecy not only organizes social relations but does so in hierarchical ways. Possessors of strategic secrets are probably considered superior to nonpossessors; but nonpossessors of dark secrets may be considered, or consider themselves, to be morally superior to possessors. It can thereby reinforce existing hierarchies or bring about new ones that can potentially subvert existing structures. Thus, secrecy can interact with the structures of an organization and specifically the formal and informal hierarchies in different ways. The classic texts point out how secrecy may spur the attribution and sense of privilege, superiority, status, exclusivity, and independence. Outsiders may regard those perceived to keep secrets to be special, while simultaneously the keeping of secrets can make insiders feel special and distinct from others. All of this is indicative of the ways in which secrecy interrelates with power.

In approaching secrecy as constitutive of organizations, namely as organizing social relations in particular ways and thereby shaping organizational behavior, relations, and actions, we can see its significance above and beyond the concealment of valuable knowledge, as is so often assumed in discussions of dark and strategic secrecy. These ways of "organizing secrecy" are important in and of themselves. But they do not exhaust what is important. To them, we must add "secrecy as organizing." This allows an understanding of the ways in which secrecy interacts with different organizational aspects that can be central to the workings, if not the very constitution, of organizations. In following this approach, less importance is placed on the kind of knowledge concealed than on the significance that the process of concealment has for organizations. However, the implication of this should not be taken to be that there are two separate domains of secrecy—the informational/functional and the organizational. It is rather that these two aspects of secrecy are always intertwined. They are conceptually distinct, in the sense that one refers to the thing being kept secret and the other to the processes of keeping the thing secret. But empirically they are always linked.

Thus Weber's insight that organizational secrecy does not exist for "purely functional" reasons does not mean that functional reasons for secrecy do not exist, but that they exist alongside and are inseparable from various other reasons (i.e., they are not "pure"). For example, military or commercial secrecy may take place for clear reasons of functional value—namely to protect valuable information—and simultaneously or only incidentally create certain social formations, hierarchies, and bring about a sense of specialness. Yet it may be—as Schein implies—that the creation of group identity is primary and the informational aspects secondary. Informational and organizational aspects may coalesce in different ways. For example, as we discuss in detail in the next chapter, organizations that habitually keep secrets for obvious functional reasons may, precisely because secrecy becomes socially habituated, keep information secret even when it has no real value. Or, to take the obverse case, the ways in which secrecy serves to create groups, networks, and cliques may be read as playing a role in the functional protection of information by making members of these social formations less likely to reveal secrets. Jackall's observation of the significance of secrecy for managerial circles, both in terms of creating bonds as well as disciplining individual members, points to this. In order to understand secrecy in its complexity it is therefore important not to discard an understanding of its informational and functional value but to locate these within the wider organizational issues we have identified. In so doing, we can also shed more light on the organizational dynamics of dark and strategic secrecy, namely why actors may engage in or disclose them.

In our discussion in this chapter, we have treated formal, informal, and public secrecy together, and it is our contention that they are intimately related. But as indicated in the previous chapter these can usefully be separated out for heuristic purposes in order to examine their operations in greater detail. Having provided both a theoretical vocabulary for studying secrecy and an appreciation of what secrecy in organizations can mean, we are ready to consider formal and informal secrecy in the next two chapters. After that, we bring the two together again to explain how the bricks and mortar of secrecy erect the organizational architecture we claim.

CHAPTER 3

Walls and Corridors
Organizing Formal Secrecy

A STUDY OF ESPIONAGE FICTION suggests that its enduring popularity is largely based upon the fact that

> to imagine becoming part of a secret organization is a compelling fantasy . . . as a particularly strong image of belonging. To belong to a clandestine organization seems to carry with it a profound involvement, a relationship to other members of the organization deeper than that characteristic of other kinds of organizations because it requires life-and-death loyalty.[1]

It is noteworthy that this account explicitly links the appeal of espionage fiction to organizational life, in what we might call the drama of the official secret. It is true that one end of the genre, exemplified by James Bond books and movies, depicts espionage in terms of action, but at the other, as in the classic novels of John le Carré, a quite different picture of the secret world is evoked. Here, the emphasis is on the meetings, power plays, moral dilemmas, and moral ambiguities within bureaucratic state agencies that are recognizable versions of our everyday experience of organizations. Yet it is secrecy that renders these stories exciting and dramatic in two different but clearly related ways. On the one hand, novels such as those of le Carré seem to offer an authentic,[2] or at least plausible, depiction of the secret intelligence world, and thus they provide readers with the vicarious thrill of experiencing what that world is like. On the other hand, central to those and many other espionage novels is betrayal, for example, by double agents, and it is this that is a primary source both of their moral charge and consequently, their dramatic appeal.

What links these two aspects of espionage fiction is not simply that they are about secrets but that they are about that primary quality of secrecy: the creation of boundaries. By giving a glimpse of the secret intelligence world espionage fiction allows the reader to cross the boundary and enter it. In depicting betrayal they show the breaking of boundaries and highlight the vulnerability inherent in the keeping of secrets, namely the possibility of their revelation. In this chapter we examine a series of interrelated ways in which the boundary of secrecy may be erected, maintained, and, on occasion, crossed and broken. Specifically, we focus on formal forms of secrecy. Secrecy is about both the concealment and sharing of information, and the boundaries or walls of formal secrecy enable a way of doing both. Their walls conceal knowledge but they also define the corridors between rooms through which secrets may legitimately pass.

What these walls and corridors share—what makes the secrecy involved "formal"—are processes to keep secrets, processes that at their most generic are rational-legal in character.[3] That immediately flags up that at least part of what is at stake is the "official secrets" of the Weberian bureaucracy, most obviously the state bureaucracy. But state secrets are not the only ones to have legal protection— corporations are also able to protect trade secrets and may be required by law to protect information. Beyond that, we are concerned with the deployment of organizational rules and regulations, whether or not enshrined within law *per se*. In Erving Goffman's terminology, we are primarily concerned with strategic secrecy. Military and intelligence cases may be seen as paradigmatic or ideal-typical—and furnish many of the examples that we use—but we argue that they bear a more or less close resemblance to analogous cases (such as commercial research and development) as well as to more everyday or commonplace situations.

We begin by outlining some of the main ways that formal secrecy operates, focusing first upon law and the configuration of secret knowledge as property, and second on regulatory processes in organizations. We then consider some of the dilemmas entailed in formal secrecy, specifically the paradox of the "need to know" principle and the possibility of culturally ingrained secrecy.

HOW FORMAL SECRETS ARE CREATED, KEPT, AND BROKEN

Let us consider the ways in which boundaries are erected around knowledge so as to render it secret. Organizations create boundaries in all sorts of ways and for all sorts of reasons, and doing so may be regarded as a generic organizational process, at least in rational-legal organizations.[4]

Boundaries are also central to secrecy. So here we are concerned with the overlap between these two: with the boundaries of rational-legal secrecy. As such, both law and regulation are relevant.

Law and Property

Writing of trade secrets, Sissela Bok points out that to use this term "is to invoke for it the protection of due property. . . . Like property, trade secrets can be bought and sold, stolen and recaptured, even lost for good."[5] The basic function of the law in this context is to render knowledge into economic property so as to acquire or keep ownership of a valued informational asset.[6]

Perhaps unsurprisingly, most of the existing organizational literature that conceives of secrecy in this formal way is concerned with ownership of technical innovations.[7] In this context organizational theorist David Teece developed the concept of "regimes of appropriability" to explain the means by which an organization may successfully keep ownership of its knowledge.[8] Legal protections are one of these methods, including laws governing trade secrets and intellectual property. Such protections do not necessarily involve secrecy, however: patents, for example, normally involve the public disclosure of the invention to be patented but place restrictions on who may freely or "properly" use them. Secret methods are therefore a subset of the legal appropriation of knowledge and include not only trade secrets but also nondisclosure and noncompete agreements.[9] They are not necessarily successful, as Teece points out: "Trade secret protection is possible . . . only if a firm can put its product before the public and still keep the underlying technology secret."[10] There can be many difficulties of enforcing the legal protection of knowledge through trade secrets.[11]

The nature and dilemmas of these areas of law are clearly the subject of an enormous literature in their own right.[12] But the question of legal technicalities is secondary to the underlying issue we are concerned with here, which is that the very concept of any attempt to protect secrets through law is predicated upon an understanding of them as something to be appropriated as property.[13] Although this is most obvious in terms of trade secrets, the same is true for strategic and financial secrets, military secrets, and the management of information privacy.[14]

It is a truism of legal and political philosophy that property is contingent upon legal definition and protection.[15] Without such definition and protection, property is entirely contingent upon coercion: the capacity simply to hold on to some asset (as might be the case in criminal gangs, for example). Configured as property, entitlement becomes a matter of legitimate rights defined, in modern societies, by rational-legal authority. This is implicit or explicit in the word *property* and the many terms cognate with it. There is a "propriety" to property; it is rightly or correctly held. One has a "title" to property because one is "entitled" to hold it. And companies holding such rights are said to produce "proprietary" products, those that may bear a particular trade name, for example. Associated with property entitlements are protections and penalties for violations. Thus, someone who discloses state secrets may be prosecuted and punished, as in the case of Chelsea Manning (then known as Bradley Manning) and the WikiLeaks disclosures in 2010. A company that misappropriates the trade secrets of another may be sued, as may an individual who violates a nondisclosure agreement. For example, the British engineering firm Dyson is currently suing the German corporation Bosch, alleging that a former Dyson engineer passed on secrets about a new form of electric motor.[16]

But the very existence of violations of secrecy points to the vulnerability of the law as a protector of secrets. Indeed, formal secrets entail a particularly *high* degree of vulnerability. Why? Precisely because of their formal character, they are typically recorded and have a tangible and therefore readily discloseable form: a document, a communiqué, a formula, a blueprint. It is not until something is rendered as property than the possibility of its theft exists. This is very obvious when we consider that some of the most potent secrets are "deniable knowledge"—the instruction being given off the record, rather than a written memorandum giving the same instruction. This is akin to Goffman's insight about the way that hinting at knowledge is an effective way in which secrets may be communicated.

From this, two things flow. One is that despite the association of formal secrecy with proper secrecy in the senses of entitlement and propriety, it is emphatically not the case that formal secrecy is to be regarded as a stronger or "more real' form of secrecy. The second issue is that precisely because of the fragilities associated with formal secrecy in its legal sense, organizations typically make use of processes other than law in order to maintain formal secrecy. After all, the availability of legal redress hardly helps once a secret has been revealed. If, for example, military secrets are leaked with consequences on the battlefield, those consequences are hardly mitigated by visiting dire punishments upon the person who has leaked the secret. It may be that such punishments act as a deterrent, but history suggests that even in societies that inflict barbaric punishments, deterrence is not total. It is true that in commercial situations financial redress for, for example, trade secrecy violations may in some way compensate for those violations. But the process is likely to be a long and costly one. The battles between Apple and Samsung over alleged patent[17] violations (the so-called smartphone wars) have raged over several years, and have entailed at least fifty separate cases in several legal jurisdictions.

Organizational Regulation

Everyone who worked at Bletchley Park (BP) had the experience of being required to sign the Official Secrets Act (OSA) and, more vividly, of receiving very stern instructions on the matter of secrecy. There are some stories, probably apocryphal, of new recruits being told, with a pistol on display, that security breaches would result in being shot! Slightly less dramatically, "We were told in no uncertain terms that this [signing the OSA] was a very important thing and we would go to the Tower if we breathed a word."[18] This may be regarded as a case of the most basic organizational process in formal secrecy—the creation of a legal barrier to disclosure outside of the organizations. But, that in itself offers only a limited protection. In addition, Bletchley Park created multiple compartments inside the organization so that different sections or subsections worked in isolation from each other and did not speak about their work outside of it. Thus, in addition to the boundary between the inside and the outside of the organizations, there were multiple internal boundaries. These boundaries were created by the two interrelated processes of ignorance and silence. Those in one compartment were ignorant of what went on in another compartment, and that was maintained by a silence of those within one compartment when interacting with those from another.

In the previous chapter, we drew attention to the spatial metaphors that characterize the way we talk about secrecy in organizations, and compartments are one way of apprehending this. But it is misleading if taken to connote a series of hermetically sealed boxes equivalent to work groups. At Bletchley Park, for example, there were a series of "concentric circles"[19] that were not identical with, although they related to, work sections;[20] thus they defined the legitimate corridors linking different compartments that needed to share secret knowledge.

The significance of the metaphor of concentric circles rather than simply compartments is that it suggests—and this was indeed the case at BP—that some people or groups were more central and others more peripheral: there was a hierarchy based not on formal rank (which at BP was often indeterminate) but upon access to secrets. The principle hierarchy in the case of BP had to do with access to the Ultra secret (meaning, primarily, the secret that Enigma ciphers were being read): "The Ultra community at BP saw itself as—perhaps was—an elite within an elite."[21] This is revealing for two reasons. First, it points to a specific way in which secrecy creates feelings of "specialness" among those in the know. Second is the notion of a conscious knowledge of and identification with a group (i.e., it *saw itself* as an elite).

Thus we can see several attributes of formal secrecy at work here. There is a legal boundary between inside and outside. There is a complex configuration of multiple insides and outsides within the organization. There is a hierarchy of access associated with status. And there is the basis of a sense of special individual and group identity based upon that status.

It may be speculated that such practices of compartmentalization and concentric circles, characterized by the twin processes of ignorance and silence, remain the case within state intelligence agencies. At all events, we know that something similar obtains within other organizations concerned with military secrets, such as the Lockheed Skunk Works. For example:

Before the government would sign a contract with me I had to submit for approval a security plan, detailing how we would tighten all the hatches of what was already one of the most secure operations in the defense industry. Hell, we already operated without windows and behind thick, eavesdrop-proof walls. We had special bank-vault conference rooms, lined with lead and steel, for very sensitive discussion about very secret matters. Still, the Air Force required me to change our entire security system, imposing the kinds of strictures and regulations that would drive us all nuts in either the short or long run. Every piece of paper dealing with the project had to be stamped top secret, indexed in a special security filing system, and locked away. . . . They imposed a strictly enforce two-man rule: no engineer or shop worker could be left alone in a room with a blueprint. If one machinist had to go to the toilet, the co-worker had to lock up the blueprint until his colleague returned.[22]

What we can see here is how the precondition of a legal obligation (the contract) was the creation of organizational procedures and practices to compartmentalize access to secrets within the organization by creating literal (and in this case lead-lined) walls. In this way, the risk of revelation is reduced because that risk arises, as Simmel notes, from the "frequency and contacts" with outsiders because these "carry with them too great temptation to disclose what might otherwise be hidden."[23] In this case too can be found the issue of prestige as "even our rivals would acknowledge that whoever ran the Skunk Works had the most prestigious job in aerospace"[24] and of group identity: "Most of us had worked together intimately under tremendous pressures for more than a quarter century. Working isolated, under rules of tight security, instilled a camaraderie probably unique in the American workplace."[25]

It should not be thought that these processes of compartmentalization are confined to military and intelligence organizations. The organization theorist Julia Liebeskind details a wide range of commercial settings in which similar or even identical practices are prevalent that she calls "structural isolation," meaning in particular spatial restrictions on access to secrets. To give just a few of the many examples she provides:

An agribusiness firm (which I will call AgriCo here) where I conducted interviews for this study operates a large commodity-trading business. On any given day, AgriCo buys and sells commodity futures contracts worth many millions of dollars. Were its trading positions revealed to outsiders, it could suffer enormous financial losses. To protect this information, AgriCo organizes all its trading activities, and stores all its trading records, within a single, large room. Almost no-one apart from the trading staff is permitted to enter this room, and the windows of this room are protected to prevent anyone from looking in from neighboring buildings. Similarly, at CloneCo [a biotechnology firm] discovery research activities are protected by a system of locked laboratories. Each research scientist has a card key that allows them access only to those laboratories where they are directly involved in research.[26]

Although spatial compartmentalization within organizations is one important way in which boundaries around secret knowledge are erected, it is by no means the only one. Indeed, it might be seen as a subset of the wider process of the compartmentalization of social interactions. As we saw in the BP case, there were prohibitions of people speaking about their work to those outside their section (for example, during social interactions at mealtimes). In this and in other cases, such as Lockheed, this prohibition extended to family members. In the commercial cases discussed by Liebeskind, some organizations had rules prohibiting or proscribing out-of-work interactions with employees of rival firms and even, in the case of CloneCo, participation in scientific projects with academic partners, despite the fact that "these collaborations are valuable to the firm, allowing it to access the knowledge of external experts. However, collaborations inevitably result in leakage of information to outsiders, despite the precision with which contracts are specified."[27]

This latter case is interesting for two reasons. First, it shows a dilemma involved in secrecy, namely the organizational price to be paid for not being able to share knowledge openly. Second, it underscores a point made earlier about the limitations of attempting to use purely legal means (in this case, the contracts) to erect boundaries around secrets. For, however tightly these are written, leakage is "inevitable." The same limitation applies to legal agreements such as nondisclosure agreements specifying that former employees will not reveal secrets to their new employers[28] and noncompete agreements between firms. However, because these cases involve extra-organizational actors, there is no possibility of using intra-organizational rules of enforcement.

In addition to control over the physical and social interactions of people in these various ways, a key regulatory mechanism in formal secrecy is control over documents (whether physical or electronic), for instance, in the form of data protection laws. For this reason formal secrets are especially vulnerable to deliberate or accidental disclosure precisely because they typically take the form of tangible records. Within military and intelligence organizations, the classification of documents on the basis of ascending hierarchies of access (e.g., "secret," "top secret") is commonplace, and the same terminology is sometimes employed within commercial settings. Access to such documents is again compartmentalized in terms of where they are and who can see them, with rules specifying their movement, or the corridors through which they may pass. In the professional service firms (PSFs) studied, this meant that consultants were prohibited from working in public spaces on client projects. In fact, in a consultancy firm one of the authors previously worked for, an anecdote spread around the firm warning consultants to carefully handle secret documents in public: a project team advising the national railway company worked on the project while riding on one of the client's own trains. By accident, secret documents concerning the sales figures of the company were left on the train and were later found by the railway staff. Understandably, this led to a major crisis in the consultant–client relationship.

Some firms routinely search employees and their cars on entry and exit. Access to electronic records is restricted to authorized users within organizations, for example, by password. Clearly the field of data security is a complex, technical, and rapidly changing one.[29] For our purposes here, the point is that this is one important means through which barriers around secret knowledge are erected and rules for its sharing enacted and, moreover, a means that is ubiquitous in nearly all organizations and occupations. Thus the noted occupational sociologist Everett Hughes explains that "most occupations rest upon some bargain about receiving, guarding, and giving out communications. The license to keep this is bargain is of the essence of many occupations." This requires "the lawyer, the policemen, the physician, the reporter, the scientist, the scholar, the diplomat, the private secretary . . . to keep secret" and secure their knowledge, be it knowledge concerning their occupation, organization, or of customers and clients.[30] The secure handling of confidential information often translates into professional ethics codes as well as organizational norms aimed to discipline people's conduct. In one of the PSFs, a consultant noted that the firm "is very good in its code of conduct and ethics and that is about treating confidential information in a very good manner and that is about how you conduct yourself . . . there is quite a well-defined code of conduct, what is understood and what your responsibility is in terms of how you behave around the office and clients." Thus, the organizational regulation of documents is not simply a technical, legal matter but can go hand in hand with formal behavioral rules (i.e., codes of conduct) aimed at disciplining members' behavior.[31]

Organizational Surveillance

So far, we have characterized formal secrecy in terms of the way that law and organizational regulation govern the spaces and nature of interactions and access to knowledge. But implicit within that is another set of organizational processes that are concerned with surveillance or monitoring. Surveillance in organizations takes multiple forms and has multiple purposes, and has been the subject of an extensive literature in recent times;[32] by no means does all, or even most, of it have to do with secrecy. More commonly, organizational surveillance has to do with workrates. It may however be that this surveillance it itself undertaken secretly. An obvious example would be the use of "mystery shoppers" to monitor staff behavior in retail environments. But, our concern here is with those forms of surveillance deployed to check for breaches of formal secrecy. Secrecy is not just about creating barriers but also about policing them on an ongoing basis, itself an organizational achievement. Thus, in the Lockheed Skunk Works

We were monitored unceasingly. Toward the end of the stealth project I had nearly forty auditors living with me inside our plant, watching every move we made on all security and contract matters. . . . I had to double my administrative staff just to keep up with all these audits.[33]

The Bletchley Park case gives many illustrations of this, including background checks on personnel, ongoing lectures on the importance of security, and elaborate surveillance of staff. Employees were instructed to respond to queries from outsiders about their work with vague answers about working in an office, or for the government, or, possibly, that they worked "in communications," and that they should not make reference to working at a place called Bletchley Park (even though at the time this name would have meant nothing to most people). Special arrangements were made for postal deliveries, telegrams, telephone calls, and rail warrants so that it would not become obvious that there was (as the years went by) a huge concentration of personnel working at this one site. Security officers traveled incognito on the buses that brought staff to and from work, listening for any "loose talk"—communication other than within and through the prescribed routes or corridors.

A particular concern was whether those living in the surrounding area might have somehow gained knowledge of what was being done at BP.[34] Thus, for example, this extract from a report from a security officer in 1941:

During the course of my investigation I have visited nearly every hotel, public house, and club in Bletchley and the surrounding districts. . . . I do not believe that any information as to the nature of the duties undertaken [at BP] has been imparted to [local residents]. The greater majority are very patriotic and [are] satisfied that whatever is done is all for the good of the country. There are some however who have a different idea and refer to the civil employees as persons who have dodged out of London, either to avoid the air raids or being called upon for military service. On the other hand there are a few people who have a shrewd idea as to what may be going on, by referring to some of the employees as Doctors of Science, Mathematicians, and Professors from various Universities who are undertaking work of great national importance. . . .[35]

The quaint language and remote historical setting may make this seem a rather untypical example. If so, consider this account of life at Proctor & Gamble, which shows a not dissimilar picture:

One brand group . . . went to lunch at a Cincinnati restaurant and discussed a commercial that was already on the air. Late that day the brand manager got a call from his boss to discuss a "security violation." He was scolded for talking about the advertisement at a public restaurant. "Security people go to restaurants because P&G is convinced that corporate spies sit around to hear our conversations," he said. "They hope that by harassing you enough, you'll comply with the rules." Some security officers do little besides ride airplanes between Cincinnati,

New York and Chicago to make sure that P&G and its advertising agency representatives do not talk shop in flight. Internal phone calls are monitored too. One former officer recalls how he was interrogated by his bosses because the phone records showed that he had returned a phone call to a Wall Street analyst.[36]

The use of security officers inside and outside the workplace is only one, and perhaps rare, form of surveillance. More ubiquitous are checks on the access of, or the attempted unauthorized accessing of, records—typically nowadays achieved through automated auditing of computer use. Technological surveillance of organizations has become increasingly sophisticated, so that "smart buildings" can monitor the whereabouts of employees throughout the day. In 2014 Hitachi announced the invention of the *Business Microscope*, which allows not just monitoring of movements but of interactions.[37] The system requires all employees in an organization to wear a digital ID badge containing devices that monitor who is talking to whom and for how long and how close they stand to each other, and includes biometric measures of how energetic the conversation is. In the context of what was said earlier about regulating both spatial movements and social interactions within organizations, this is clearly a powerful tool for policing secrecy.

Attempts to regulate social interactions can also be understood in terms of the limitations of legal means of keeping formal secrets. Liebeskind draws a distinction between forms of knowledge that are legally protectable and those that are not. She identifies as particularly unamenable to legal protection the less tangible forms of organizational knowledge that are uncodified or tacit.[38] Teece also points out that tacit knowledge of employees is much harder for rival companies to imitate than tangible product knowledge, but by the same token it is effectively impossible to give legal definition and protection to.[39] "Organizations do not 'own' the 'intellectual assets' of employees,"[40] for all that these intangible assets may be strategically crucial.

Thus far, we have presented an understanding of formal secrecy in terms of the rational-legal protection of certain knowledge deemed to be secret. We have shown that this is more complex than might be thought because it entails the erection of boundaries not just between the organization and the outside world, but a potentially quite elaborate "geometry" of compartmentalization and associated mechanisms of surveillance or policing of the boundaries. Even so, what we have explained could readily be understood within the framework of a conventional approach to secrecy as a relatively straightforward matter of the deployment of rational means to protect assets. But, as we will now see, this is not so.

BEYOND RATIONALITY:
DILEMMAS OF FORMAL SECRECY

Let us consider two related ways in which the decision to keep secrets in organizations departs from a straightforward rationality. The first is concerned with the indeterminate and paradoxical question of what to keep secret. The second is the situation in which the answer to that question encompasses everything.

The Need-to-Know Paradox

At the heart of compartmentalization is a common security principle: access to secrets must be on a need-to-know basis. The two are directly linked:

Need-to-know mentality is brought about by the organizational practice of information and secrecy compartmentalization. Compartmentalization involves compartmentalizing secrets or slicing secrets into parts so no one individual can put the secrets together to comprehend a 'bigger picture". When compartmentalized this way, many people know many different and unique slices of information.[41]

But it is perhaps obvious that this principle is highly contradictory: how is it known whether there is a need to know? Unless you already know something, you don't know whether you need to know it, but if you already know it, but don't need to know it, then it is impossible to cease to know it.

The consequence of the indeterminacy, if not outright paradox, of need-to-know is that it cannot offer the rational basis for compartmentalization that it appears to. This can be illustrated by the Bletchley Park case, where the need-to-know principle was paramount. One result was that several cases have since come to light in which groups within Bletchley Park were working on the same, or similar, problems in isolation. For example, one of the naval ciphers proved impossible to decode until a chance meeting with someone working on Army codes revealed that his group had broken the same system months before. More pungently, the head of the group working on one of the Japanese ciphers learned, not at the time, but decades later that another group had been working on a closely related cipher. The two groups were not just both based at Bletchley Park, they were based on the same corridor of the same building.[42]

This issue may be understood in terms of the dilemma of knowledge-sharing in the context of formal secrecy. Liebeskind's example of the prohibition of work with external academics at CloneCo is a related case: what might be beneficial exchanges of knowledge are rendered illicit by the rules about secrecy. She gives several other examples of similar prohibitions and their effect of stifling innovation and/or increasing coordination costs. In all of these cases a lack of knowledge-sharing may preclude learning, and may also foster costly duplication.

There is no ultimate solution to this issue in the sense of finding some optimal extent of compartmentalization versus secret-sharing. Each attempt generates a further problem. An interesting and revealing example can be found in the response of the US security agencies in the aftermath of the 2001 Twin Towers terrorist attack in New York City:

One of the essential steps in reform following the 9/11 attacks was overcoming the bureaucratic and technical hurdles to the sharing of information within the federal government. In its final report, the Commission urged abandoning the "'need-to-know' culture of information protection" in favour of a "'need-to-share' culture" that rewards information sharing. By doing this, the Commission argued, analyst and investigators would have a better chance of "connecting the dots" to anticipate impending threats.[43]

But it was the erosion of compartmentalization in order to facilitate knowledge-sharing that subsequently allowed Chelsea Manning access to the enormous volume of secret information leaked to WikiLeaks. Indeed:

somewhere between 500,000 and 600,000 military and diplomatic personnel had access to the SIPRNet system that Manning tapped. The government actually doesn't know precisely how many people overall have security clearances to access classified information.[44]

One way to think about this issue is that the compartmentalization of formal secrecy requires the erection of hard barriers around access to knowledge, that is, a definite and rigid line between those in the know and those not. But the need-to-know principle cannot deliver a hard delineation between those two groups. Understood in this way, a different and important phenomenon arises, which is that however rigidly the barriers are erected and however rigorously they are policed, they are never fully effective and may be subverted. The issue here is not that of leaking secrets, but how people find ways of working that cut across the secret barrier. For example, at Bletchley Park

it was laid down (fortunately the rule was never strictly obeyed) that Hut 3 workers were not allowed to discuss their work with Hut 6 workers, nor to have direct access to the Hut 6 Decoding Room. In practice it was always of great importance that members of Hut 3 Watch should be able to take corrupt decodes personally to the decoders, a procedure which naturally gave better results than the contacts at third-hand via official channels.[45]

The reason this is so important is that it illustrates how around the formal procedures of formal secrecy there lie informal practices. These practices are not those of informal secrecy (in fact, they are about informal disclosures of formal secrets). Rather they are examples of the kind of informal practices that attend all kinds of formal rules, whether about secrecy or anything else. It has been well described in organization studies, especially in the bureaucratic dysfunctionalism literature,[46] that despite the notion that rule-following produces optimal outcomes, in fact people make organizations work "better" by bending or flouting formal rules. This, indeed, is why when workforces "work to rule" they do so with the intention and effect of disrupting the organization. In general terms, this is about the limitations of rational-legal principles of organization. In terms of the need-to-know principle, the implication is that the informal flouting of the official boundaries of who needs to know may occur precisely because it does not offer an objective or rational basis to decide who needs to have access to secrets and who does not.

Finally, we return to another example of informal violations of formal secrets, namely the case of pay (the same could apply to other kinds of terms of employment). Pay secrecy in organizations is relatively well documented, and we discussed it in chapter 2 as an example of strategic secrecy. But it is a different kind of case than most of those discussed in this chapter, in that it is not like a trade or intelligence secret to be protected from external scrutiny (although that may also be a factor) and has more to do with internal management of the organization, as in Rosabeth Moss Kanter's classic study of Indesco.[47] Within such contexts, informal discussions of formally secret pay levels may be frequent. This was the case in our studies of PSFs in which internal competition was intense, and level of pay had a huge significance as an indicator of one's relative standing within that competition. As a result pay levels were routinely revealed on an unofficial basis. As one respondent put it: "The salary range is that deep dark secret [lowers his voice and speaks in an ironic manner], whatever it is, whatever anyone else earns, it is all supposed to be secret." What one might say about these cases is that they illustrate not just indeterminacy about the need to know but radically different conceptions of it. For the organization, only senior managers need to know about pay rates, but for individuals within the organization there is a very pressing need to know. Thus here there was not just a bending of the rules in order to "get the job done" (as in the Bletchley Park example) but a wholesale flouting of the rules for reasons completely unrelated to the work itself.

Cultures of Secrecy

A second set of reasons why we need to understand formal secrecy in a more complex way relates to its cultural nature and implications. Elsewhere we have asserted that it is inadequate to think that things are kept secret because they are valuable. Rather, things may be regarded as valuable because they are kept secret. In chapter 1, we quoted Max Weber to the effect that bureaucracies are disposed to keep secrets above and beyond purely functional reasons, or, as the noted Weberian scholar Reinhard Bendix expresses it, in the absence of "plausible reasons."[48] We have also referred to one of Simmel's fundamental insights about secrecy, namely that it has an appeal above and beyond the content of secrets themselves. In other words, it is not enough simply to consider the mechanisms of formal secrecy (compartmentalization, surveillance) as if it were self-evident why they are deployed.

Michael Herman occupies an unusual position in having been a senior practitioner in the UK's intelligence community[49] who subsequently became a leading scholar in the intelligence studies field. He points out (echoing and invoking Simmel) that the very existence of strict secrecy bestows upon intelligence practitioners a feeling of "specialness" into which newcomers are inducted through peculiar rituals, secret language, and elaborate precautions. He suggests that a deeply ingrained and life-long sense of being a member of a privileged inner circle develops.[50] The consequence of such a culture can be to make secrecy the default position so that "secrecy is often overdone; special codewords and limited distributions become departments' badges and means of protecting and extending their territory."[51] In a similar way, a study of secrecy in complex organizations notes that "the use of secrecy tends to be self-reinforcing and self-perpetuating. . . . Every bit of information is judged to be valuable and hence classified as secret."[52] In this analysis, too, what is at issue is a shift in cultural norms (expressed as a shift from norms of rationality to those of distrust).

The first aspect of such cultures is that secrecy becomes something that is either for purposes other than protecting something valuable (e.g., its purpose may be to advance departmental interests) or that is simply an end in itself, an ingrained practice so that secrecy becomes the default setting within an organization. Weber describes this tendency toward over-classification as "the transformation of official information into classified material by means of the notorious concept of the 'service secret.'"[53] Cultures of secrecy may indeed become so strong that organizations regard as secret material that is actually in the public domain.[54] More generally, secrecy may be applied even when there is little or no reason. Examples of this may be found in some of the cases we have already discussed. Thus in the Proctor & Gamble study it may be recalled that it was considered a security violation to discuss a commercial that had already been aired![55] And in the Lockheed Skunk Works project:

Keith Beswick, head of our flight test operations, designed a coffee mug for his crew with a clever logo showing the nose of Have Blue peeking from one end of a big cloud with a skunk's tail sticking out the back end. Because of the picture of the airplane's nose, security classified the mugs as top secret. Beswick and his people had to lock them away in a safe between coffee breaks.[56]

The second aspect of this is more complex. Just as things that are not valuable may be made secret, so may those things kept secret take on a disproportionate value. In terms of the logics of secrecy this is related to the *mysterium* dimension of secrecy (whereas most of what has been covered in this chapter relates to the logics of *secretus* and *arcanum*). Daniel Ellsberg recalls briefing Henry Kissinger, the former US Secretary of State, about the effects of having access to secret intelligence:

You will forget there ever was a time when you didn't have it, and you'll be aware only of the fact that you have it now and most others don't . . . and that all those other people are fools. . . . It will have become very hard for you to learn from anybody who doesn't have these clearances. Because you'll be thinking as you listen to them: "What would this man be telling me if he knew what I know?"

Elsewhere, on the same theme, he notes:

You will deal with a person who doesn't have those clearances only from the point of view of what you want him to believe and what impression you want him to go away with. . . . You'll give up trying to assess what he has to say. The danger is, you'll become something like a moron. You'll become incapable of learning from most people in the world, no matter how much experience they may have in their particular area that may be greater than yours.[57]

The US Commission on Protecting and Reducing Government Secrecy came to similar conclusions after the Twin Towers attack: "In a culture of secrecy, that which is not secret is easily disregarded or dismissed. . . . Secrecy can be a source of dangerous innocence."[58]

An interesting, almost extraordinary, twist on this can be found in the case of Bletchley Park, where the material was so secret that its recipients (e.g., military commanders) were not allowed to know its provenance. Thus, in the early days, the intelligence was sometimes not used by the military because they did not realize that it *was* intelligence and they therefore discounted its value. A fiction was invented that it came not from the decoding of signals but from a human agent (given the code name "Boniface") in order to reassure recipients that this was indeed secret intelligence and so should be taken seriously, while concealing the deeper secret of the breaking of Enigma.[59]

This idea, that what is kept secret must be inherently more important than what is not kept secret, is one that has been widely reported in politicians' memoirs when they recall the effect of being admitted to intelligence secrets. As Michael Herman puts it, in ways that in part echo Ellsberg: "Its [intelligence's] position with government rests on its special source; the authority of 'if you knew what I know'. The thrill of secret knowledge makes Ministers read intelligence in their evening boxes,[60] even if they leave more mundane items to the next morning. If intelligence has any single, defining characteristic in the eyes of governments and publics it is this secrecy and the mystique it attracts."[61]

The mystique of secret intelligence resonates with the more general cultural charge of espionage, but it also relates to the idea we discussed in previous chapters that secrets seems to have a special epistemological and ontological status; that somehow they contain a truth that is "more real," "more true," or at least "more complete" than non-secret knowledge. This accounts in part for the enduring appeal of conspiracy theories.[62] We noted in chapter 1 that these are partly explicable in terms of a kind of paranoia about secrecy and power elites, but they also relate to—and require—the idea that the real truth of certain events is secret.

It might perhaps be thought that though the mystique of secrecy may be very strong for state intelligence, it is much less so for the more routine secrets of ordinary organizational life. That is intuitively true. It is hard to imagine much of a thrill being gained from access to company records on customers and employees. Or is it? Which of us, left alone in an office and seeing a file marked "Secret" and/or bearing our name or that of a colleague would not be tempted to look inside? It has become increasingly popular for people to pay to access their credit rating records, and at least part of the impetus must be to discover what information is held about us. In any case, it is not simply intelligence agencies that may fall prey to cultures of secrecy. For example, In Britain, the National Health Service has been repeatedly criticized for exactly this,[63] and, following recent scandals, has been called on by politicians to develop a new culture of openness.[64]

The idea that secrecy in itself bestows value can have one particular and at first sight perverse effect that is encapsulated in the adage, if you want to hide something put it where everyone can see it. In other words, precisely because people think that what is secret must be valuable, they will ignore the value of that which is, apparently, not secret. An example comes from the Skunk Works project:

Only five of us were cleared for top secret and above, and over the years we had worked on tremendously sensitive projects without ever suffering a leak or any known losses to espionage. In fact, Kelly evolved his own unorthodox security methods, which worked beautifully in the early days of the 1950s. We never stamped a security classification of any paperwork. That way, nobody was curious to read it.[65]

So, in summary, one part of what we have to understand about formal secrecy above and beyond the way that barriers are erected around knowledge is the indeterminacy of what needs to be kept secret, and the possibility of a default response that everything needs to be kept secret. As a final example of this we return to Bletchley Park. Once the secret of its work became public, former employees were released from their obligation of silence. Yet many maintained it, so ingrained was the habit. Particularly delicious are those cases where spouses both worked there but never told each other:

My husband John and I had been married for 30 years or more when one spring we visited a stately home. . . . The magnolia trees were in full bloom. John said, "there were two such lovely magnolias where I was stationed for a time during the war". "Oh" said I, "I knew two such trees too—beside a lake". "Really," said John—same lake, same magnolias at Bletchley Park. In all those years we had kept the secret from one another!![66]

CONCLUSION

At the heart of formal secrecy in organizations lies an inflection of a more generic organizational process: compartmentalization. But it is compartmentalization of a specific sort, namely around secrets. And these are secrets of a particular sort: those legitimately held in a rational-legal way. What we have sought to explain is how this creates a kind of organizational geometry in which lines between compartments—whether thought of as boxes or concentric circles—run through, across, and around organizations. We can think of these compartments as creating walls of varying opacity within organizations, but as with all walls these delineate rooms and also the corridors between them. Formal secrecy both erects barriers around secret knowledge but also proscribes the connections between people and groups in organizations by specifying the terms under which secrets may be shared and with whom.

Formal secrecy is not, therefore, a binary line between the inside and outside of an organization, with secrets held by those within and concealed from those outside. That is just the most basic part of it. In addition, laws and organizational regulations governing, for example, access to data, physical access to facilities, or interactions with and disclosures to other people are central processes. Together, at least in complex organizational settings, these rational-legal processes create a kind of spider's web of demarcations around secrets and between people who may have access to these secrets. The content of these secrets will, of course, encompass a very wide variety of things—we have given examples ranging from signals intelligence secrets at Bletchley Park, the Stealth Fighter project at Lockheed, pay rates in professional services firms to innovations in biotechnology firms. But, as explained in the introduction, these things, though for many purposes interesting and important in themselves, are not our primary focus, which is to understand the underlying features of the secrecy process that maintains or seeks to maintain them as secrets.

We have further argued that this formal secrecy, for all that it may be understood simply as a rational way to protect valuable knowledge, is by no means the clear-cut, rational process that might be expected in this understanding. In particular, we have pointed out the central paradox entailed in the creation of secret compartments within organizations: that it relies upon a need-to-know principle that is essentially indeterminate. Moreover, or perhaps as a special case of that general issue, organizations may come to adopt a posture of indiscriminate secrecy so that everything, no matter how trivial, is treated as secret. One consequence of this may be to regard what is secret (and, at the extreme, only what is secret) as inherently valuable simply because it *is* secret.

This possibility links directly to the many ways in which secrecy may be seductive. One version of this is to regard what is secret as being more true than other forms of knowledge—the "proof" being that someone thinks it is worth keeping secret. A slightly different version, which we again disavow, is that the formal secrecy discussed in this chapter is real secrecy or proper secrecy or more secret than the kinds of informal secrecy discussed in the next chapter. This is precisely to fall prey to the *mysterium* of the official secret, and it is an error not least because formal secrecy is in some ways much more vulnerable to disclosure because it typically involves tangible records that may be accidentally lost or deliberately revealed.

Finally, it is important to note another facet of formal secrecy. We have referred to the temptations to hint at or reveal secrets and to the risks of accidental disclosure, but beyond all that is the issue with which we started the chapter: the drama of espionage. Here what is at stake is deliberate disclosure, typically for reasons of ideology or financial gain or, in the case of whistleblowing, for ethical reasons. It is this possibility that accounts for precisely the processes of formal secrecy in organizations that we have been considering in this chapter. It suggests that the key way that secrecy is experienced is as fear and vulnerability. One might regard formal secrecy as a way that organizations seek to institutionalize a response to this fear. At its heart lies the paradox that, in doing so, they generate further fear, with each secret document and database creating a new vulnerability; each new precaution creating the possibility of a new kind of betrayal; each new rule creating the possibility of a new infringement.

CHAPTER 4

Open and Closed Doors

Organizing Informal and Public Secrecy

DOORS PLAY AN IMPORTANT ROLE in social imaginations and expressions of secrecy. A door constitutes a threshold: a point of entry into
the inside, of exit to the outside, and a barrier between the two. A door
can be open, closed, locked, made out of opaque, unbreakable material,
such as iron and steel, or out of glass and thus be transparent. But what
and who is behind the door? Who has the key to open it and grant one
access to the inside? How is the door closed when exiting the inside—
locked, left open for others to get a glimpse of the inside, or slammed? In
one scene in Franz Kafka's *The Trial*, a priest tells Josef K. about a man
who seeks to enter the interior of the law but a door keeper does not grant
him access. Until his end the man awaits entry yet is not allowed to pass
through the door. This parable "Before the Law" leads to interesting questions about myth, authority, and secrecy. Is the law kept hidden except to
initiates? Or is the man not allowed in so that he keeps believing in the
myth of a functioning and all too powerful system of law that does not
actually exist? Is the door to the law open as the law is empty, without
content?[1] It also highlights the role of the door in secrecy. Through the
door one becomes enrolled into secrecy or excluded from it, its existence
marking the transition between secret and non-secret worlds. Doors are
points of passage through which one must pass to be admitted to secrets
or through which secrets may leak or be seen: they connect the inside and
the outside of secrecy.

As with the walls of secrecy discussed in the previous chapter, its doors
are not just metaphorical but may be literal. One office building in the
public service firm (PSF) studies was characterized by both an absence and
an abundance of doors: to enter the building a key card was necessary that
was granted only to organizational members or had to be picked up by a
member. Once inside there was a labyrinth of dark hallways, stairways,
and elevators along with more doors that needed individually granted key

cards. Although the consultants worked in large open-plan, "doorless" offices, the managers and partners worked in individual offices of different sizes: the more senior ones had offices with wooden doors and walls, the less senior ones offices with glass doors and walls.[2] Meetings took place in enclosed spaces without any natural light or in smaller rooms next to the open-place offices where anybody walking by could look inside. The distribution of offices and the possession of keys to open and close doors symbolized not only a person's position in the hierarchy[3] but also her or his access to secrets. This recalls Elias Canetti's observation of how power manifests itself through "keeping the key" to secrets;[4] we return to keys and locks in the next chapter.

When thinking of secrets in such organizations as professional service firms, formal secrecy relating to client confidentiality might be the first thing to come to mind. Indeed, before being allowed to pass the entry barriers into the organizational inside, every consultant and also researcher had to sign a confidentiality agreement aiming to protect information concerning clients and the firm itself. But alongside such formal secrecy, there were webs of informal and public secrecy that reinforced and at times undermined it.

This chapter discusses the significance of informal and public secrecy for organizations by outlining how they operate, shape, and are experienced in organizational life. We begin by focusing on informal secrecy, pointing to its wide-ranging nature and core characteristics, such as informal enrolment, trust, and normative control. Then we turn to public secrecy, its mode of functioning and prevalence in organizations. In the final part of the chapter we discuss how there can be organizational cultures of secrecies—pluralized to denote the multiple forms of secrecy that might be in play.

INFORMAL SECRECY

Compared to formal secrecy, informal secrecy constitutes a more fluid, adaptable, and indeterminate phenomenon. Intentional concealment takes place in unofficial and largely unwritten ways and is not subject to formal rules and laws. Such secrets cannot be subject to appropriation in the form of legal property rights. To use the metaphor of the door, in the case of formal secrecy the door between the inside and outside is more clearly demarcated; in order to be let inside one has to sign in with the doorkeeper or security guard. In the case of informal secrecy, the door can take all sorts of shapes and sizes: from a revolving door with continual flows moving in and out, a sliding door through which different people are let into different sections of the inside, to the sealed door that remains entirely hidden from the outside. At one end of the spectrum, informal secrecy can be of casual nature: the sharing and breaching of secrets takes place at a high rate, membership is not carefully selected, and the secret may even be created with the very intention of it being spread to outsiders. An example of such casual informal secrecy is confidential gossip.[5] At the other end of the spectrum, informal secrecy is shared by a close group of individuals, membership is highly restricted, and rituals mark group life. Such situations are often described as "a firm within a firm" [6] in which a tightly knit group secretively controls and possibly even subverts an organization. Nevertheless, despite this variety, we can identify some common facets that they share.

How Informal Secrets Are Created, Kept, and Broken

Informal secrecy takes place when the actors involved are aware of the need to conceal certain information and thus differentiate between the insiders and outsiders who may be privy to or excluded from it. In the case of formal secrecy, the explicit enrolment of, for example, signing an official document ensures this awareness; in the case of informal secrecy the person introducing a new member to the secret expresses what, how, and in front of whom the information is supposed to remain concealed. Socialization takes place informally through secrecy-sharing moves between the insider and new member.[7] In the interactions with the consultants at the professional service firms, informal secrecy was shared in explicit and implicit ways through the use of expressions, such as "That is off the record" and "Let me close the door [before answering this question]." In some instances when consultants shared sensitive information, such as their plans to leave the company, they literally closed the door of the meeting room, lowered their voices, and looked around through one of the glass doors to check whether someone else could see and hear them. These may not necessarily have simply been precautions against being overhead. They can also be seen as secrecy-sharing moves designed to signal that the information about to be communicated was supposed to be kept "on the quiet." Sometimes they gave indication of who the outsider is supposed to be. In one meeting with internal human resource managers at one firm, the managers joked that they would report what was said during the meeting to "John—the CEO—afterward, obviously," identifying him as an outsider.

Membership initiation may be accompanied by ritualistic practices, such as giving a promise or participating in social or sporting events. At the PSFs, the latter events were important vehicles for initiating membership to the firms' leadership team and their secrets. These rituals and secrecy-sharing moves function as potent markers of the boundary between being and not being in the know. The sharing of formal secrets might also involve such informal rituals. Apart from ensuring awareness about the need to engage in secrecy, such rituals, especially promises, create an emotional and moral burden to the extent that by swearing to them one's personal integrity and sincerity are defined in terms of one's ability to hold and not disclose the secret. For informal secrecy, ritualistic forms of initiating membership take on a particular importance as, in contrast to formal secrecy, they lack the legal protection of secrets and hence legal sanctioning following any breach of contract. Typically informal secrecy takes place within verbal communication; this is part of what constitutes its informality, in contrast to the recording of formal secrecy. It is true that in organizations other media, such as email and texting, may be used; when this happens, as with formal secrecy, it creates vulnerabilities. It is increasingly understood that such communications may come to light causing embarrassment or even scandal and do not constitute private and untraceable communication.[8] This is well illustrated by the 2015 high-profile case in the United States of the hacking of Sony Pictures' emails revealing jokes and insults about movie stars and others.[9] Recording an informal secret to some degree formalizes it, especially if an email account is that of an organization, making it subject to organizational and possibly legal rules.

Membership of informal secrecy groups is achieved by personal selection rather than granted in accordance with some formal rules, for example, clearance levels that correspond to hierarchy. However, there may be systematic membership criteria for the in-group, for example, belonging to a certain social class[10] or relating to gender[11] and race. The sharing of a common experience can provide the basis for informal secrecy between individuals. For example, with the introduction in most countries of restrictions on workplace smoking, smokers' huddles could be sites for informal sharing of information, including secrets.[12] Individuals with invisible stigmas, such as homosexuals in heterosexually dominated cultures, are more likely to share their secret with others who seem either sympathetic toward them or in a similar position.[13] Indeed the sharing of informal secrets can occur in the form of a mutual exchange of secrets; in this way, both parties are vulnerable and need to trust each other. Moreover, membership initiation might be unintentional. A secret might be revealed by accident to another so that the interactional secrecy-sharing move takes place only after the information has already been passed on. This is a common experience in daily organizational life—some information is passed and only afterward is an injunction to treat it as confidential is given (signaled verbally by re-marks such as "That's not to be repeated, by the way"). Informal secrecy networks are also likely to transcend organizational boundaries and carry over into personal friendships conducted outside working hours.

Informal secrecy typically requires some level of trust—what Georg Simmel calls, with telling emphasis, "reciprocal *confidence*."[14] At the most generic level, trust entails having the confidence to confide in another.[15] In the context of secrecy the word *confidence* takes on a literal meaning because secrecy is concerned with the confidential holding of information. Members may test outsiders to assess whether they are sufficiently trust-worthy to gain access to informal secrets. At one PSF, in the first meeting with a partner and director the researcher was asked to disclose the name of the other firm she was studying. The researcher refrained from giving the name, pointing to the confidentiality agreement she had signed with the other firm and the fact that she had "given them her word" not to dis-close the firm's identity. That a competing company provided her access and that she kept her word helped to signal her trustworthiness.

Although trust may foster secrecy, secrecy can also reinforce trust by the ways in which insiders rely on each other to keep up a continuous concealment. Given the absence of legal enforcement, informal secrecy is much more heavily dependent upon trust as its primary regulatory mechanism than formal secrecy, in the same way that trust is more generally central to control in informal contexts.[16] Related to this are the socially negotiated informal norms, beliefs, morals, or conventions that regulate informal secrecy—that is, normative forms of control[17] that indirectly attempt to shape individuals' behavior, outlook, and experience. As Simmel notes, secrecy has a "disciplinary influence" on those who are party to it.[18]

Let us take the example of the frontstage and backstage self that professionalism is based on and regulates through normative control. In the previous chapter we mentioned that professionalism is particularly important for dealing with clients' formal secrets. It signals trustworthiness, being in control of oneself and thus the client's confidential information; additionally, in formal terms it ensures legal compliance. Yet its disciplinary effects can also ensure that, say, individuals' gossip about difficult clients, which consultants often shared during cigarette and coffee breaks, is kept confidential.[19] Thus, normative control can intersect with and regulate both formal and informal secrecy. A key way in which this control is exercised is through exclusion and inclusion mechanisms.[20] The threat of exclusion serves the exercise of norm regulation, making individuals more likely to adhere to the rules of secrecy. At the PSFs, an important criterion for membership and promotion in organizations, particularly to leadership levels, consisted of one's ability to display a professional self[21] and therefore to engage in informal secrecy in front of clients. For example, jokes that could be made within the firms would not be permissible if clients were present. Those who demonstrated themselves to be unreliable by flouting such norms would quickly find themselves excluded from the promotion race and possibly from continued employment. Even without such explicit penalties, individuals seen as untrustworthy will soon be excluded from confidential conversations.

The revelation of informally held secrets can vary considerably depending on how extended or restricted they are, and this has very much to do with context and the nature of relations. Although normative control can have strong disciplinary effects on members, the fluid and indeterminate nature of informal secrecy can make it prone to accidental revelations. This points to the inherent dilemma of informal secrecy: it is as easily revealed as it is shared. It would be easy for an informal secret to slip out by mentioning it to the wrong person. Because membership is not officially recorded, it is much less clear who the outsiders are and what information needs to be kept secret. Sanctions such as social exclusion, discrimination, ridicule, criticism, or inducement of shame can follow the breach of informal secrecy. Yet it can also be the case that informal secrets are *expected* to be passed on. It is commonplace for gossip to be passed on in confidence without any real expectation that this injunction will be respected. Rather, the expectation is that it will not be passed to "inappropriate" people (for example, the person who is the subject of gossip). The betrayal of an informal secret may therefore not be so much a matter of telling outsiders but of telling the wrong sort of insiders. Here we see very clearly the role of secrecy in creating in- and out-groups, so that betrayal comes not from telling the secret but from telling it to someone who is not in the in-group, namely to outsider insiders. This is the topic of the next section.

Informal Secrecy:
Organizing Social Relations, Groups, and Cliques

Any kind of information can be subject to informal secrecy. Some of it may appear trivial, for instance, confidential gossip about an organizational member's love life outside of work. But the information concerning the leadership's future strategy might be so strategically important that it cannot even be written down because the very codification creates vulnerabilities. Does this mean that the latter kind of informal secrecy is to be treated as more organizationally important than the former?

Our answer is no. There is nothing inherent to one piece of information that makes it more or less relevant to an organization and its members; its specific relevance results from the organizational context it takes place in. Let us take the example of informal secrecy about an organizational member's love life. In the celebrated American television series *The Sopranos*, the boss of the New Jersey-based mafia clan, Corrado "Junior" Soprano, seeks to keep his sexual interests, namely that he enjoys giving oral sex to his female partner, hidden. As he explains in one scene, such secrecy is necessary because, if revealed, this information would undermine his authority in the clan and induce a sense of shame (as happened in the series). This shows that although the information itself seems trivial, this might not be the case for the person keeping it secret as well as for his or her relationship to others in the organization.[22] Seemingly minor pieces of gossip might become very significant and damaging, as has been recognized in practitioner literature on leadership.[23] The scandal around the informally secret extramarital affair of the former Director of the US's Central Intelligence Agency, David Petraeus, provides a potent illustration of this. In itself, having an affair might not be regarded as a matter of great importance within an organization, but in this context it was regarded as a possible (formal) security threat because an outsider might have gained access to the secret inner circles of power.

Whatever its content may be, we focus here on the way that informal secrecy organizes social relations, that is, shapes, undermines, or reinforces them. Informal secrecy contributes to the formation, maintenance, and/ or splitting of cliques, networks, or in-groups between and within organizational units. For example, Melville Dalton describes the significance of cliques:

From the cafeteria to the showers they meet and gossip about their home departments and their dissatisfactions. . . . This relatively aimless association is important in plant affairs. As small unattached gossip groups moving freely around the firm, these cliques are both a point of leaks from the functional groups as well as a source of information for them.[24]

As this quote implies, such effects may be in line with or may cut across the formal organizational structure. In his study of *Organizational Culture and Identity*, the organizational sociologist Martin Parker shows how informal secrecy structures relations between organizational departments at one company he studied. Here the finance department was seen "as a powerful and secretive department," in which people "are keeping their area as an empire and they want to keep it as a secret."[25]

Informal secrecy can take place vertically, producing and reinforcing hierarchical differences. At one of the PSFs the leadership team was seen as secretive. They shared little information "about where the company is going to in the future," "hid behind emails," and made decisions "in a room somewhere," unknown and inaccessible to the consultants. For the members of the leadership team, such secrecy served to create a degree of bonding:

The more senior you are, it becomes an even more strong group that you want to be part of, the whole leadership group and so there are very strict rules. There is a certain brotherhood, certain rules that you have to buy into in order to be part of it. . . . [The rules are of] not really speaking the absolute truth.

Being a member of the leadership meant that one knew the "truth" but concealed it in front of others. Sharing this "truth" created a "brotherhood" and clearly separated the leadership from others. Note the powerful symbolism of the language here: apart from highlighting the ways in which secrecy can have gender implications ("*brother*hood"),[26] the quote could very well come from Simmel's study of secret societies!

Moreover, there was a team responsible for the leadership's communication, managing "who should say what to whom and when" and hence also what should *not* be talked about. As Canetti notes, the handling of communication, especially being "sparing of words" can be a powerful way to create hierarchy.[27] Consultants realized that the leadership's communication was managed and concealed more than it revealed; while flooded with emails on "things that do not matter," they recognized that "where the company is going . . . nobody is telling [us] that." In this way informal secrecy—the sharing of information with some but not others—was a potent way in which hierarchy was enacted within the firm.

Informal secrecy of groups can manifest itself in their various practices, decision-making processes, and meetings.[28] Within the PSF just mentioned the internal "round table" review meetings at which the leadership decided upon the performance of the consultants and their career advancement was officially depicted as "an open forum" but took place in a "closed room." This led to different organizational myths and rumors,[29] such as speculations that consultants are "force ranked" (i.e., that their performance is ranked in a preset distribution): "I have heard that they force rank people in teams into rating levels . . . but we were never told the full story." Whether an outsider received confidential information about such meetings depended on their ties to those attending the meeting. This meant that one had to be part of a leader's clique. This illustrates how informal secrecy can be closely associated with the very widely explored organizational phenomena of networking and social capital that we saw in Dalton's discussion of cliques.[30] It was of great importance for the consultants to be part of the "right networks," that is, the networks that included influential senior managers and mentors.[31] In this way, the consultants received firsthand information about upcoming project roles and career opportunities and could hope that the leader of the clique would engage in confidential conversations with others prior to official meetings so as to build coalitions around promoting them.

This shows how the mechanisms of social exclusion and inclusion entail power effects. Not being part of the circle of those inducted into secrecy, though knowing that it exists (it is manifest not latent secrecy), can make individuals look up to those who are in the know, create a sense of dependency, and also cause them to ask themselves what they have to do in order to be part of this circle. Informal secrecy can make manifest social distinctions not only in hierarchy levels but also sphere of influence and favoritism in organizations. Here we can see how informal secrecy greatly intersects with decision-making processes, coalition building, and other forms of politicking endemic within organizations.[32] One common practice is discussed by Robert Michels in relation to political parties. He notes that prior to official meetings and debates, people often "discuss *en petit comité* questions of the greatest importance" so that outsiders are confronted with "accomplished facts."[33] Such premeetings are a familiar part of organizational life, as is the tactic, when a contentious issue arises within a meeting, of deciding to continue the discussion "offline." In his study of a telecommunications firm, Steve Feldman describes how organizational actors may purposefully conceal information as to influence how people make sense of a certain situation and thus the kinds of decisions they make.[34] Such agenda-control tactics have long been recognized as a part of "non-decisional" power[35] and are a form of information control common within organizational politics, along with use of the filters of "confidential" and "restricted."[36] This latter tactic is illustrated by Andrew Pettigrew's study of computer programmers in which, in the absence of written records, programmers used their secret knowledge to advance their group interests as a form of knowledge-hiding.[37]

At the same time, there are many barriers to employees' informal secrecy. High levels of competition and surveillance may counteract it, whether as an intentional or unintentional outcome of management practices. In particular, competition (e.g., for promotion) can undermine the development of the trust necessary for the sharing of informal secrets. That surveillance can act as a counteracting force to secrecy is apparent in the case of the PSF offices. Their open-plan design and glass walls made the informal exchanges necessary for the sharing of secrets difficult because individuals felt surveilled: "[it is like] there is . . . a magnetoscope," as one put it. Indeed, the offices were "deadly silent." As we stressed in chapter 1, at the core of secrecy is the concealment and also the *sharing* of information. Thus the absence of communication—"deadly silence"—does not provide a fruitful basis for informal secrecy. Yet it may also displace the activity of informal secrecy so that if, as in this case, the office is heavily surveilled it may move to nonwork spaces such as after-work socializing. But here, too, matters are complex, because within the PSFs such socializing was also often under surveillance. Often these were company events held in the presence of the leadership, making it more difficult for the employees to engage in informal secrecy.[38] Here the role of alcohol that the companies typically sponsored is interesting. In line with the saying *in vino veritas*, such drinking sessions encouraged the consultants to open up and perhaps "confide" in the leadership, but to do so in ways that, for successful employees at least, needed to be controlled and "appropriate."

In another of the PSFs, new trainees were sent early on in their corporate lives to a residential course in which heavy drinking was the norm and it was understood by all that this was a semi-official way of promoting socialization into the inner workings of the firm. Indeed the research suggested that they were a key moment in the formation of knowledge about the firm.[39] Again these were to an extent, backstage interactions, but they did have some degree of sanction, and in that sense were managed albeit still informal. In other cases there were backstage spaces where the sharing of informal secrecy among consultants took place in ways invisible to and even resistant to management, sometimes at the same events with a further backstage so that semi-official interactions were accompanied by unofficial ones in other parts of the venue. One might regard this complex shifting of informal secrecy from the surveilled workplace to the second backstage behind the nonwork backstage as a way to regain a sense of autonomy in much the same way as with Erving Goffman's findings in total institutions. Indeed, Sissela Bok describes how secrecy can constitute a "safety valve . . . in the midst of communal life"[40]—something that can be particularly important for employees in disciplinary environments because informal secrecy allows them to uphold a second world in which they feel in control and perhaps more authentically themselves in contrast to the first world in which they are being controlled. For instance, employees would frequently hide their future plans to leave the company in front of management:[41] "If my boss asked me: . . . 'Do you want to get to the top of this organization?' Then I would say: 'Yes,' but I might tell him the truth." Such informal secrecy, which the employees shared with each other and with the researcher, allowed them to present themselves in a positive light in front of their superiors. Yet it also fulfilled the function of distancing themselves from the disciplinary nature of the work by developing "some selfhood and personal autonomy beyond the grasp of the organization."[42]

Informal secrecy can also fulfill a different purpose: it can serve to hide aspects of oneself that one is ashamed about, such as invisible stigmas. This is an attempt to use secrecy to integrate oneself into a group rather than as a tactic to separate oneself from it. One manager of a PSF remarked on the need to conceal that he is medicated for his "compulsive sleeping disorder" because he felt "embarrassed about this condition." He would share it only with people with whom he has moved "beyond the professional relationship" and thus felt he could trust. Such secrecy can be highly important in the context of leadership that is often predicated upon physical performance, and thus illness or other physical problems may dramatically affect the aura and authority of leaders.[43] A related example is that in some workplaces women keep secret the early stages of pregnancy for fear of discrimination or adverse comment.[44]

Because informal secrecy can operate as a form of resistance, it may serve to significantly subvert the formal hierarchy and rules. This can explain why it is often associated with the illegitimate and unethical and, from the management's point of view, be approached as an organizational threat to be countered through surveillance. In his study *Managing the Shopfloor*, David Collinson refers to how the "hidden economy of the shopfloor," that is, the appropriation of production, may be informally shared among workers and create a bonding in opposition to management.[45] At one PSF, one analyst group particularly engaged in informal secrecy. The members of this group "talk[ed] about everything," including the evaluations and remuneration the firm gave them. This sharing led to the creation of a tight in-group that subverted the firm's formal pay secrecy. The group's informal secrecy was against the interest of the leadership, because the latter sought to maintain a fog of informal secrecy around itself and its decisions at the review meetings: "There is this senior manager who said that you guys know each other far too much and you talk to each other too much." Indeed, the analyst group's close bonding made them appear as "a collective voice" rather than as individuals competing with each other, which was the dominant ethos of the firm. So informal secrecy among employees can bring about and/or contribute to a bonding that provides a basis to subvert and oppose formal rules. It can even, as noted in chapter 2, be the basis of overt industrial action, such as secretly organized wildcat strikes.

PUBLIC SECRECY

Public secrecy constitutes a more complicated and subtle sort of informal secrecy. To use the metaphor of the door again, similarly to informal secrecy, public secrecy does not entail an official doorkeeper who defines and regulates access to the inside and where one has to sign in. However, in contrast to the different sizes and shapes of informal secrecy's doors, here the door is necessarily open and transparent, that is, everybody can potentially see and pass through it. This open yet simultaneously barred access captures public secrecy's ambiguous, even paradoxical, nature: something is generally known but cannot be acknowledged.[46] Public secrecy entails an inherent tension of knowing and not-knowing.[47]

By way of illustration, consider the example of Chelsea Manning's WikiLeaks disclosures. In one way these are an example of the revelation of formal (state) secrets. Yet the disclosure of diplomatic cables by WikiLeaks showed that widely shared and understood "truths" about international relations must nevertheless not be openly said even to those perfectly well aware of them. US diplomats were not allowed to publicly speak about the cables because this would have confirmed their existence. In public discussions of WikiLeaks involving US officials, "everyone knew" that WikiLeaks had disclosed cables stemming from the US State Department, yet US officials could not articulate this. More generally, it was striking that many of the WikiLeaks disclosures, for example, about US officials' attitudes to various governments, only confirmed what "we all knew": "The only surprising thing about the WikiLeaks revelations is that they contain no surprises," as the contemporary philosopher Slavoj Žižek commented.[48] Much of the information leaking out (e.g., concerning the Iraq war, Russian corruption, or Arabian disapproval of the Iranian regime) had been part of public knowledge, though without being clearly stated and revealed. Yet the fact that these things were in some sense known does not undermine the way that their not being *stated* was a matter of very high value—as shown by the furious reaction of the US authorities to the disclosures. This points to the way that public secrecy was in play. Indeed, diplomacy in international relations can be considered a prime example of such secrecy as tact, the keeping up of an image, and the management of situations overridden with contradictions are particularly important.[49] But how are public secrets created, kept, and broken in organizations and how do they shape organizational life?

How Public Secrets Are Created, Kept, and Broken

Public secrecy is a form of informal secrecy but is distinctive in not being articulated or revealed. There is not an explicit sharing of information or a definable moment of informal enrollment. Rather, public secrets need to be "picked up" through interactions within a process of socialization. To be a member means to be aware that there exists this transparent open door that creates a fine line between the inside and outside, marked by rules concerning what can be articulated and expressed and what cannot. One way in which actors become aware of public secrecy is through observing others, noting what is openly said and what is left unspoken, even though the members of the social situation are aware of it. There might also be what Goffman terms "hinted communication," through which an in-group member gives the outsider more or less subtle indications as to what can be said and what not. For instance, in *The Corporate Closet*, James Woods describes how homosexuals in heterosexually dominated organizations may "want others to be aware of their sexuality . . . but strike a low profile." Making others aware yet not having to openly speak about one's sexual orientation is achieved by "making suggestive remarks, encouraging their peers to read between the lines."[50] The result is some kind of "counterfeit secrecy"[51] or what we term "public secrecy":

[There is] an arrangement in which others know that an individual is gay, but collude in the mutual pretense that they do not. In these situations, both parties to an interaction know a secret but maintain the outward appearance that they are unaware of it.[52]

At the PSFs individuals repeatedly referred to "unspoken rules," and one of them noted that "the whole definition of right and wrong [came] from the unspoken." This absent-present web of rules and definitions had to be discovered by the consultants when joining the firms—something that they often struggled with: having no "guidance [on] how to act . . . what to expect and what people expect from you" was difficult. Failing to grasp the existing yet not openly spoken about expectations made one consultant feel "blind." In some cases in which consultants failed to pick up some of these rules, a close colleague pulled them aside and explained to them what they can say and do and what not. In another of the PSFs, an employee who was dismissed was puzzled because her appraisals had consistently shown her performance to be "satisfactory."[53] Yet it was a public secret, which she had not picked up, that within the firm's culture "satisfactory" really meant "not good enough." Such a failure to be aware of secrecy at work is not an artefact of concealment—that is, it was not that she had been deliberately excluded—but instead a reflection of the haziness of public secrecy with its twin features of knowing and not-knowing.

This haziness means that public secrets are not owned as a possession but are shared, though in an unstated manner, by virtue of membership of a community and to some extent define what full membership of that community consists of. Public secrecy is therefore not restricted—that is central to its status as being public. Certainly it will be of interest only to particular groups, but within those groups knowledge is in principle extended across the group as a whole. There is no restriction to a privileged, need-to-know segment of the organization, nor could there be because the secret is unspoken. The only way in which public secrets can be protected is by silence or, more precisely, the "conspiracy of silence" that Eviatar Zerubavel refers to, because every member of a group in a particular situation needs to ignore a certain issue. This involves a meta-secrecy in that part of the secret is the knowledge that this silence is expected. As is the case for the other forms of secrecy, actors' reflexivity—that is, their knowledge of and ability to control themselves and specifically their images in interaction—is necessary, and this is achieved through the exercise of normative control.[54]

One way in which such controlled appearances of silence take place is through "looking the other way" and "turning a blind eye,"[55] whereby the very act of "turning" signals that one is not actually blind (unlike the employee mentioned earlier who failed to understand the workings of public secrecy) but aware of what not to know, see, and talk about.[56] At one PSF, there was an "open secret that nobody follows the time directive" and that the practice of "ghosting," the underreporting of working hours, was widespread.[57] As one HR manager noted: "I know and that is so well known. The policy is that you have to record the hours you are working. But I know that the practice is different.". When she checked up on consultants' reporting of hours, everybody knew that the reports were not correct: "They would not want the eye-contact with me . . . [and] I just say 'that file looks good' [but] . . . I don't believe that." Through not looking at the other and simply passing the files, public secrecy about the ghosting of working hours was taking place between the consultants and HR managers.

Because the public secret is shared in an extended way, its betrayal does not consist of revealing it to those who should not know it, but by speaking of it to those who already know it. If consultants told the HR manager that the project manager expected them to "ghost" hours, the HR manager would have to treat this as "a sackable offense"—something that all parties to the situation tried to avoid. Violation consists of saying what should not be said to insiders, rather than to outsiders to whom the secret would be of no interest. The sanction for breaking the public secret can vary from being seen as not fitting in in some nebulous way to being excluded from membership.

Public Secrecy: Organizing Social Relations and Situations
Given the fluid and open nature of public secrecy, its significance does not lie so much in creating a bonding and closeness within an in-group but rather the ways in which it shapes how actors make sense of and behave in situations characterized by contradictions. Specifically, its underlying tension of knowing and not-knowing allows these contradictions to be dealt with and maintained. This can take place across and within the organizational hierarchy as well as between the formal and informal or within the latter realm. The scandals around the Oil-For-Food program of the United Nations exemplify public secrecy between the formal and informal realm. There was much rumored gossip and documented evidence in the form of cables that the program led to bribery actions between the Iraqi government and food marketers, among others, the Australian Wheat Board. The Australian government "knew not to know" this:

Although these [the cables] arrived in the building they were not enacted. Senior bureaucrats knew that the Minister did not want to have them brought to his attention, operating as he was on a "need not to know" basis. . . . The rumored gossip that circulated in those cables, faxes and e-mails that was received but never attended to, because it was never *formally* acknowledged, could be denied the status of an issue. It was, literally, constructed as a non-issue.[58]

The workings of public secrecy are present here because the issue existed, yet, through the efforts of all members in the ministry to refrain from acknowledging it, it was made into a "non-issue." This highlights the role leadership can play in bringing about public secrecy. By "never attend[ing] to" the issue, leaders signaled to others what is supposed to be known, can be talked about and what cannot. Here we can see how public secrecy defines the scope of discourse, that is, how actors make sense of, or in front of others interpret and act, in a particular situation. This example also underlines how "by keeping certain information from becoming public, it is designed to make people who have it less threatening, thereby tacitly stabilizing existing power structures."[59] We saw in the previous chapter how formal secrecy operates on the need-to-know principle, which presents the paradox of not knowing what you need to know. Public secrecy could be said to operate on a "need-not-to-know" basis and contains the opposite paradox—that you need to know what it is you need not to know!

Public secrecy can also take place within the informal realm and among people of the same hierarchical level, as Woods's example of the unacknowledged awareness of homosexuality apparent in interactions between colleagues shows. That informal interactions between employees and leaders are shaped by public secrecy is described by a consultant at one PSF:

Sometimes it feels like everyone knows what is going on. So, I would go to my manager and say: "I have noticed this and that. . . . Can I help you with that?" . . . They know that I am saying this because I want to be perceived as proactive and I know that, but at the same time it means that that is what you have to do in order to do well. . . . It is a kind of game and everyone knows it.

That such seemingly authentic interactions take on the character of a "game" was a widespread yet simultaneously unacknowledged knowledge—a public secret that consultants were, however, expected to know and engage in "in order to do well."

Although, as with any kind of informal secrecy, it is difficult to discern whether public secrecy takes place intentionally or becomes unintentionally ingrained into an organizational culture, it certainly has a purpose that lies in allowing for the coexistence of contradictory realities. Such a coexistence provides spaces to maneuver, manage appearances, and stabilize existing orders. As Taussig argues, "It is precisely the role of . . . public secrecy to control and hence to harness the great powers of con tradiction so that ideology can function."[60] In this context, the public secret concerning ghosting of time sheets is illuminating in that along with the official reports, some consultants had "a separate spreadsheet where you recall the actual hours." The project management unofficially took into account this separate document and gave the consultants some hours off if they overworked. This document would "never be given to HR"; in front of HR and the senior leadership consultants were expected to engage in public secrecy. The coexistence of the two realities meant that officially the firm could maintain toward outsiders and themselves the appearance of complying with the European Working Time Directive while simultaneously allowing for the unacknowledged reality of ghosting and overwork.[61] Woods's description of the ways in which homosexuality is dealt with in organizations also underlines how public secrecy stabilizes the existing order; because the existence of homosexuality is known yet remains unacknowledged, it is possible for the dominant heterosexual norms to be reproduced.

Public secrecy can assume the "fetish" character described by Taussig. The notion of ghosting and the ghost underlines this; it is a dead figure, a secondary image that appears to the living and captures how what is absent (i.e., dead) can become all the more present. Indeed, at one PSF there existed a degree of fascination and celebration yet also irritation and discontent about the long working hours. The very fact that these hours were ghosted arguably contributed to this fetish, and thus the unacknowledged existing culture of working officially unreported long hours. At the same time, the cases of public secrecy highlight its inherent vulnerability to exposure. It requires only one consultant to speak out to HR or one senior bureaucrat to require the Minister to officially acknowledge the cables for the public secret to lose its secretiveness and become public without being secret. Following this, public secrecy not only fosters but also requires the presence of normative control so that organizational members refrain from exposing and thereby breaking the already known secret.

CULTURES OF SECRECIES

In the previous chapter we showed that there can be cultures of secrecy in which information of no particular value is made subject to formal secrecy. These cultures highlight that secrecy cannot simply be explained by the need to protect valuable information but instead, or in addition, by the ways in which it gives rise to a sense of specialness and mystique. On the basis of our discussion of informal and public secrecy, we can further see why secrecy might be strongly embedded in organizations, reinforcing the ways organizational cultures bring about such forms of secrecy and vice versa. Informal and public secrecy build on and foster norms and values concerning what can be shared and openly talked about and what cannot, as well as with whom one can share information and with whom one cannot. This is the case because normative control is required for protecting and sustaining these forms of secrecy. In this sense, informal and public secrecy can be considered to be both a medium and an outcome of normative control.

Because these norms and values make up the basic belief systems and assumptions that operate in organizations, secrecy or, more precisely, the different kinds of secrecies, can become deeply ingrained within organizational cultures. These cultures are sustained by the ways in which certain roles and relations may become associated with secrecy as well as by organizational rituals and general stories, myths, rumors, and gossip. To say that there is a culture of secrecy means that informal and public secrecy do not constitute singular events scattered around organizations but are embedded in wider patterns of how individuals behave, make sense of, and experience organizational life. Their potential significance for organizational cultures highlights why they are not to be regarded as trivial and any less "real" than formal secrecy.

In particular, informal secrecy can be intertwined with cultural assumptions and beliefs around leadership, so that what defines a leader can be based on secrecy. Not only does secrecy serve to signal and symbolize being knowledgeable and thus in a better position to make decisions than those who do not hold secrets (as discussed in chapter 2), but it also contributes to a degree of mystique around leaders. Thus, the required "sacredness" of leaders, namely that which differentiates them from followers, might be explained through informal secrecy and its creation of an enigmatic and magical appearance of those perceived as keeping secrets.[62] There can be a dynamic relationship between leadership and secrecy in that by virtue of being a leader, someone may be regarded as having access to and holding (both informal and formal) secrets—something that in turn reinforces their position as a leader. That such an interrelation with secrecy is deeply ingrained into our basic assumptions of leadership is explicit in the titles of popular leadership books, such as the *Jack Welch and the G.E. Way: Management Insights and Leadership Secrets of the Legendary CEO* or *The Warren Buffett CEO: Secrets from the Berkshire Hathaway Managers*.[63] We can explain this connection between informal secrecy and leadership in the light of historically ingrained, cultural assumptions deriving from the idea of the *arcanii imperium*, that the powerful hold secrets, as described by Canetti. In a similar way to how formal secrecy forms an important part of the public image of espionage, informal secrecy may relate to wider cultural understandings of leadership, for example, images of Machiavellian tacticians or puppet masters.

Secrecy may be greatly embedded in cultures involving experts and expert knowledge. For instance, it is widely observed that engineers and technicians in organizations seek to cultivate and keep a mystique and distinctiveness.[64] Such differentiation is likely to be maintained through the deployment of informal (and formal) secrecy, and can be further linked to the symbolic value attached to expert, especially scientific, knowledge in modern societies. Just as the mystique of leadership secrets connects to a wider imagination, so too does the mystique of the omniscient scientist. Public secrecy may also become strongly embedded in organizational cultures, especially when it relates to wider cultural assumptions and taboos. This is exemplified in Woods's discussion of homosexuality, in which the general dominant norms and values of heterosexuality shape and are reproduced through the workings of public secrecy in organizations.

Although the emergence of cultures of secrecies needs to be seen within specific historical, cultural, and societal contexts, the nature of the organizational relations also contributes to bringing about and sustaining cultures of secrecies. Complex, politicized, and conflictual organizational settings are likely to be characterized by cultures of secrecies, given the ways in which secrecy intersects with coalition building, politicking, and networking. In such environments, what is shared, openly communicated, and what remains hidden constitutes a contested and political matter. Thus informal patterns of concealing and sharing information and their effects on forming and creating organizational bonds are likely to emerge in and pervade such settings. Indeed the 1986 *Challenger* space shuttle disaster can be partially explained by the (sub-)culture of secrecy among the engineers, which meant that they did not openly communicate information to other organizational members in order to maintain their expert status and power.[65] Apart from such occupational subcultures, in other cases, especially where there are high levels of labor conflict, secrecy among employees may be central, so that a worker who "talks to management" is considered a sell-out or even traitorous.

Thus we draw a distinction between secrecy in organizations and cultures of secrecies in organizations. Just as an organization may hold formal secrets without becoming prey to a culture of secrecy, so too may informal (and public) secrecy be present without being culturally dominant. It's probably fair to say that all organizations have some examples of informal secrecy, for example, confidential gossip or public secrecy where things that are unsayable and yet widely known. Only in some cases will this give rise to cultures in which informal secrecy is rife to the point of being habituated—for example, if open discussion of issues is heavily sanctioned by management, we might expect a proliferation of informal and public secrecy. In such situations informal secrecy becomes not just a passing or sporadic behavior but the first recourse and therefore standard practice within an organization.

CONCLUSION

In this chapter we examined the ways in which informal and public secrecy occur within and shape organizational life. In many ways, these forms of secrecy overlap with formal secrecy: they are, after all, all versions of secrecy, and the distinction between these different versions is a largely heuristic one. As the metaphor of the door highlights, they all involve a passing point between an inside and outside that brings about specific social differentiations and organizations of social relations. Yet the "material" out of which the door is made, how access through the door is granted and regulated, the flow between the inside and outside, and how the inside behind the door relates to the larger organizational architecture can greatly differ both between and within these sorts of secrecies. This has something to do with the more indeterminate and fluid nature of informal and public secrecy, and the way that they rely on trust and normative control. Informal secrecy in particular has the potency to bring about close in-groups with strong emotional bonds. Moreover, given that formal rules and laws are not required, informal and public secrecy are likely to be more widespread in organizations than formal secrecy because they touch, in principle, all interactions.

Whereas formal secrecy takes place largely in line with organizational structure, informal and public secrecy can occur in line with or cut across the structure, forming and maintaining various groups, cliques, coalitions, and networks in organizations. We have explained how informal and public secrecy may intersect with a plethora of organizational phenomena, such as leadership, decision-making processes, resistance, politicking, networking, and the maintenance of contradictory realities and the keeping up of a certain image. We have depicted how secrecy is woven very deeply into the everyday life of organizations and may be found in just about any activity and aspect of them. Indeed, because informal and public secrecy enforce and are based on norms and values, they can be embedded in organizational culture of secrecies. That is, the various organizational cultures, subcultures and countercultures may be permeated with and reinforced through the workings of secrecies. This further highlights that the way people behave and make sense of and experience organizational life can be greatly shaped by informal and public secrecy. The various doors through which people and secret knowledge may pass, or may not pass, or pass when they are not meant to, or through which they may simultaneously pass and not pass, when taken together with the organizational geometry of formal secrecy outlined in the previous chapter, contribute to a complex architecture. It is to this that we now turn.

CHAPTER 5

The Hidden Architecture
of Organizational Life

IN *THE HOUSE OF THE DEAD*, Fyodor Dostoyevsky's autobiographical novel about a Siberian prison camp, the narrator observes that

when our barrack was locked it suddenly took on a peculiar aspect—that of a real dwelling-place, a home . . . during the daytime . . . officers of the watch . . . are liable to come into the prison, and for this reason the convicts behave slightly differently, as though not quite at their ease . . . and in a state of some anxiety. But no sooner was the barrack locked than all the men would sit down calmly, each in his own place, and practically all would begin to work at some handicraft or other.[1]

We can read this story as having three interrelated aspects. One is literal: a physical door is closed and a key turned in a lock. The second is phenomenological and metaphorical: the meaning of the space changed from being a barracks to being like a home. And this is also an organizational shift, from prison to dwelling place. The third aspect might be called one of social dynamics: the feelings and behaviors of the prisoners change from anxiety to calmness, and new activities are undertaken. What brings these three aspects together is that the locking of the door renders the room an unsurveilled space, hidden from the view of the prison guards and in that sense secret from them, albeit shared by the inmates themselves.

In this chapter we pursue in more detail the idea of secrecy as a hidden architecture and its significance. This architecture we call "epistemic" in that it is concerned with the barriers to and conduits of knowledge. Although secrecy is often thought of as if it were the absence of communication, this is not so; it is both about hiding and sharing knowledge. Indeed, the epistemic architecture entails the creation of boundaries around and within organizations, as well as flows of secrets through them. It is not a static architecture, though. At the very moment that a secret is made, the possibility of its revelation is also present. Given this inherent vulnerability of secrecy, this architecture is an ongoing accomplishment, requiring regular maintenance, and potentially being continually changed, just as a building is maintained and modified over time.

We approach the various aspects of epistemic architecture in a particular way. For important analytical purposes, we do not separate them out because we suggest that they operate simultaneously. What might be called the structures of secrecy, whether this be locked laboratories or networks sharing confidential gossip, are therefore inseparable from the social dynamics of secrecy in terms of the meaning and impact for organizational members. Secrecy is both made by social action and is a maker of social action. Structure and action are therefore not to be treated as a dualism but rather as a duality, namely as a recursive and reproductive relation.[2] We may trust someone enough to tell them a secret, but in telling them that secret we create a bond of trust between us: the two things happen—and can only happen—simultaneously. So what we call the "hidden architecture of organizational life" is all at once about the different domains of organizations: from structure, culture, to experience. In the following we explore the ways—literal, metaphorical, phenomenological, and social— that secrecy creates and is created by organizations.

BOUNDARIES:
PERIMETERS, WALLS, COMPARTMENTS, ROOMS

The idea that there is a dividing line between an organization and the outside world is a pervasive one within organization studies, and in some ways foundational to a discipline that has organization as its object. Traditionally, and still commonly, this line is understood naturalistically. Like the distinction between objects or between an organism and its environment, so too might there be thought to be an objective boundary between organization and environment. Much recent organization studies has replaced this view with a variety of conceptualizations of the boundary as fluid, negotiated and socially constructed.[3] Secrecy might be considered in this light, as one of the ways that the existence of organization as a demarcated entity is enacted.

Thus if you had approached Bletchley Park (BP) during World War II you would have encountered a fence patrolled by military personnel. There was no sign saying "Top Secret," and had there been so this would have partially undermined its effectiveness: the very fact that there was secret work going on was a secret.[4] This tangible perimeter marked the boundary between the inside of the organization, where secrets were held, and the outside world. That may be an extreme example, but it is common enough for access to organizations to be policed by security passes and other physical barriers. Not all of these are about secrecy, but they may be intimately related to it, for example, restricting access to areas where employment files are stored. Similarly, the kinds of conversations employees may have about confidential matters will be different if they are in a public zone such as a reception area, which may contain outsiders, than when they are in controlled areas where no outsiders are allowed.

The idea of the public versus the private is significant for how secrecy is commonly thought of. Whereas public and communal spaces stand for openness, visibility, and transparency, the more private spaces, such as dark rooms behind closed doors or underground chambers, are typically associated with secrecy. Yet such a split ignores the ways in which public space may precisely offer the required anonymity to engage in secrecy—one may only think of the ways in which movies on Cold War espionage often depict public parks as sites of exchange between secret agents. Furthermore, the increasing use of glass in the architectural designs, such as the external facades, of corporate buildings may be interpreted as a move toward overcoming the barrier between the inside and outside, and thus toward greater transparency. Yet glass can distort and produce images so that, despite the illusion of openness, the outsider may know little about what goes on internally.[5] Similar to the idea of camouflage, organizations may also design offices and choose their location in a way that draws attention away from or at least not to them. The so-called anti-tower or invisible tower to be built in Seoul, South Korea, which through the use of a high-tech LED façade system reflects its surrounding and creates an invisible and transparent illusion, is an extreme example of such blending into the environment.[6]

The physical boundaries associated with secrecy go far beyond the simple perimeter between inside and outside, however. They may also permeate the inside of organizations, erecting a potentially complex series of internal compartments. As we saw in previous chapters, firms may re-strict access to laboratories, trading rooms, and office spaces and hence segment their workforces according to who may enter these spaces. Even in the Lockheed Skunk Works, we found lead-lined rooms that allowed secret discussions to take place. At Bletchley Park, staff were allowed to enter only their own workspaces or communal areas like the canteen The anthropologist Hugh Gusterson conducted a fascinating ethnographic study of the US's Lawrence Livermore nuclear weapons laboratory and examined secrecy in some detail.[7] The laboratory was divided into an elaborate series of zones or boxes within boxes, with a color coding de-noting the level of security clearance needed and entry requiring a pass of the corresponding color. White zones were open to the general public, red zones were for nonclassified work and required only a minor security check to obtain a pass, and green areas were for classified research work and needed extensive security vetting. There were then further levels of exclusion up to the small blue area where the most sensitive information was handled.[8] So this cutting-up of organizational space according to ac-cess to secret knowledge created a literal architecture of internal partitions.

But although physical boundaries can be seen as a literal architecture (albeit having a symbolic meaning) of walls and restricted access areas, they are only one and perhaps not even the most important form of boundary.[9] Alongside them can be found social boundaries such as the organizational regulation of who may talk to whom and about what. Here, indeed, an architectural metaphor is often used in everyday life: Chinese walls.[10] This term is most frequently found in the financial services industry, to refer to restrictions on information flows between different sections that may have conflicts of interest, such as corporate advice and brokerage departments in an investment bank. Similarly, editorial and advertising departments in the news media, auditing and consulting departments in accountancy firms, or representatives of adversarial clients within law firms may all be parti-tioned by Chinese walls. Such walls are policed not by armed guards but by organizational rules, training, and monitoring, and in some cases are the subject of legal enforcement.

These metaphorical walls—even when less well-defined than formal-ized Chinese walls—in principle affect how people behave in organizations, but the extent to which they do so is likely to rest not so much on the effectiveness of organizational and legal rules but the extent to which they are culturally embedded. What matters is what people think, believe, and feel. Secrecy is therefore linked not just to physical and organizational structures but also to social dynamics and, specifically cultural and sub-cultural dynamics.

At its most basic level, the idea of an organizational culture is predicated upon the construction of a boundary between insiders and outsiders. This is why physical perimeters also have a symbolic meaning, because being able to cross them is one of the most tangible markers of belonging. The more general ways that distinctive organizational cultures are enacted are numerous,[11] but clearly having access to secret knowledge is one potent way: the insiders know what is "really" going on, and can participate in the "behind the doors" discussions. In Gusterson's nuclear laboratory study, those who did not have the green badge denoting access to classified material and areas were "not a full adult member of the laboratory" and, in an especially evocative expression, were considered as being "in a leper colony."[12]

Such visible badging of group membership as defined by access to secrets is of course not typical of organizations, and will normally be more subtle. But even if different in form, similar dynamics can be in play. As we saw in chapter 4, organizational life is replete with ways that communication occurs on a confidential basis, off the record, between you and me or even—invoking the architecture metaphor—behind closed doors or within these walls. That information is being shared in a secretive way, for restricted consumption, matters in that in many contexts it is impossible to function fully and effectively if not included within such secrets. This might be especially true in relation to public secrecy, where pretty much unspoken things are both known and not-known by participants. Public secrets are things that it is assumed everyone knows, so to be outside the boundary of such knowledge is not simply to be cut off from this or that network, but to be estranged from the very foundations of belongingness: as with the scientist lacking security clearance to not be "a full adult member" of the community.

This sense of boundaries around or within organizations cuts across the formal and informal versions of secrecy. It applies as much to restricting access to confidential data as it does to restricting access to confidential gossip, for example. This is important because despite the heuristic separation of formal and informal we have drawn, the two are deeply connected. It is not just a matter of them interacting, but that they exist simultaneously and there can be a constant slippage between them.[13] It is a common experience to see this in meetings where there is a formal record of proceedings in the form of minutes. Something will be said which is perceived as sensitive, followed by the injunction "don't minute that" (i.e., not to write it in the formal record of the meeting), usually accompanied by laughter. Such interactions are revealing of the way that certain things are known as informal and perhaps public secrets, and when said in what is a formal context the participants know and understand this. The laughter is precisely an expression of this shared knowing, and an indicator of the tension and perhaps the pleasure it engenders. In such situations we have the simultaneous production of informal and formal domains: they do not simply exist side by side but are mutually constitutive.

That there is a dynamic relation between the different variants of secrecy is also apparent where informal secrecy turns into formal secrecy. For example, in a small organization actors may keep information informally secret, but as the organization and hence also the scale of secrecy (i.e., the number of insiders) grows, the members may seek to officially record and regulate secrecy. The reasons for this transformation may relate to the need for enforced restriction and coordination provided by official laws and rules because there might be too little trust between organizational members, given membership size and staff turnover. Insiders may also feel the need to legitimatize the existence of and engagement in secrecy (e.g., to newcomers)—something that formal secrecy is more likely to offer, because informal secrecy is often associated with ethical wrongdoing.

Yet this does not necessarily mean that in such cases one kind of secrecy replaces the other. John Lanchester's novel *Capital* depicts an investment banker worrying about the size of his annual bonus:

His employer . . . did not make it straightforward, and there were many considerations at work to do with the size of the company's profits . . . many of them not at all transparent, and some of them based on subjective judgments. . . . There was an element of deliberate mystification about the process, which was in the hands of the compensation committee, sometimes known as the Politburo. What it boiled down to was, there was no way of being confident about what the size of your bonus was going to be.[14]

This story captures the *entanglement* of a formal, committee-based system with more informal judgments which combine to mystify. In the book, the banker frequently tries to gain hints as to what his bonus will be to no avail, provoking continued anxiety until the secret is finally revealed at which point the whole process begins again.

In a similar way, in one of the professional service firm (PSF) cases, successful applicants were assigned "offer grades," which is to say a ranking (A, B, C, etc.) of the quality of the accepted applicant. This was a formal secret, as knowledge of it was confined to those with bureaucratic access, namely the HR managers, to the offer grades and was recorded in employee files. However, the existence of offer grades was officially denied and had the character of a public secret in that it was widely understood, but rarely if ever discussed within the firm, that some staff had been marked down from the beginning as of higher status than others. But it was also an informal secret, in that those marked down in this way were given various "coded signals," and on occasion told "in terms" albeit "off the record," that they were among those regarded as having particularly good prospects. Moreover, the researcher was himself told, as an informal secret, that offer grades did exist but were not to be talked about openly. Yet clearly this conversation shows how they could be spoken about openly: the issue was to whom and in what context. So, again, what can be seen is a complex entanglement of formal, informal, and public secrecy.

This becomes important when considering the role of secrecy in creating insiders and outsiders, because the true insider has knowledge of both formal and informal secrets and an understanding of how they intersect. In the example of off-the-record comments in meetings, the interaction works only because those involved share this double knowledge: to an outsider it would often not be clear why the comment should not be recorded and why the participants laughed (a laughter that might be described as knowing). An outsider could not participate effectively in this interaction.

In the French language, there are two verbs for the English to know: one is *savoir* and the other is *connaître*. *Savoir* applies mainly to those things we know intellectually (such as facts), while *connaître* to those things we know experientially (such as people). To function effectively as an organizational insider, one needs to know in both of these senses. That is why, the researcher was told about the existence of offer grades and that they were not to be discussed: to function effectively in his project with the HR managers he needed to know (intellectually) that they existed, but to function effectively in the firm as a whole he needed to know (experientially) with whom they could and could not be discussed.

Appreciating what can and cannot be said, and to whom, also points up the importance of time. The metaphor of architecture is most obviously a spatial one, but architectures are also temporal in that buildings evolve and change over time. Organizational insiders and outsiders are not simply defined by a binary opposition between those who are and are not employed at a particular moment. Rather, insiders of long standing may acquire a depth and complexity of knowledge that makes them more deeply or profoundly insiders than recent joiners. It is common to hear that someone who has been around an organization for a long time "knows where the bodies are buried," and this metaphor is, precisely, an acknowledgment that there are some secret truths "buried" in the organization that newcomers are not aware of.

This temporality of organizational membership can be found in Gusterson's nuclear weapons laboratory study that reports a distinction based upon whether and how often a physicist has been through the entire cycle of conceiving a nuclear device through to its testing. Testing is a kind of initiation ritual after which one joins the club of true insiders, with those who have been through the process several times being the most esteemed.[15] So, here, insiders are of various sorts, characterized by longevity and experience. Similarly, at Bletchley Park, there were distinctions of prestige based on whether someone had been present during the early "glory years" of the initial codebreaking breakthroughs or had arrived later.[16] More generally and informally, it is commonplace in organizations for certain individuals to be known (and often admired) for always being in the know, the first to hear things, hooked into the grapevine.

This issue also speaks to the way that secrecy connects to hierarchy and therefore to the vertical boundaries within organizations. This may often be a matter of organizational seniority: the higher your grade, the higher your clearance to be in possession of secrets. However, it also relates to the capacity to span boundaries. In a highly compartmentalized organization, relatively few people, and these the senior ones, have knowledge of what is happening within the different compartments, having a "bird's-eye view" of all or most of what is going on. This is not necessarily straightforward though, because secrecy can cut across hierarchies. For example, the decision by the United Kingdom to build its own atomic weapons after the Second World War was not known to most cabinet ministers at the time, although junior technicians working on the project were necessarily in the know. Moreover, as detailed in chapter 4, informal groups, such as the cliques of leaders and consultants, may also cut across hierarchies. Although secrecy relates to the hierarchical structure of organizations, it may have its own hierarchies that depart from this: the epistemic architecture of organizations is not identical with their organizational charts, but interrelates with these in variable ways. This is apparent in cases of systematic corruption, which involve a hidden web of relations, exchanges, and dependencies that cut across the official hierarchy and operate within and outside the organization.[17] In the 2006 corruption scandal of Siemens, this web spanned from the company's managers and employees to external consultants and government officials.[18] Although an extreme case, it highlights how the familiar boxes and lines of an organizational chart may be quite misleading because, as noted in chapter 3, secrecy more commonly enacts a series of overlapping concentric circles.

PERMEABILITY:

DOORS, CORRIDORS, WINDOWS, CONDUITS

We have talked so far about boundaries as if they were rigid and impregnable, acting as solid demarcators around secrets and, at the same time, between insiders and outsiders. But this is far too simplistic. At the most basic level, secrets do leak even from the most security-conscious organizations, whether as a result of deliberate espionage or revelation, or because of accidental disclosure; hence the surveillance and policing of organiza-

tional secrecy. In fact, the policing of boundaries even in highly secure organizations may be less rigorous than might be expected. In Gusterson's
study, for example, he observes that despite strict rules that security passes
should never be left unattended, this was frequently ignored in practice.[19]
Moreover, Gusterson himself managed—unintentionally—to enter areas
of the weapons factory for which he did not have a pass.[20]

Similarly, Chinese walls are notable for being repeatedly breached.
Indeed, some of the most significant financial and corporate scandals of
recent years are a result of this—Enron in 2001, for example[21]—as Nobel
Prize-winning economist Joseph Stiglitz has argued.[22] The reasons for such
breaches are complex and various, but though sometimes animated by
straightforward greed, seem often to have to do with perpetrators' perceptions of having a duty to clients that overrides commitment to organizational rules. This seems to have been the case with Arthur Andersen,[23]
Enron's auditors, and also in a study of Chinese walls in German investment banks.[24] In other words, identities may not be coextensive with organizational boundaries but rather—in the case, for example, of professional
identity—transcend them.

Thinking of the more informal kinds of secrecy, one sees that organizational groups are especially permeable.[25] Their membership is informally
defined, and security relies upon participants knowing who may and may
not be entrusted with secrets, or knowing who is or it not trustworthy.
This is likely to be imprecise and relatively weakly regulated, especially in
the case of confidential gossip groups. Yet in other ways this weak regulation makes such groups secure, because there is no record of their activities which are easily deniable as a result. In terms of the metaphor of
architecture, we may think of such things as unintended cracks in the wall.

In relation to the permeability of organizational barriers, more can be
at stake. Because secrecy is a way of communicating as well as concealing knowledge, this makes it inherently fragile: walls may not have ears
but they have doors leading to corridors. Benjamin Franklin coined the
aphorism "Three may keep a secret, if two of them are dead,"[26] the joke
being that whenever a secret is shared it becomes insecure, but to the extent that they are *necessarily* shared they are always insecure. As secrets
flow around organizations, as they must for communication to occur, it is

always possible that they will flow out. People leaving firms, for example, cease to be insiders but carry with them the secrets they learned when they were, and enforcing confidentiality may be impractical. So this, although unintended, arises not from a secret slipping through the boundary but from the necessity of secrets being shared.

Just as the barriers around secrets can take physical forms, so too can the conduits through which secrets are shared. For example, the computer networks within which data are held and circulated have various forms of physicality, including cabling. Indeed, one of the commonest ways in which organizational secrets leak out is the simple one of a laptop or flash drive being lost or stolen. For example, in November 2014 a Canadian government agency lost a flash drive containing sensitive information, including Social Security data, for more than 500,000 people,[27] and there have been hundreds if not thousands of such cases worldwide.[28] This exemplifies the particular vulnerability of secrets that are recorded, in contrast to those that are only verbally shared. The existence of records makes for the possibility of them being obtained or accessed by someone who is not authorized to see them. Computer technology exacerbates this vulnerability precisely because it is possible for large amounts of information to be concentrated in a single place and in highly portable form.[29] The same information if contained in paper files would be very much less likely to be lost or stolen. For the same reason, recent years have seen massive increases in cyber-espionage by individuals, corporations, and states because the computer networks in which information flows represent the weakest point of organizational secrecy.

There are other ways, too, that barriers are permeable. One can think of the walls as having not just doors but frosted glass windows through which secrets may be partially glimpsed. Public secrecy might be thought of in very much this way: both secret and not secret, known and not-known. In an ongoing high-profile scandal in the United Kingdom, it became known after his death in 2011 that a well-known media personality, Jimmy Saville, was a prolific, predatory sexual abuser of children. And it has emerged that to many in his employing organization, the British Broadcasting Company (BBC), this was an open or public secret.[30] So this is, in some respects, a story about organizational secrecy, and indeed the

BBC has been accused of having had a "culture of secrecy" that allowed Saville's crimes to occur.[31] Cases like this are very hard to analyze, lying as they do somewhere on the edge of secrecy, and perhaps the metaphor of something half-seen through a frosted window captures this.

Even in less complex and contentious cases, this kind of frosted glass permeability can be found. One of the temptations of secrecy is for those in the know to hint at their knowledge. Conversely, it is commonplace for people in organizations to speculate about the hidden agendas of other people or groups. The dynamics of this are variable and, of course, context specific. Normally, the speculations are of a malign intent, with the hidden agenda being, for example, plans to axe jobs. But sometimes they can be part of a benign or even adoring fantasy that "they" (perhaps those leading the organization) have things under control and are acting for the good of all (which might be part of the leadership mystique discussed in chapter 4).

This interplay between groups who are in the know and those who are not is an almost perennial feature of organizations. For example, in one of the PSFs one of the younger partners, who was widely admired for his career success, was known to act as an unofficial conduit between the partner group and selected non-partners giving partial information about plans and developments in the firm that were supposed to be confidential to the partners. This naturally meant that those non-partners with whom he associated were seen by others as having a particular insight as well, and so were prized as contacts for those outside the partner's circle. In fact, this might be seen as a good example of how an informal group sharing confidential information gets created, including the kind of concentric circles within such networks formed of those closer or further to the source of information. This can be regarded as the informal analogy to something like the colored zones and passes in Gusterson's nuclear laboratory study, albeit that the markers are more subtle.

Hinting at or half-revealing secrets is not just a feature of internal organizational relations or of the micro-processes of interaction. It can also be seen at the macro level of how organizations manage their relations with external audiences. Secrecy, in terms of the specialness and mysterious aura it creates, may be used to sell products.[32] Apple is well known for its "technological dramas" and mysterious staging of products prior to market introduction— designed to positively influence both investors and potential consumers.[33] That "secrecy helps to sell" is also apparent in the hysterical consumer crowds, eagerly waiting in long lines to be among the first to read the newest book of J. K. Rowling's *Harry Potter* series. The use of secrecy in this way is not a straightforward matter of complete concealment, though. It has become quite common for companies like Apple[34] or Samsung[35] to drop hints in the media over long periods of time of new products that will be coming out, performing a kind of "striptease" to entice future customers. The *Harry Potter* case is a good illustration of the complex mix of secrecy and hinting:

It consisted of a complete black out on advanced information. The book's title, pagination, and price were kept under wraps until two weeks before publication. Review copies were withheld, no author interviews were allowed, and foreign translations were deferred for fear of injudicious leaks. Juicy plot details, including the death of a key character and Harry's sexual awakening, were drip fed to a slavering press corps prior to the launch. Printers and distributors were required to sign strict confidentiality agreements. Booksellers were bound by a ruthlessly policed embargo, though some were allowed to display the tantalizing volume in locked cages for a brief period just before. . . . And in a stroke of retro genius, several advance copies were "accidently" sold from an unnamed Wal-Mart in deepest West Virginia, though one of the "lucky" children was miraculously tracked down by the world's press and splashed across every front page worth its salt.[36]

It is the *mysterium* or mystique of secrecy that makes it enticing for customers to get a glimpse of the *arcanum* of what is hidden. In a similar way, but for very different reasons, intelligence agencies frequently hint at the terrorist plots that they have dealt with or suspect exist without giving details of secret information. This too is a way of managing external relations by urging public vigilance or, alternatively, seeking public support and budgets for the agencies' activities.

LIVING WITH SECRECY

So far we have mainly talked about how secrecy, its boundaries and conduits, is constituted by social actions and relations. In this section we focus on the constitutive role of secrecy. What does it mean to live in or with this hidden architecture? The most basic issue here, identified by Simmel, is the considerable possibilities that secrecy offers for a sense of individual and group identity, especially that related to specialness: "Secrecy gives the person enshrouded by it an exceptional position . . . which is in principle quite independent of its . . . content, but it naturally heightened in the degree in which the exclusively possessed secret is significant and comprehensive."[37] This also explains the reciprocal relationship between secrecy and elites. Formal secrecy offers, by definition, explicit markers of this specialness denoted by levels of clearance giving access to particular material or physical access to restricted sites such as laboratories. Because they are explicit, such markers may be apparent to both insiders and outsiders within an organization because members are aware of the differential access that each has.

We have noted several examples of this, such as, in chapter 3, Michael Herman's account of being a member of a "privileged inner circle,"[38] and the status attached to the Lockheed Skunk Works. We also saw how, in the Bletchley Park case, those who had access to the secret that Enigma had been broken saw themselves as constituting "an elite within an elite." Apart from obviously being indicative of that sense of specialness, tangentially it reveals something else: even those outside of the Enigma secret, but party to the wider secrecy of BP were understood as being an elite of sorts. In another example, a BP staff member did not know about Enigma but did know in advance about the 1944 D-Day landings.[39] She reports feeling "special" when she came off duty and returned to her accommodation, shared with civilians who had no such knowledge, a feeling reinforced when the landings happened and her fellow lodgers heard the news on the radio. Perhaps it is the case that such feelings explain, in part, the existence of cultures of secrecy, in that secrecy can be not just "ingrained" but almost addictive?

Certainly the experience of knowing secrets may provoke not just a feeling of specialness but of excitement. Daniel Ellsberg, in his memoir of his time as a Pentagon consultant, recalls how being privy to "the inside dope made you feel important, fully engaged, on an adrenaline high. . . . Clearly it was addictive."[40] Having a top secret safe in one's office created an excitement: "I could still remember the feeling I had the first time I was reading something . . . stamped "Top Secret" . . . my heart beginning to pound, my breath coming short." It is interesting that these symptoms are also those of anxiety or fear and indeed the quote continues: ". . . the notion that someone was looking over my shoulder . . . I had to make them look like an ordinary manuscript."[41]

That is important because it illustrates that to speak of secrecy bestowing a sense of specialness is not to say that this specialness is experienced positively. Indeed, it may well be experienced as burdensome. This was the case for some at Bletchley Park, in that some employees were afraid they might talk in their sleep, and others refused to have operations for fear of disclosing classified information when coming round from the anaesthetic.[42]

But the burden of secrecy may not just be about the fear of disclosure; it may also be about the temptations to disclose secrets. The two may be related: one way to unburden oneself is to reveal secrets. It relates to the issue of specialness, because by revealing, or hinting at, one's secret knowledge it is possible to make oneself look important in the eyes of others. Simmel describes how "there is desire to signalize one's own superiority as compared with . . . others."[43] At Bletchley Park there was a particular impetus to do so, because in a time of war when others were in the armed forces, how could a young civilian (as many employed there were) justify his noncombatant status? Indeed, throughout the war there were instances of BP staff doing just this, despite the many injunctions to resist the temptation to tell even family members what they were doing. It is for this reason that intelligence services, up to the present day, seek to recruit people who are psychologically comfortable with not receiving external recognition for their work.

The burdening temptation of disclosure can also exist where secrecy is felt to compromise one's moral integrity and honesty. The experience of secrecy is then strongly ethically charged by feelings of guilt, fidelity, and loyalty between insiders and outsiders. Whistleblowers like Ellsberg describe the tension of feeling trapped between the promise they gave to insiders and their wish to be honest and truthful toward outsiders.

All of these issues—feeling special, burdened, or tempted to disclose secrets—are predicated upon the underlying idea that there is a clear line between those in the know and those not. However, a much more complex situation obtains precisely because of the way that secrecy in organizations typically entails multiple compartmentalization, the complex organizational geometry, as we dubbed it in chapter 3. This means that very few people are in possession of the "whole truth." Instead, different people within the organization have access to segments of knowledge rather than to the big picture. This is true not just in formal organizations but is a common attribute of resistance and terrorist organizations that often work in cells in which, in order to enhance security if a member is captured, no individual knows more than a few contacts. Thus, paradoxically, possession of some secret knowledge has the effect not of rendering members aware of their special status of being in the know but of provoking a realization of their ignorance. The perpetual puzzlement of Josef K. in Franz Kafka's *The Trial* captures precisely that: in a world of multiple secrets, nothing makes sense.

The novelist C. P. Snow, who had been involved in the British atomic weapons program during and after World War II, fictionalized these experiences in *The New Men*.[44] Snow was an acute and realistic observer of organizational life[45] and makes several observations about the experience of secrecy, including that

if one had to live close to official secrets . . . one knew what it must be like to be a paranoiac. The beautiful detective-story spider-web of suspicion, the facts of everyday clearer-edged than they have ever been, no glue of sense to stick them in their place.[46]

He evokes a world in which people live in a fog of secrecy, a world where people use code names, false names, disclose facts selectively, and are all the time preoccupied with the fear of illicit disclosures. The experience is one of disorientation rather than one of self-assured insiders (even though Snow's fictional *alter ego* is a senior civil servant). And this is precisely related to compartmentalization because it emerges from the fragmentation of knowledge into segments that very few, if any, have complete access to. This may not always be as dramatic as Snow's portrayal, but it remains a logical if unexpected feature of partial knowledge of secrets in that it alerts one to the fact that there are secrets one is not aware of more fully than would be the case for someone who has no secret knowledge at all.

Martin Parker's study of organizational culture also uses the image of a fog of secrecy, which has the effect of making people feel "blind."[47] It is an image that speaks particularly well to cases of public secrecy given the contradictory realities and implicit and unstated rules involved.

But the experience described by Snow is also likely to befall outsiders of secrecy (indeed, it shows that even as an insider one might still feel like an outsider). Being an outsider can take two forms: one in which one is unaware of the existence of secrecy and thus remains experientially unaffected by it; another in which secrecy's existence is known, or at least suspected. In the latter case, the sense of being excluded while simultaneously attributing some kind of specialness to insiders is likely to occur. However, such exclusion can be perceived as unfair and even illegitimate, especially when political decisions that directly affect outsiders are concerned or misconduct is suspected. Thus, outsiders may be drawn to uncover secrets by, so to speak, tearing down the walls of secrecy. As discussed in chapter 2, this characterizes the current push toward greater transparency. Seeking to uncover secrets can be part of efforts to undermine the power relations secrecy can give rise to, that is, between those in the know and those who do not know. Outsiders, say members of one organizational department, might also react to the existence of secrecy of another department by refraining from sharing information themselves. Here we may think of the "secrecy race" regarding military armament that took place during the Cold War between the United States and the Soviet Union.[48] The outsiders' experience can also bring about the kind of paranoia Snow describes and that often accompanies conspiracy theory. Conspiracy is based on the idea that behind the fog, there are "masters" in the know, pulling the strings, and determining the course of action.[49] But individuals might also prefer to remain outsiders, or outsider-insiders in the case of public secrecy, so that they do not have to carry the burden of keeping secrets, for instance, if this involves being committed to a particular group of insiders and/or potentially harmful information.

This further highlights how, for insiders, the experience of secrecy may be a negative one. Julia Liebeskind argues that employees in commercial firms with high degrees of secrecy may well be disaffected, both in a general way because of the implication of low trust, and more specifically by the onerous and possibly intrusive regulation and surveillance of their work.[50] The science fiction author John Wyndham depicts this succinctly in his novel *Trouble with Lichen*, set in an innovative biochemical firm whose head "maintained that secrecy, unless it was absolutely necessary, lowered efficiency and deteriorated the sense of corporate endeavor."[51] Other negatives of secrecy were experienced by the scientists in Hugh Gusterson's laboratory who felt a perennial tension between their work and home lives, with their spouses resenting the distance that work secrecy created within families.[52] Daniel Ellsberg describes this in relation to his daughter, who helped him collect classified material from the Pentagon. When he asked her not to tell anyone what they did, "Mary felt very burdened by the obligation to keep something from her mother, which she'd never been asked to do before."[53]

All these experiences may not be very strongly present in the case of the routine organizational situations of, for example, data protection. Even so, there are many everyday dilemmas and difficulties that arise from, for example, inadvertent forwarding of emails to people inside or outside an organization who should not have sight of them. Within health care there are requirements on staff—and not just clinicians but, for example, receptionists—to respect confidentiality.[54] At the same time, however, various kinds of information sharing about patients (for example, their medical records) is not just allowable but necessary to deliver effective health care. Secrecy here is not simply a matter of the confidentiality of an individual clinician–patient encounter but a matter of rules governing which groups may have access to records and under what circumstances. Where patients and staff live within the same community this may be especially important because of the possibility of accidental disclosures in social situations. Although these cases are in some ways different from military secrets, they give rise to similar or related issues. For example, staff conversations in the corridors or elevators of a hospital may inadvertently breach medical confidentiality[55] in ways not dissimilar to those in which Bletchley Park staff might inadvertently reveal information in the canteen or on public transport.

Similar observations might be made in a wide array of occupational settings[56]—education, social work, legal work, financial services, among many others—and in many cases, such as medicine, psychotherapy, the priesthood, and the law, may be foundational to codes of professional ethics. To take one of these cases, that of psychotherapy, secrecy occupies a central place because therapists are routinely privy to the innermost thoughts, fears, and, indeed, secrets of clients.[57] This imposes stringent legal requirements upon psychotherapists,[58] which is an example of formal secrecy, including security of documentary records.[59] It also requires careful management of encounters between therapists and clients outside of sessions, such as accidental social meetings,[60] which may be regarded as being an aspect of the maintenance of secrecy in informal settings. Moreover, psychotherapists' access to secrets about clients is also accompanied, at least potentially, by some of the other experiences we have discussed. The perils of countertransference are well known in psychotherapy; but one specific version of this is that the therapist feels special by virtue of the trust and knowledge placed in him or her when a client confides secrets. At the same time, this knowledge may be experienced as burdensome if the therapist finds it to be troubling or disturbing in some way, a process known as "vicarious traumatization."[61]

The comparison between everyday organizational life and cases of high security is warranted in another way. Although we have referred to the potential excitement of reading top secret files, and to a feeling of specialness that may occur in such settings, it does not follow that people in these organizations feel a conscious and continuous awareness of secrecy any more than a hospital receptionist does. The social and psychological effects of secrecy are more subtle than this: in a high-security organization, precisely because it is such an organization, secrecy is an everyday experience except, perhaps, on first encounter, at moments of drama, or on retrospective reflection. In fact, one feature of organizational secrecy is its ubiquity or "omnipresence," which is so great that it may go almost unnoticed.[62] Just as those in high-security organizations may not notice secrecy because it is familiar, so too might those of us who work in more "normal" organizations not notice the secrecy that we experience because for *us* that is the normality. But this does not mean that its effects are insignificant—in the same way that psychodynamic processes in organizations are ubiquitous, unnoticed, and yet highly significant.[63]

Informal secrecy has a particular capacity to be heavily emotionally charged. Here membership of the in-group involves being personally "chosen" and requires a greater degree of reciprocal trust than the more bureaucratically orchestrated procedures associated with formal secrecy. Membership has to do with individual character rather than rational-legal position or role. Indeed the fact that informal secrecy is sustained through normative control implies that the "hearts and minds" of the insiders may be entangled in keeping the secret. But there is no causal law here: one can readily imagine that the opposite might be the case, namely that the emotional involvement is low in more casual cases of informal secrecy (and public secrecy) so that the sense of a common identity and bonding among insiders may be weak.

That informal secrecy may sometimes be more casual and less tangibly marked than formal secrecy also means that the experience of specialness is likely to occur only if insiders can expect outsiders to perceive them as special. To take the example of the mystique of leadership, for such a mystique to be attributed to a leader, followers need to perceive the leader as holding secrets and thus being in the know. Again, the kind of specialness such secrecy can give rise to does not necessarily have to be a straightforwardly positive one. As Sigmund Freud in his famous piece *The Uncanny* notes, there is a close connection between the uncanny and the secret.[64] This connection points to the potentially unsettling and eerie nature of secrecy. We can see how this applies to organizational members' relation to leaders, such as in the PSF cases, who are often both admired and looked up to yet are also experienced as mysterious, enigmatic, and therefore peculiar.

In order to bestow a sense of specialness to insiders, informal secrecy has to be manifest for outsiders—this explains why insiders in informal secrecy may be especially prone to hint at their knowledge to outsiders. In Gusterson's nuclear laboratory in-group membership is very easy to see: it is denoted by the color of one's pass and the zones one can enter. In informal secrecy, group members must find other ways to signal their status to outsiders, entailing a complex and subtle social negotiation.

The line between hinting at secret knowledge and actually revealing secrets is a very fine one,[65] and this inflects the issue of the burden of informal secrecy in a particular way. In our PSF research, we often heard expressions like "I would probably get shot for saying that" or "They would kill me if they found out." Again the issue here is the relative fuzziness of the boundary around informal secrets—just what can be said and to whom is not nearly so clear as it is with formal secrets. Admittedly, even there, as in the weapons laboratory case, it can be "cognitively complicated to remember what information fits into which category and can or can't be shared."[66] However, at least in principle, when in doubt the employee can refer to security officers for guidance. In the case of informal—and especially public secrecy—the opaque rules and lack of instructions of what is required of insiders make this a matter of subtle negotiation.

Living with secrecy, then, may be experienced in a range of ways, both positive and negative. It may engender feelings of belonging, specialness, and exclusion or it may be burdensome or even disorientating. The same is true of many other things that people do in organizations. But secrecy gives a particular flavor to these experiences because of its imbrication with profound themes of loyalty, trust, and betrayal. In our everyday work tasks we might feel anxiety that we might fail and let people down; it is only in the context of secrecy that we might fear that we have betrayed people.

ARCHITECTURAL STYLES

Throughout this book we have often used examples of what are, in an obvious, commonsensical way, secretive organizations: intelligence agencies, military research facilities, high-tech skunk works. We have also provided many examples of other kinds of organizations and, we hope, successfully suggested that what applies to obviously secretive organizations applies *mutatis mutandi* to organizations more generally. There is another dimension to this that we have emphasized as well: secrecy is not necessarily about protecting knowledge that is important or valuable, but that secrecy makes that knowledge take on a value by virtue of being secret. It is expressed nicely by Hugh Gusterson:

Secrets often turn out to be surprisingly mundane and unexciting once they are revealed. . . . Still, regardless of whether they are secret because they are important or important because they are secret, secrets are exciting. Secrecy is a means by which power constructs itself as power, and the knowledge of secrets is a perquisite of power.[67]

Thus it should not be thought *a priori* that organizations that deal with obviously important secrets are different from, or more secretive than, those that do not. All organizations engage in secrecy in some way and to some degree.

With this reemphasized, let us now discuss some of the reasons why secrecy is likely to be more significant in some contexts than in others. To use the architecture metaphor, all buildings have an architecture, but its form will vary widely according to function, history, fashion, and any number of other things.[68] Most obvious of these is function. Louis Sullivan's maxim that "form follows function" was the credo of modernist architects: the way a building is designed should be based upon the function or purpose intended for its use. From that perspective, organizations that have many secrets to keep are most characterized by having the kind of architecture we have discussed. And, indeed, we do not intend to suggest that secrets are kept for no reason other than secrecy itself. Organizations such as intelligence and military agencies or technically innovative firms are very likely to engage in secrecy, especially formal secrecy, and for these organizations this is far from trivial.[69]

It is no coincidence that modernist architecture provides a metaphor for a functionalist understanding of secrecy in organizations. Both are characterized by rationalism. In the case of architecture a building exists to perform a particular function, no more and no less. In the case of the functionalist understanding of secrecy—what we call the "informational approach"—secrecy is straightforwardly a matter of protecting valuable knowledge. That is not unimportant, but it is insufficient in itself, just as modernist architecture does not exhaust the possibilities of architecture; indeed, many modernist buildings exhibit forms of ornamentation that do not have an obvious function. Secrecy exists as ornamentation as well as function in organizations.

It is likely that secrecy is related to organizational complexity. A "great deal of corporate secrecy is maintained not by conscious design but by the mere fact that the corporation is so complex."[70] This is underlined by

the observations of secrecy in the context of high levels of role segmentation and compartmentalization found in complex organizations.[71] This
implies that just as secrecy has as one of its effects the compartmentalization of organizations, so too does compartmentalization have the effect of
engendering secrecy. The compartmentalization is therefore both a structural feature of complex organizations and also a cultural feature because
compartments typically give rise to subcultural identities and practices.[72]
Architecturally, this would be to say that function follows form rather
than form follows function.

Moreover, it seems plausible, especially regarding the more informal
kinds of secrecy, that secrecy is found in organizations characterized by
conflicts of various kinds and the fear and uncertainty that these engender. In several of the studies we have drawn upon this is so: cases of in-
terdepartmental conflict[73] and of power struggles between managers and
workers.[74] Within such contexts, political cliques, actual and suspected
hidden agendas, and informal groups sharing information or engaging in
speculation are likely to be especially rife. Architecturally, we might think
of these complex and/or conflicted organizations as having a variety of
non-modernist styles. Perhaps they bring to mind the elaborate grandeur
of a great Gothic cathedral, or the drama of Italian baroque. Perhaps,
instead, they can be thought of as intimate and ornate rococo structures.

Finally, there are those cases we have identified in which secrecy is
likely to be found because of an overarching culture of secrecy. Here form
and function are de-differentiated in that everything is treated as secret.
The purpose of secrecy is secrecy itself. Architecturally this would most
closely resemble a postmodern style in which form is adopted for its own
sake. In some architecture of this style, function and ornamentation become de-differentiated with, for example, heating pipes and elevators
placed on the outside of buildings.[75] This represents the ultimate rejection of modernist rationalism in architecture, just as cultures of secrecy
entail a rejection of the idea that the keeping of secrets is a function of
their organizational value.

We can therefore see that the hidden architecture of secrecy can be
associated with a variety of styles of organizational building. It is most
prevalent in organizations that, by reason of their function or field of

operations, have many secrets to keep. Less obviously it is a feature of organizations that are complex and, especially, conflicted. But it is always present in some form and to some degree, and our argument is not that secrecy constructs just one kind of organization but that organizations of all sorts and forms are, in part, built of and around secrets.

CONCLUSION

As the quotation from Hugh Gusterson with which we began this book puts it:

At the most obvious, functional level, the laboratory's colored badges, locked trash cans, exclusion areas, and conversational restrictions are part of a system that, however erratic, exists to ensure that foreign governments do not gain access to American military secrets. Looking at the laboratory's system of secrecy with a less literal eye, however, I argue that these regulations also have a role to play in the construction of a particular social order within the laboratory and a particular relationship between laboratory scientists and the outside world.[76]

In this chapter, we have shown how the social order of organizations is constructed by secrecy. We have used the metaphor of an epistemic architecture to depict the construction of what is inside and outside organizations and how organizations are internally partitioned. This creates pathways through which secret knowledge flows, and shows how the boundaries between insiders and outsiders are erected, maintained, and potentially broken. Indeed, the doors, corridors, or cablings through which secrets flow and are passed are coexistent with social relations between organizational actors, whether that means bureaucratic protocols of access or trust-based networks. This architecture is epistemic both in structuring the places where secret knowledge is held and shared and in structuring its knowers. Here the architecture metaphor breaks down, because there is no architect of these organizational buildings other than the people who inhabit, bring to life, and ultimately *are* them.

The forms of epistemic architecture are as variable as the forms that actual buildings take, but they share some basic characteristics. Regardless of their architectural style, all buildings are recognizable as buildings. We find repetitive patterns in the way that secrecy works in organizations:

separations of knowledge and with them separations of people; connections of knowledge and with them connections of people. We can therefore see remarkably similar features of specialness, excitement, burden, and disorientation whether we are talking about weapons laboratories, finance houses, PSFs, or psychotherapists. If we have labored this point it is in order to urge that secrecy is omnipresent. Unnoticed, perhaps—because this is a hidden architecture—but working away around us every day and worked at by us every day.

The most basic of these features is the possibility of a distinctive sense of individual or group identity. I or we are important, special, or different because we have access to this secret knowledge that others are denied or unaware of. This is the core insight derived from Simmel and taken up by Goffman, Edgar Schein, and others that explains why secrecy in organizations has such powerful resonances. But, here, we have also indicated that that power may not necessarily have a positive valence. It may be experienced as burdensome. It may simply not offer *enough* satisfaction, causing the secret holder to hint at or reveal knowledge to enhance the sense of specialness. Or it may be disorientating or, at least, troubling precisely because compartmentalization slices and dices knowledge. If secrecy is a spider's web, then few if any in the organization have the place of the spider sitting at the center with all parts of the web accessible. Instead, individuals are in some way adrift in, to use another of the metaphors, the cloaking fog of secrecy. This experience can also befall outsiders of secrecy who may struggle with the sense of exclusion, seek to tear down secrecy's facades, or alternatively feel relieved by not having to carry the burdens secrecy brings with it.

We are not suggesting that secrecy is the only way that organizational architectures are enacted. On the contrary, the boundaries and conduits of organizational life are made up of very many different aspects, as are group and individual identities. If we think, for example, of boundaries around professions, these are made of a multiplicity of materials, including legal entitlement to practice, training in technical knowledge, and a wide range of behavioral regulations. But some aspects do relate to secrecy: formal requirements to maintain client confidentiality or informal norms to conceal sexual attraction between colleagues that would be regarded as unprofessional. Secrecy should therefore be regarded as woven into the very wide array of social practices through which organizations are made and reproduced. Yet, that said, it is not "just another" such practice. Secrecy offers particular and potent ways to construct complex organizational architectures.

One might ask why secrecy enacts so elaborate an architecture, and here we come back to its inherent fragility. Georg Simmel once again provides the key insight here when he says "Secrecy involves a tension which, at the moment of revelation, finds its release."[77] There is a pressure at work in secrecy. Like electricity or water in buildings, secret knowledge must always be penned in to proscribed places and forced to flow around prescribed routes. At any moment it will break loose and at that moment ceases to exist as secret knowledge, becoming just knowledge. It requires a continuous organizational effort to keep it corralled. We might normally think of architecture's primary purpose as being to keep the outside world out—to hold at bay the rain, wind, heat, and cold that continually threaten to break in—and the inside world of shelter and comfort in. The hidden architecture of organizational life is similarly continually in peril because the tension of secrecy seeks its release and the barriers between inside and outside are at risk of being overwhelmed. In Dostoyevsky's prison, the locking of the barracks immediately turns it into a secret home. When the door is unlocked again, the secret home just as quickly disappears. Its existence is entirely dependent upon it being kept hidden from outside view.

Conclusion
Finishing Touches

THE CENTRAL ARGUMENT of this book has been that secrecy fundamentally shapes the making and remaking of work organizations—that
is, the hidden architecture of organizations. By regulating what is said and
not said, by and to whom, secrecy organizes social relations. At the same
time as it brings about organizational structures and cultures, secrecy is
embedded in them. Rather than constituting a singular phenomenon that
an organization does or does not exhibit, secrecy is deeply interwoven into
the very social fabric that knits together organizations in the first place.
This means that it both cuts across and is directly relevant to a variety
of organizational phenomena. The approach we have developed seeks to
establish secrecy not as a property of organizations but as a core characteristic and process of organization itself.

When speaking of secrecy, we in fact have secrecies in mind. There is
not one single kind of secrecy; it can take on various shapes and forms. In
particular we have distinguished between formal and informal, including
public, secrecy. This distinction refers to how secrets are created, kept, and
broken. It captures the different ways in which secrecy shapes and is shaped
by organizational interactions, relations and behavior. Although in some
organizational contexts one form of secrecy might be more prevalent than
another, more often than not they coexist and perhaps be even intertwined.

In approaching secrecy through the lens of organizing, the book has
shifted the focus from the information that is hidden to processes of intentional hiding, their conditions and consequences; in short, from secrets to secrecy. It is not adequate to regard secrecy simply in terms of the
information it conceals, such as dark or strategic information. Instead,
or additionally, we must grasp its significance for organizing given the
epistemic cabling and compartmentalization it involves. Any analysis of
secrecy needs to take into account its varied implications for social differentiation, bonding, the creation and cementing of group identities, and

the exercise of power, along with the social psychological experiences involved. Indeed, the fascination of secrecy has something to do with the feelings it evokes. It is a phenomenon that can produce strong reactions: from the painful sense of betrayal to the alluring feelings of specialness and superiority to the burdens of guilt and responsibility. It can engender awe and fear. Secrecy is therefore not to be approached in a dry, technical manner. The concept should not be used as just another tool to apply to a particular aspect of organizations. In drawing on references to secrecy from a wide range of sources, including novels and films, we have tried to give a flavor of the colorful ways in which secrecy both brings organizations to life while also being ingrained into organizational life.

In this concluding chapter we explain why and how secrecy matters for understanding organizations. We begin by discussing what it means to add secrecy to the analytical repertoire of organization theory. Here we outline what discussions not only of secrecy but of organizations more generally can gain from incorporating the insights advanced in this book. But we also want to meet an obvious objection to this claim. Though we have given many illustrations of secrecy in organizations, there are surely significant problems when it comes to studying it empirically. So we provide some discussion and suggestions about how this might be achieved before concluding with an invitation to others to explore further the theme of secrecy.

BRINGING SECRECY IN

Our interest in organizational secrecy has been driven by our passionate belief that research should aspire to understand the richness and complexities of organizational life by giving a "realistic" account of it. This is a heavily freighted term to use, but we believe that although what is kept secret, how, and why is socially constructed, it remains the case that at particular places and times secrets exist as a fact of organizational life. It is only in this way that we can make critical contributions to debates on organizations and their various implications for individuals and society at large. If secrecy is present in organizational life—as our numerous examples from empirical studies and elsewhere have suggested—its significance should be taken into account when studying organizations.

Research needs to acknowledge the pervasiveness of organizational secrecy by refraining from treating it as a marginal or anomalous phenomenon, and in so doing, see how what remains hidden fundamentally shapes, if not makes, organizations.

In approaching secrecy as a form of organizing, we can paint a more nuanced picture of why people keep or disclose secrets as well as how this affects insiders and outsiders. Far from being self-evidently defined through economic and legal concepts, formal secrets are subject to the indeterminacy of what needs to be kept secret. Related to this is the dilemma of the need of organizational compartmentalization for reducing the risk of revelation versus the need to share secrets for the effective functioning of organizations. This highlights that formal secrecy is a complex and contested social process that involves more than simply determining what knowledge is to be kept hidden and signing legal contracts. We have also questioned the apparently obvious idea that formal secrecy is somehow stronger in the sense of providing a better protection of knowledge than informal secrecy, or even a more real form of secrecy. The codification of knowledge produces vulnerabilities so that precisely when strategic matters deemed as highly important are involved, people may prefer to engage in informal secrecy, which is less traceable. Furthermore, because informal secrecy has a greater potential to create tight social bonds given that it is based on individual membership selection and normative control, insiders of informal secrecy may feel more bound to maintain it than they do formal secrecy.

These insights are directly relevant to debates about knowledge-sharing and -hiding. The attractions of secrecy may help to explain why organizational silos remain stubbornly resistant to organizational endeavors to enhance knowledge-sharing. Moreover, whereas secrecy in the form of knowledge-hiding is often seen as stifling creativity and innovative processes,[1] our analysis shows how the reverse may also be the case. Secrecy is not only about knowledge-hiding, but also about sharing knowledge in social formations such as groups, cliques, and networks. Such social formations can foster creative thinking to the extent that they develop separate rules and norms and provide members with a sense of autonomy vis-à-vis the existing organizational hierarchy and structure. The feelings of importance and specialness acquired by working in secret may also allow members to cope with the uncertainty concerning how an idea or product in the making will be evaluated by outsiders—something that is especially prevalent at the beginning of creative processes. Thus, contra to discussions favoring openness as inevitably desirable, secrecy can in fact spur the sharing of knowledge and therefore aid rather than undermine creativity.[2]

The social psychological dimensions of secrecy are also relevant for understanding situations in which it is deemed important for commercial or other reasons for an organization to guard secrets, whether internally or externally. They shed light on the ways in which people may gain a sense of importance by hinting at, and thus potentially compromising, their possession of secrets. Alternatively, the burden of secrecy may motivate people to reveal organizational secrets—for example, in the case of whistleblowing—with effects that may be either reprehensible or laudable depending on the particular case and how it is viewed.

This core idea of the special nature of secret knowledge has another consequence. People can be prone to treat it differently, believing that it is more relevant and real than other knowledge, with the *mysterium* of secrets leading to them being elevated to a special ontological status. This can mean that there is a greater risk that insiders of secrecy, such as leaders in public and private organizations, become overconfident in their strategic decisions; they feel themselves to know better and more than outsiders and thus refrain from consulting others. Similarly, it can mean that outsiders of secrecy-sharing groups and organizations place too much trust in the insiders' apparently superior knowledge and therefore ability to make the right decisions. To take an extreme example, these processes can be of political significance in times of crisis when people may feel compelled to trust politicians' decisions on the basis that "we don't know what they know." But this can also explain how the opposite can occur: a spiral of distrust can emerge, when outsiders come to perceive a lack of knowledge among, or misinformation from, insiders to whom they previously ascribed access to secrets and thus having special insights (as seems apparent in the case of the US intervention in the Iraq War in 2003). And it can explain the eternal appeal of conspiracy theories in which it is believed that the secret truth is concealed by shadowy, powerful elites.

The link between secrecy (in its different variants), social differentiation, and the sense of specialness—the allure of secrecy—is important for understanding the rise of organizational cultures of secrecy in which secrecy becomes the end in itself. It shows how regardless of the value of the information involved, secrecy can become a default mode in organizations. Indeed, the sense that another organization or group inside the organization engages in secrecy may spur the hiding of knowledge among those perceived as outsiders. Here secrecy takes place for symbolic rather than simply strategic reasons. The idea of a culture of secrecy is important to keep in mind in discussions of dark secrecy, which often treat secrecy in terms of a few "bad apples" who disfigure otherwise ethical organizations. Such an account neglects the ways that dark secrecy may be culturally embedded and institutionalized within organizations. The insight is directly significant for the ongoing debates on transparency and democratic accountability. If organizations seek to be more, or even fully, transparent in the way often urged on publicly accountable organizations in particular, then the powerful allure of secrets and their cultural embeddedness become highly relevant. Attempts at organizational transparency may be resisted, precisely because secrecy has the possibility to bestow a strong sense of belonging and specialness.[3]

In drawing attention to why and how people can be so strongly invested in the keeping of secrets, we can explain why transparency measures may not only be difficult to enforce but also be based on an illusory understanding of organizational dynamics.[4] This can create dilemmas, especially in public organizations where transparency needs to be particularly strongly espoused in public, yet daily organizational life itself might be deeply bound up with secrecy.[5] Indeed, under the veil of transparency initiatives, which usually focus on very specific organizational issues, informal secrecy may foster and/or organizations may introduce even stricter and intricate forms of formal secrecy, thus circumventing the transparency efforts. This may occur precisely as actors seek to maintain a sense of being in control as opposed to being controlled through externally imposed transparency programs.

In this context, the distinction we have drawn between formal, informal and public secrecy becomes crucial: the avowed policy of organizations may be one of transparency while the informal practices remain secretive. People may engage in informal secrecy for image creation by decoupling the information they provide to outsiders from their actions and/or actively misinform outsiders.[6] In such cases, public secrecy is also likely to be prevalent because it allows those involved to deal with the contradictory reality of both publicly adhering to the transparency measurements while simultaneously circumventing them. Moreover, the distinction has implications for the issue of accountability. In the case of formal secrecy insiders become more accountable because the fact that they are in the know, and what they know, is tangible, whereas in the case of informal and public secrecy one can pretend not to know or have known anything. A notorious example of this is the debates around what Germans knew about the death camps in the Second World War.[7] Thus the burdening and binding aspects of secrecy—in its legal, social, and emotional senses—can explain why actors may intentionally seek not to know certain secrets. In the case of the Holocaust, the use of euphemisms such as "the final solution" even in the minutes of formal meetings precisely expresses this.

Given that last example, it seems important to reemphasize our view of secrecy as being neither good nor evil. Secrecy is an inherent, or as Simmel puts it, a universal feature of social life that will not entirely disappear, no matter which transparency and public accountability measures are taken. We need to be cautious about the dualistic categorization of transparency and public accountability as ethically desirable as opposed to secrecy as problematic as if, as the former US President John F. Kennedy famously put it, "The very word 'secrecy' is repugnant in a free and open society."[8] Such a categorization fails to see how secrecy and transparency overlap. Secrecy can involve forms of organizational surveillance, that is, attempts to make transparent members' actions. Furthermore, it does not sufficiently account for the political and normative nature of transparency discourses and practices. Transparency in terms of the striving toward informational control is what defines total institutions. In such cases, engaging in secrecy can provide a space of autonomy. It is this (what we regard as) politically desirable aspect of secrecy that we hope to bring into debates about transparency and accountability that are typically primarily focused on secrecy's undoubtedly existing dark sides. Indeed, in the current climate of debates about big data, secrecy may have become a necessary form of resistance and protection.

Beyond such issues of individual autonomy and resistance, it seems to us that there are good arguments for organizations, including the state, to engage in secrecy. There are legitimate issues of commercial confidentiality and state security that are not helped by approaching secrecy and transparency/accountability as binaries. The key issue is what things, for what reasons, and within what groups secrets are kept or revealed. We have even suggested that an all-out demand for transparency may actually negate accountability and enhance secrecy: in a world where everything is publicly available the volume of information would be so great that it would be easy to hide inconvenient truths. To reprise the example we gave in chapter 2, this can be seen in the way that when customers sign up for, say, mobile phone apps or Internet services, they are required to consent to multiple, complex terms and conditions of service that may run to thousands of clauses. In practice, of course, few if any of us read them—we just tick the box and only later may discover the consequences. If that does happen, and we complain, the service provider is protected by the fact that it has been completely open and the user was fully informed of the terms and conditions and agreed to them. Here transparency paradoxically allows the hiding of information, and the accountability implied by consumer agreement is bogus.

Uncovering Organizations: The Hidden Architecture

Our aim has been to add secrecy to the analytical repertoire of organization studies by showing that, despite its marginal treatment in the field, it is widespread and in a certain way constitutive of organizations. We want to encourage researchers not only to study secrecy per se—although that would be welcome—but also to deploy the notion of secrecy when studying a wide range of organizational phenomena. Given the manifold ways in which secrecy shapes and is shaped by organizational behavior, interactions, and relationships, it is directly relevant for the study of a broad array of topics, for example, those of change, innovation, politics, and leadership. Unless it is believed that these and other examples occur in a fully open and transparent way, then it must be the case that an attention to secrecy will supplement their analysis. The agenda we therefore seek to promote is to insinuate into organization research the question of how secrecy impinges on such staple topics.

For instance, in studies of change management a focus on secrecy can help to understand how decision making may be shaped by actors' belonging to an exclusive network, formed around the sharing of informal secrets and involving strong forms of normative control. Similarly, research on organizational politics can gain from including secrecy in the analysis so as to understand how, say, a department seeks to exert control over other departments through classifying information as secret—something that reinforces members' sense of belonging to that department, making them emotionally invested in keeping the secret in front of members of other departments, but also contributing to struggles over resources and decisions. Moreover, studies of gender, race, and class may incorporate our insights so as to further understand how forms of discrimination and "othering" take place and are fostered through secrecy's construction of insiders versus outsiders. Our insights can also contribute to studies of innovation, for instance, by explaining why actors are particularly likely to conceal information about new innovative products when there is a strong group identity formed and maintained through normative control processes involving a rich array of ritualistic practices. And studies of leadership can gain from incorporating secrecy into their analysis because it sheds light on how the distinction between the leader and follower is often based on secrecy given the differential knowledge, or the perception thereof, involved; the aura and performance of leadership may be greatly built on the possibly illusory idea that the leader holds secrets and therefore knows more than others.

In addition to incorporating the concept of secrecy into different areas of organizational analysis, we propose that the focus on the hidden architecture helps to understand organizational life more generally. The insight that secrecy constitutes a form of organizing adds a new dimension to central debates about what constitutes organizations. Let us turn to some classic definitions of organizations to see how this is the case. In the foundational text *Administrative Behavior*, Economics Nobel Prize-winner Herbert Simon defines an organization as "patterns of communications and relations among a group of human beings, including the processes for making and implementing decisions."[9] This can be enriched by understanding how organizational secrecy and the boundaries it constructs shape such patterns of communication and social relations on the basis of which decision making takes place. Here it is important to reemphasize that secrecy is not to be seen as in opposition to communication. Instead we have shown how it structures communication by setting barriers around what is said and what is not, by whom and to whom, and thereby, as with communication in general, constitutes organizations.[10] And in its public form secrecy paradoxically allows communication by the resolute noncommunication of important knowledge.

In another landmark piece, *Organizations*, James March and Herbert Simon refer to organizations as "systems of coordinated action among individuals and groups whose preferences, information, interests, or knowledge differ."[11] Again our focus on secrecy as bringing about the hidden architecture of organizations is directly relevant here. Not only does secrecy coordinate actions through the "decided order"[12] in terms of the boundaries of groups and organizational membership it produces, but also it is one primary mechanism in which differentials of knowledge and information are created.

The picture we seek to paint of organizations is not a static one (as these definitions might make it seem). Secrecy as much as organizations and their architecture is processual, emergent and ongoing.[13] Secrecy is not a one-off event, nor are organizations fixed entities. The organizational architecture it creates are changing because the boundaries between insiders and outsiders need continual maintenance yet can easily break and shift given the inherent vulnerability to revelation. Moreover, there is a recursive relationship between secrecy as organizing and secrecy in organizations. At the same time as secrecy makes, remakes, and potentially unmakes organizations, organizations also bring about and embed secrecy.

Bringing secrecy into these core definitions of organizations involves moving from envisioning organizations in terms of what is visible to their more hidden aspects. Organizations are constituted both by those things that can be seen and heard as well as those things that actors intentionally conceal. This distinction between the visible and hidden is not to be equated with formal and informal. The hidden processes can take place as much in the official realm (i.e., formal secrecy) as in the informal one (i.e., informal and public secrecy). Organizational researchers have long delved into things that are in some way not immediately visible (for example cultures, motivations, tacit knowledge), but what we are urging here is an attention to those things that are more or less intentionally concealed.

Despite all this, we do not claim or aim to add a new "approach" to organization studies. The field certainly does not lack in multiple schools and specialized subfields! Instead our intention is to incorporate secrecy across different, already existing approaches. We are wary about the obsession of continually making claims of newness that seems to have become mandatory in the field. Secrecy is not a new phenomenon, nor is it necessarily more or less relevant today, nor is the interest in it entirely new. Part and parcel of our efforts has been to connect to foundational theorizations, such as those of Weber, Goffman, and Simmel, as well as to classic studies of organizations such as those of Dalton, Moore, Schein, and many others. Because organization studies as a discipline is in many ways in thrall to the new, it tends to be forgetful of its rich intellectual heritage. We see giving attention to secrecy as one way of tapping into some of the neglected veins of that heritage.

RESEARCHING SECRECY

Let us suppose that all arguments put forward in this book are accepted. Still, it might be asked: how can we study that which is intentionally kept hidden? Empirical investigations of organizational secrecy are by definition difficult, because "after all, it is much easier to study what people do discuss than what they do not" and thus keep secret.[14] This is perhaps the main reason why the phenomenon has remained a neglected research terrain. However, it may also be that the very ubiquity of secrecy means that researchers do not even notice it.[15] If so, the first value of identifying the concept of organizational secrecy lies in sensitizing researchers to its possibility as they conduct empirical research. Thus, it is not so much a matter of studying organizational secrecy *per se* but of being attuned to its potential relevance to the primary object of study, whatever that might be.

Research access to formal secrets is likely to be difficult to achieve (or, at least, in a way that will allow ready publication of the findings). Certainly formal secrets, such as those relating to trade protection or national security, will either be concealed from researchers altogether or be subject to stringent legal safeguards. In such cases the only realistic research methods will be to some degree historical in character. This is possible to the extent that formal secrets may well have a finite life and cease to require or have legal protection after this time. For example, a number of studies exist of state intelligence agencies based upon information that was once secret but has subsequently been declassified.[16] The study of Bletchley Park from which we have drawn some examples is one such case. In a similar way, commercially sensitive research might be conducted subject to a time-delay agreement that expires when the sensitivity no longer exists. A further strategy may be to interview individuals who have recently exited the organization under study. Although they may still be subject to previously signed confidentiality agreements, their willingness to provide insights not on the content but on the process of secrecy is likely to be higher (as one often sees in, for example, the memoirs of former politicians). Indeed, it may be possible for researchers to access secrecy when it is manifest without accessing secrets themselves. Here the distinction of secrets and secrecy has an importance because it means that the secrecy process can be researched even where the secret content is inaccessible. For example, the interrelation of secrecy and the creation of a strong group identity resulting from being part a new product development group may be researchable without knowing anything about the new product. A good example in this regard is Gusterson, who discusses in considerable detail the rituals of secrecy within the nuclear weapons laboratory he studied without having to reveal anything about the technical secrets which these rituals related to.

Researching informal secrecy, including its public variant, poses challenges that are both lesser and greater than for formal secrecy. The challenges are less because informal secrecy is by definition not protected by the same kind of legal sanctions as formal secrecy. But they are greater because it is not necessarily a matter of gaining knowledge of concrete, discrete pieces of information but may require a more subtle and less tangible understanding of how shared meaning is created. This means that in-depth participant observation is necessary; only in this way can familiarity and trust with organizational members be established and organizational secrets be shared with researchers as if they were organizational members. The researcher has to become part of the in-group, which, specifically for informal secrecy, requires a certain level of trust, established through closeness, mirroring the process of informal secrecy itself. As Schein notes in relation to his work on secrecy and in-groups, "You had to be a real insider to know."[17] Indeed, it is not surprising that his and the other studies, such as those of Jackall and Dalton, were based on extensive field involvements. In some ways, public secrecy may be easier to research, because we have here "an unstable and uncapturable blending . . . of concealment and revelation of secret that for all its secretness is not really a secret."[18] However, although the secret is public, researchers need to become or be made aware of its presence by the hints, subtle clues, and peoples' efforts of knowingly not knowing. This requires researchers not only to be familiar with the operating norms and values, which public secrecy tries to protect, but also to observe and participate in interactions between organizational members.

At the same time, the researcher, especially when participating in various groups, needs to be cautious in not revealing secrets to other groups and thus to be reflexive about the tension involved in secrecy.[19] Discretion, confidentiality, and the protection of sources are particularly relevant when studying secrecy because, as our analysis has shown, secrecy and power are so interrelated. This means that by gaining access to secrets the researcher becomes implicated in the very power dynamics secrecy gives rise to. Although any kind of research involvement and the knowledge it produces is political, in relation to secrecy the researcher has to be especially aware of and carefully handle the dynamics, such as those concerning social differentiation and attributions of superiority, that this can involve.[20]

Organizational secrecy also poses questions regarding overreliance of interviews in empirical research. Paradoxically, it may call for a more careful listening to what is not said. This implies that an awareness of the "strategic absences, [the secret's] resort to riddle and tone," as Taussig puts it in relation to public secrecy is required.[21] One perhaps slightly fanciful way to imagine such research activity would be in terms of the decoding or deciphering of messages[22] or conducting a "kryptonymy" (as psychoanalysts have termed the search for and interpretation of those things that are deeply hidden in, yet fundamentally shape our psychic life).[23] Although a sophisticated analysis, such as a textual, conversational, or discourse analysis, can certainly be revealing, what we envision here is that researchers, in addition to their "natural" engagement in the field, become sensitive to the potential presence of secrecy. Here part of the difficulty is to determine why informants do not share certain information with the researcher or other organizational members: is it because they do not actually know it themselves or because they intentionally try to conceal it? Apart from directly asking informants, being attentive to their presentation of self in interaction—blushing, hesitations, voice lowering, and long pauses before answers—may give clues about the presence of secrecy. At the same time, one needs to be cautious about outsiders' attribution of secrecy when it is not present; organizational members may refer to nonexistent secrets because this makes them feel special. In these and other cases, the triangulation of sources in terms of the accounts of different organizational members or other data will help in verifying or making more plausible any findings concerning secrecy.

Sensitivity toward the presence of secrecy also calls for researchers to be reflexive about how information sharing in the interview is shaped by the existing group relations and potentially by the workings of secrecy within a specific organizational context. This is of course the case in any research interview, but more so when secrecy is at stake. Clearly the way in which concepts of secrecy are brought to bear will vary considerably according to the research context, and a sensitization to self-conduct in specific contexts is necessary. Secrecy will manifest itself in different ways that may not be immediately obvious within these different settings. Our point throughout has been that we need to notice secrecy in organizations and, when we notice it, recognize its varied significance for organizational life.

As we have worked on this book and discussed the ideas within it with others, what has been remarkable is how, once attuned to it, we and they have noticed on a daily basis how ubiquitous secrecy at work is. In so many of our interactions there are imprecations to treat this or that piece of information or event as confidential—it happens in formal meeting rooms quite as much as in corridor conversations, and relates to everything from institutional decision making to promotion prospects to our colleagues' private lives. When we set our students' exams we are required not to use email but to keep the questions on a secure flash drive; when we mark them, the students' identities are anonymized to prevent prejudice or favoritism. Our networked institutional documents are password protected to conceal them from the view of outsiders. When we discuss ideas with policymakers or corporations we frequently do so under rules of non-disclosure. When we conduct or seek funding for empirical research we abide by ethics codes that require the anonymization and secure storage of data. Before entering a research site we normally sign a confidentiality agreement with the organization, and if conducting research interviews or administering questionnaires the first step is always to give assurances of confidentiality. When we submit papers to peer-reviewed academic journals for double-blind review, our identities are kept secret from those who review them, just as the identity of the reviewers is kept secret from us (yet both authors and reviewers speculate about, and no doubt sometimes guess, one anothers' identity). Once looked for, secrecy in its many forms appears all around us, structuring our working world and shaping our interactions within that world. In recognizing it in our own organizational experience we are surely obliged to acknowledge it when we study the organizational experiences of others.

THE END OF THE TOUR

In this book we have conducted a tour—perhaps like that given by guides in a stately home—of the cryptic, concealed, and secluded spaces of organizational life. By delving into the shadows of organizations, our aim has been to bring the workings of secrecy into the light. On this tour we have encountered the intriguing dynamics of secrecy and its multifaceted social and emotional implications for individuals and organizations. This has allowed us to develop an understanding of how secrecy organizes social relations and thus can be constitutive of organizations. There are, of course, more sights and sites of organizational secrecy to visit: in a tour of a stately home, some areas are not on view and other areas might arouse such interest that one returns for a second or third visit. For all we have tried to accomplish, our tour has been one of exploration, guided by those who have explored these sequestered walls, hidden attics and obscure turrets before us; and offering to those who may wish to follow the analytical keys to open the doors to the hidden architecture of organizational life that is the work of secrecy and within which secrecy is at work.

Notes

INTRODUCTION

1. The various literatures relating to secrecy utilize the terms *information* and *knowledge* variously or indiscriminately. In this book we use the terms interchangeably to reflect this (because it would be very cumbersome to disaggregate the usages) but mainly because both information and knowledge may equally be subject to secrecy. It is true that it is often held, especially in computer science, that information becomes knowledge when acted upon in some way, and so, in this sense, because to keep a secret is to act, then any information that is secret must in fact be knowledge. However, in the organizational literature the meaning, distinction, and relationship of knowledge and information is the subject of considerable debate (see, e.g., Blackler, 1995; Tsoukas & Vladimirou, 2001), which is beyond the scope of this book.

2. Throughout this book we use *organization studies* as a generic term to encompass what in different communities is called variously *organization theory*, *organization behavior*, *organization analysis*, or, indeed, *organization studies*.

3. Liebeskind (1997: 625) stated that "an extensive literature search revealed that there is very little in the current business, organizational theory or institutional economics literature on the issue of organizational secrecy." Ten years later, introducing a short special section on the topic, Jones (2008: 95) noted that "secrets are rarely studied by organizational scholars," and one of the contributions points out that "secrets in organizations are pervasive [but] have not been studied in any systematic way" (Anand & Rosen, 2008: 97).

4. Schein (1985/2000), Jackall (1988).

5. Mone & McKinlay (1993), Weick (1996), Greenwood & Hinings (2002), Starbuck (2003), Czarniawska (2008), Gabriel (2010), Grey (2010), Suddaby et al. (2011).

6. Collinson (1992), Woods (1993), Rich & Janos (1994), Gusterson (1998), Žižek (2011).

7. Bok (1989: 6).

8. Bok (1989: 11).

9. Brewis et al. (2006).

10. Marx (1999), Nissenbaum (1999).

11. Teich et al. (1999), Scott & Rains (2005), Rains & Scott (2007), Frois (2009), Coleman (2013), Dobusch & Schoeneborn (2015).

12. http://www.experienceproject.com/.

13. Land (2008: 1195).

14. Martin (1990).
15. Morrison & Milliken (2000).
16. See, e.g., Baker & Faulkner (1993), Erickson (1981), Parker (2008), Stohl & Stohl (2011), Schoeneborn & Scherer (2012), Scott (2013).
17. It is true that one of our empirical sources is an organization whose existence was at the time secret from the general public. But, first, its existence became publicly known, and, second, it was not clandestine in the sense of being hidden from the authorities—indeed, it was a state organization.
18. Simmel (1906: 463; emphasis added).
19. Bok (1989: 14), see also Birchall (2011a).
20. Although as we later suggest, the converse is possible: there can be processes of secrecy with no actual secrets being hidden.
21. *The Huffington Post* (2011).
22. Zerubavel (2006).
23. Dufresne & Offstein (2008: 103, emphasis added).
24. Horn (2011).
25. Horn (2011: 109).
26. Horn (2011: 108).
27. Luhrmann (1989: 138).
28. See the literature on the "communication as constitutive of organizations" (CCO) perspective, e.g., Ashcraft et al. (2009), Cooren et al. (2011), Brummans et al. (2014).
29. We avoid the terms *information architecture* and *knowledge architecture*, which are widely used in computer science, because of their technical meanings. By *epistemic architecture* we denote a social and organizational architecture related specifically to secret knowledge.
30. Scott (2009: 277).
31. Those wanting to see full methodological details should refer to the studies themselves.
32. Grey & Sturdy (2008, 2009, 2010), Grey (2012, 2013, 2014).
33. We appreciate that this abbreviation nowadays is likely to connote British Petroleum, but we use it in the interests of concision and hope that readers will come to find it familiar.
34. Anderson-Gough, Grey, & Robson (1998, 2000, 2001, 2002, 2005, 2006), Costas (2012, 2013), Costas & Fleming (2009), Costas & Grey (2014), Costas & Kärreman (2013, 2015), Grey (1994, 1998).
35. Costas & Kärreman (2015).
36. Costas & Grey (2014).
37. Grey (1998).
38. Anderson-Gough, Grey, & Robson (2000).
39. Grey (1994).
40. Costas (2012).

CHAPTER I: LAYING THE THEORETICAL FOUNDATIONS

1. Kafka (1925/2000: 90).

2. Kafka (2000: 90).

3. Kafka (2000: 94).

4. Kafka (2000: 174).

5. Weber (1922/1978: 992). At another point Weber argues: "While not peculiar to bureaucratic organizations, the concept of 'official secrets' is certainly typical of them" (1978: 225).

6. Weber (1978: 225).

7. Weber notes that "the 'secret' . . . is more safely hidden in the books of an enterprise than it is in the files of public authorities" (1978: 994).

8. Donaldson (1992).

9. This prevalence of secrecy and its interrelation with power can explain secrecy's "bad name" and why it is the target of contemporary transparency movements (see Roberts, 2006).

10. Canetti (1981: 290).

11. Canetti (1981: 293).

12. One might also argue that the obverse can be true—the wildly indiscreet person can more easily fool others and conceal secrets because everyone assumes that he or she is incapable of keeping secrets. This seems to have been the case with Guy Burgess, a member of the Cambridge spy ring that spied on the West for the Soviet Union (Boyle, 1979).

13. Canetti notes that although a "large part of the prestige of dictatorships is due to the fact that they are credited with the concentrated power of secrecy" (1981: 295), secrecy can also be prevalent in modern governments: "Scarcely was the human dictator dead . . . than the secret turned up again in the shape of the atomic bomb, more dangerous than ever" (1981: 296).

14. Michels (1958: 91).

15. Mills (1959: 294).

16. Mills (1959: 244–45).

17. Roberts (2006).

18. Horn (2011).

19. Fenster (2008: 1).

20. Simmel (1906: 464).

21. Simmel notes that "secrecy serves and intensifies . . . differentiation" (1906: 466–67).

22. Simmel defines secrecy as "consciously willed concealment" (1906: 449). This is consistent with our own definition of "intentional concealment."

23. Simmel (1906: 463).

24. Simmel (1906: 462).

25. Simmel argues that "the strong accentuated expression of all not within the circle of secrecy results in a correspondingly accentuated feeling of personal possession . . . [which] acquires its proper significance, not from the mere fact of

having, but besides that there must be the consciousness that others must forego the possession" (1906: 467). This is rather different from the inclusions and exclusions of, say, professional knowledge that outsiders might, in principle, acquire.

26. Simmel (1906: 464).

27. Simmel (1906: 486–87).

28. The Skull and Bones society is often referred to as a power elite, emphasizing the link of secrecy to power elites discussed in the previous section (see Millegan, 2004).

29. Simmel notes that "every superior personality, and every superior performance, has, for the average of mankind, something mysterious" (1906: 465).

30. He refers to the "peculiar degree of cohesion" (1906: 492) in secret societies.

31. Simmel (1906: 492).

32. Chatham House is the Royal Institute of International Affairs, a global think tank. The Chatham House Rule, originally formulated in 1927, states that "when a meeting, or part thereof, is held under the Chatham House Rule, participants are free to use the information received, but neither the identity nor the affiliation of the speaker(s), nor that of any other participant, may be revealed."

33. Simmel (1906: 465).

34. Simmel (1906: 466).

35. Simmel (1906: 466).

36. This distinction of manifest and latent secrets—also found in Goffman—was expressed in former US Secretary of Defense Donald Rumsfeld's widely but wrongly derided reference to there being known (i.e., manifest) unknowns and unknown (i.e., latent) unknowns.

37. Simmel (1906: 466).

38. Simmel (1906: 465).

39. Bourdieu (1984), Scott (1990), Zald & Lounsbury (2010).

40. In line with our general approach, we speak of information rather than knowledge here because this is the term used by Goffman. For Goffman, information refers not only to that what is or can be communicated through words but also what we communicate in "non-verbal, presumably unintentional" (1959/1990: 18) ways, e.g., through our facial expressions.

41. Goffman (1959/1990: 72).

42. Let us exemplify this through the example of a waiter. He or she might emphasize his or her ability to be attentive and friendly toward customers so as to be perceived as a good waiter. In the interaction with the customer, the waiter does not present his or her roles and interests outside of work—e.g., as a parent, tennis fan, or volunteer for the local community—not because he or she intentionally seeks to hide these but because this information does not contribute to producing the impression of being a good waiter. That such impression management does not involve secrecy is also apparent in that the disclosure of this information would not bring about a sense of revelation. Thus if a customer who saw the waiter at a tennis match the week before mentions this to him or her, it will not be experienced as the disclosure of secret information.

43. Goffman (1959/1990: 37). For instance, in taking on the role of the waiter, he or she may "unwittingly" (1959/1990: 37) use expressions, e.g., of smiling as soon as a customer enters the restaurant despite having a bad day.

44. Goffman (1959/1990: 56).

45. Goffman (1963/1990: 57).

46. Goffman (1959/1990: 72).

47. Goffman (1959/1990: 76).

48. Goffman (1962: 312; emphasis in original).

49. Goffman (1962: 313).

50. Goffman (1962: 314).

51. Goffman (1969: 25).

52. Goffman (1969: 42–43).

53. With respect to stigmatized individuals Goffman notes: "Even when an individual could keep an unapparent stigma secret, he will find that intimate relations with others, ratified in our society by mutual confession of invisible failings, cause him either to admit his situation to the intimate or to feel guilty for not doing so" (1963: 94).

54. Goffman (1963/1990).

55. *Guardian* (2012a).

56. Goffman (1963/1990: 141).

57. Goffman (1963/1990: 142).

58. Goffman (1963/1990: 142).

59. Goffman (1963/1990: 209).

60. In fact, in the original fairy tale, one child—unsocialized and innocent of the norms—calls out that the emperor is naked, and rest of the crowd takes up the cry. But the received version or meaning of the phrase is that no one does so.

61. Zerubavel (2006: 2).

62. Taussig (1999: 4; emphasis in original).

63. Zerubavel (2006: 3).

64. As noted previously, this is the original meaning of the story of the emperor's new clothes.

65. Zerubavel (2006: 84).

66. Taussig (1999: 159).

67. Taussig (1999: 105; emphasis in original).

68. Taussig (1999: 6).

69. Zerubavel (2006: 41).

70. Zerubavel (2006: 15).

71. Wilson (2008: 138).

72. Cf. Luhrmann (1989: 138) on how secrecy can "elicit awe," as discussed in the introduction of this book.

73. Though this does not mean that taboos necessarily involve public secrecy; people might have internalized them to such an extent that they are no longer conscious of them.

74. Zerubavel (2006: 20).

75. E.g.. medical and scientific discourse. See Foucault (1979).

76. E.g.. separate bathing and toilet facilities for men and women. See Foucault (1979).

77. Taussig (1990: 5).

78. Manning (1960).

79. Goffman (1959/1990: 30).

CHAPTER 2: BRICKS AND MORTAR

1. In chapter 5 we argue that this boundary between organization and environment is, in part, an artifact of secrecy rather than a self-evident line.

2. Bok (1984: 23).

3. Rich & Janos (1994: 7–8).

4. Katila et al. (2008).

5. *New York Times* (2005).

6. Hannah (2005, 2007).

7. E.g., Schuster & Colletti (1973), Colella et al. (2007).

8. Pfeffer (1981: 201).

9. Colella et al. (2007).

10. Colella et al. (2007: 56).

11. For an extensive discussion of organizational misconduct, defined as "behavior in or by an organization that a social-control agent judges to transgress a line separating right from wrong; where such a line can separate legal, ethical, and socially responsible behavior from their antitheses," see Greve at al. (2010: 56).

12. *Financial Times* (2011).

13. *Spiegel* (2010).

14. *New York Times* (2008).

15. *Guardian* (2008).

16. *Financial Times* (2006).

17. Leeson (1997).

18. Hence the expression, first coined in relation to Watergate, that what creates scandals is "not the crime but the cover-up."

19. Freudenberg & Gramling (2011).

20. See Piotrowski (2010).

21. Knudsen (2011).

22. To give just a brief guide: Near & Miceli (1985), Wexler (1987), Gioia (1992), Miceli & Near (1992), Pompa (1992), Beamish (2000), Ashforth & Anand (2003), De Maria (2006), Ashforth et al. (2008), Lange (2008), Harrington (2009), Fleming & Zyglidopoulos (2009), Vadera et al. (2009), Piotrowski (2010), Gibson (2014).

23. Here we focus on the literature on corruption, e.g., De Maria (2006), Ashforth et al. (2008), Fleming & Zyglidopoulos (2009).

24. Vaughan (1996: 238).

25. This can be reinforced through the different financial jurisdictions across countries. There even exists a so-called financial secrecy index that ranks countries according to the opportunities their jurisdiction provides for tax evasion.

26. See, e.g., Beare (2003) and Mitchell et al. (1998).

27. http://eurodad.org/files/integration/2013/01/Secret-structures-hidden-crimes-web.pdf [Accessed January 2015].

28. Whistleblowing is defined as "the disclosure by organization members (former or current) of illegal, immoral, or illegitimate practices under the control of their employers, to persons or organizations that may be able to effect action" (Near & Miceli, 1985: 4).

29. See Vadera et al. (2009) for a recent overview of the whistleblowing literature and specifically individual and situational antecedents for whistleblowing.

30. Ellsberg (2002: 207). See Weiskopf & Willmott (2013) for an organizational analysis of the ethics of Ellsberg's whistleblowing.

31. Ellsberg (2002: 205).

32. Further ways to reduce dark secrecy are related to fostering certain ethical attitudes, cultures, and forms of leadership (e.g., Treviño & Nelson, 2007).

33. Roberts (2006), see also Sagar (2013).

34. See Fung (2007, 2013), Fenster (2006), Hood & Heald (2006), Birchall (2011a), Garsten & Lindh de Montaya (2008), Halter et al. (2009), Levay & Waks (2009), Madsen (2010), Van den Brink et al. (2010), Arellano-Gault & Lepore (2011); and for an overview of the transparency literature across the disciplines see Albu & Flyverbom (2013).

35. See Power (1997), Tsoukas (1997), Strathern (2000), Hood (2006), Garsten & Lindh de Montaya (2008), Flyverbom et al. (2011), Birchall (2011a, 2011b).

36. See also Gabriel (2005) and his discussion of the metaphor of "glass cages and glass palaces" for contemporary organizations in which transparency engenders control.

37. Sifry (2011: 14).

38. Sifry (2011: 17).

39. Sifry (2011: 135).

40. The impossibility of transparency and thus of seeing everything is pointed to by Berger and Luckmann (1967): "Although the social stock of knowledge presents the everyday world in an integrated manner, differentiated according to zones of familiarity and remoteness, it leaves the total of that world opaque. Put differently, the reality of everyday life always appears as a zone of lucidity behind which there is a background of darkness. As some zones of reality are illuminated, others are adumbrated. I cannot know everything there is to know about this reality" (1967: 44).

41. See also Davis (1998), Birkinshaw (2006), Piotrowski (2010), Florini (2011), Coombs & Holladay (2013), and Vaccaro (2012).

42. For a critical discussion of the relation between transparency and secrecy see Garsten & Lindh de Montaya (2008), Birchall (2011a, 2011b).

43. den Hond & de Bakker (2007).

44. Weber (1978: 992).

45. Simmel (1906: 464).

46. Schein (2010: 19).

47. Schein (2010: 99–100).
48. Schein (2010: 100).
49. Schein (2010: 107).
50. Dalton (1959: 53, emphasis added).
51. Dalton (1959: 52).
52. Dalton (1959: 52). For a critical discussion of the ethical basis of Dalton's study see Feldman (1996, 2004).
53. Dalton (1959: 56).
54. Dalton (1959: 53).
55. Dalton (1959: 60, emphasis omitted).
56. Jackall (1988: 122).
57. Jackall (1988: 80).
58. Jackall (1988: 80).
59. Jackall (1988: 194).
60. Jackall (1988: 203).
61. Jackall (1988: 202–3).
62. Jackall (1988: 133).
63. Simmel (1906: 473).
64. Argyris (1957: 158–59).
65. Argyris (1957: 163).
66. Argyris (1957: 212).
67. Crozier (1974: 153). See Connelly et al. (2012) for knowledge-hiding more generally.
68. See Burawoy (1979).
69. Crozier (1974: 162).
70. Marx (1887/1978) and see Edwards (1979).
71. Gouldner (1954). See Scott (1992) for resistance more generally.
72. Dalton (1959: 266).
73. Jackall (1988: 122).
74. Moore (1962: 69).
75. Moore (1962: 70).
76. Moore (1962: 70).
77. Moore (1962: 74).
78. The dictum *scientia potentia est*. In fact what Bacon wrote was *ipsa scientia potestas est* ("Knowledge itself is power").
79. French & Raven (1959). The original formulation identified expert power, and informational power was later added.
80. Lukes (2005).
81. Feldman & March (1981: 174).
82. Of course, for such attributions to take place secrecy needs to be manifest rather than latent, i.e., the outsiders need to be aware of the fact that the other person is holding a secret.
83. Berger & Luckmann (1967: 66).
84. Berger & Luckmann (1967: 85).

85. Lukes (2005).
86. Foucault (1980).
87. Shenhav (1999).
88. Miller & Rose (1994).
89. See also Luhrmann (1989).
90. As a minor illustration of this, in the research for the Bletchley Park study, the researcher occasionally came across files in the archive that were marked as still being classified and therefore unavailable for public view. The effect was always to produce a sense of great curiosity as to what it might contain and the assumption that, somehow, it must be of great interest.

CHAPTER 3: WALLS AND CORRIDORS

1. Cawelti & Rosenberg (1987: 14).
2. Le Carré has repeatedly rejected the idea that his novels depict the intelligence world in an authentic way, saying that had they done so he would not have been able to publish them. He says that what they offer is a depiction that is credible (*Guardian*, 2013a).
3. Formal secrecy need not always take place within a rational-legal frame. Secret societies may operate in similar ways, e.g., having written constitutions and keeping records. However, in line with our general parameters, we do not consider these here. Nor do we imply that formal secrecy is solely the purview of bureaucratic and/or formal organizations rather than, e.g., network forms. For example, a network organization may hold trade secrets, and when it does so this is rational-legal in character.
4. Townley (2008: 55–57).
5. Bok (1989: 136).
6. Cheung (1982), Scheppele (1989), Swedberg (2003), Anton & Yao (2004), Epstein (2004), Stead & Cross (2009), Information Security (2009).
7. Dougherty (2001), Katila et al. (2008), Knott & Posen (2009), Delarue & Lejeune (2011).
8. Teece (1986). See also Hurmelinna-Laukkanen & Puumalainen (2007), Hurmelinna-Laukkanen et al. (2008).
9. Maurer & Zugelder (2000: 156, 162–63).
10. Teece (1986: 287).
11. Bok (1989: 140), Liebeskind (1997: 268).
12. E.g., Milgrim (1967), Vandevoort (1971), Hutter (1981), Wiener & Cava (1988), Hettinger, (1989), Paine (1991), Bone (1998), Maurer & Zugelder (2000).
13. Liebeskind & Oliver (1998).
14. Argyres (1999), Milberg et al. (2000), Rivkin (2001), Gaa (2009).
15. See Macpherson (1978).
16. *Financial Times* (2012).
17. As noted, patents are not trade secrets, but the principle—that the costs of redress are high—holds.
18. Hill (2004: 27).

19. Calvocoressi (2001: 81–84).
20. See Grey (2012: 160–61) for a detailed explanation.
21. Calvocoressi (2001: 23).
22. Rich & Janos (1994: 42–43).
23. Simmel (1906: 467).
24. Rich & Janos (1994: 6).
25. Rich & Janos (1994: 10).
26. Liebeskind (1997: 651).
27. Liebeskind (1997: 633).
28. Hannah (2005, 2007).
29. See Whitman & Mattord (2014) for a recent overview.
30. Hughes (2009: 288–89).
31. Kunda (1992).
32. See, e.g., Sewell & Wilkinson (1992).
33. Rich & Janos (1994: 79).
34. Top-secret military and commercial installations—but not, in fact, Bletchley Park—are for this reason often sited in remote locations, an aspect of compartmentalization. See Gusterson (1998) for an example.
35. Quoted in Grey (2012: 126–27).
36. Swasy (1993) cited in Liebeskind (1997: 639).
37. CNN (2014).
38. Liebeskind (1997: 626–27).
39. Teece (1986: 287), see also Cheung (1982).
40. Connelly et al. (2011: 64).
41. Dufresne & Offstein (2008: 103).
42. See Grey (2012: 230–31).
43. Roberts (2006: 42).
44. Sifry (2011: 155).
45. Quoted in Grey (2012: 132).
46. Blau (1955).
47. Kanter (1977: 59–60).
48. Bendix (1966: 452).
49. Among other things he was a director at GCHQ, the United Kingdom's signals intelligence organization, which is the lineal descendant of Bletchley Park, and the equivalent of the United States' National Security Agency.
50. Herman (1996: 328–30).
51. Herman (1996: 93).
52. Erickson (1979: 127).
53. Weber (1978: 1418).
54. Roberts (2006: 39).
55. Liebeskind (1997: 639).
56. Rich & Janos (1994: 44).
57. Ellsberg (2002: 238).
58. Quoted in Sifry (2011: 158).

59. Grey (2012: 88).

60. British government ministers receive a daily "red box" or boxes containing paperwork to be read, some of which may be secret.

61. Herman (2001: 6).

62. Fenster (2008).

63. Craft (1994), Patrick (2012).

64. BBC (2013).

65. Rich & Janos (1994: 43).

66. Quoted in Page (2002: 70–71).

CHAPTER 4: OPEN AND CLOSED DOORS

1. This parable has led to many interpretations and debates; see Agamben (1998, 2011), Dolar (2006).

2. The parallel here with the walls of the previous chapter should be obvious. Here we have no walls (in open-plan offices), glass walls, or wooden walls. There we had steel doors for laboratories and lead-lined walls for secret discussions. This points to the varying extent of secrecy: it is not a binary opposition of secret or not.

3. Hierarchy levels in the PSFs in general drew a distinction among consultants, trainees, or qualified staff; managers; and directors and/or partners. In this context the leadership sometimes referred just to directors and/or partners and sometimes to these plus managers.

4. Canetti (1981: 292).

5. See Dalton (1959). Moreover, there is a larger literature on gossip (that has not, however, given prominence to the role of secrecy), e.g., Noon & Delbridge (1993), Kurland & Pelled (2000), Michelson & Mouly (2000), Sotirin & Gottfried (1999), Van Iterson & Clegg (2008), Waddington (2012). Here it is important to stress that informal secrecy both overlaps with and yet is distinct from gossip. It overlaps to the extent that individuals engaging in gossip can seek to keep this secretive and that gossip-sharing involves boundary creation—of the "in" and "out" crowds—and therefore "plays a vital role in group formation, regulation and perpetuation" (Noon & Delbridge, 1993: 32). However, informal secrecy differs from gossip; what defines much gossip is informal communication rather than concealment (see Bok, 1989: 91; Noon & Delbridge, 1993: 25). Gossip does not need to entail secrecy and indeed is sometimes associated with its breach: "Secrecy sets barriers between men [sic], but at the same time offers the seductive temptation to break through the barriers by gossip" (Simmel, 1906: 466; see also Bok, 1989: 91). In short, some but not all organizational gossip may be a form of informal secrecy, and some organizational gossip may involve breaches of secrecy.

6. This expression was probably first used, and is certainly closely associated with, the existence of a corrupt group of officers within the British Metropolitan (London) police in the 1960s and 1970s. See Cox (1977).

7. See also Rodriguez & Ryave (1992).

8. Weisband & Reinig (1995).

9. *Adweek* (2014).

10. Schein (2010:100) indicates this in his example of the Basel aristocracy.
11. Pilkington (1998).
12. Brewis & Grey (2008).
13. Claire et al. (2005) and also Woods (1993).
14. Simmel (1906: 470, emphasis in original).
15. See Lewicki et al. (1998), Rousseau et al. (1998).
16. Grey & Garsten (2001).
17. Kunda (1992).
18. Simmel (1906: 473). Compare with our remarks in chapter 2 about how from a Foucauldian perspective secrecy could be seen as a disciplinary practice.
19. On professionalism, normative control, and self-discipline see Anderson-Gough et al. (2005), Bergström et al. (2009), Costas & Grey (2014), Covaleski et al. (1998).
20. Keane (2008).
21. Grey (1998).
22. Further examples of such informal secrecy, particularly concerning non-work matters, include individuals concealing their sexual orientation, especially gay sexuality, for fear of discrimination or bullying (see Ragins et al., 2007). This is different from the example discussed later in the chapter of sexual orientation being held as a public secret within the workplace.
23. *Leadership Review* (2013); *Forbes* (2014).
24. Dalton (1959: 63–64).
25. Parker (2000: 137).
26. E.g., Fisher (2012: 137) on hidden networks and gender in banking.
27. Canetti (1981: 294–95).
28. See Steele (1975: 105) on secrecy and change management initiatives.
29. See Michelson & Mouly (2000) on rumor in organizations.
30. See Dirsmith & Covaleski (1995), Brass (1995), Stohl (1995), Seibert et al. (2001), Anderson-Gough et al. (2006).
31. Costas (2012).
32. See Mintzberg (1973), Pfeffer (1981), Feldman (1988), and Buchanan & Badham (1999).
33. Michels (1958: 171, emphasis in original).
34. Feldman (1988).
35. Bachrach & Baratz (1962), Lukes (2005).
36. Handy (1985: 243).
37. Pettigrew (1972), see also Connelly et al. (2012).
38. See Costas (2012).
39. Grey (1994).
40. Bok (1984: 20).
41. See Costas & Grey (2014).
42. Goffman (1962: 314).
43. Sinclair (1995).
44. Gatrell (2011).

45. Collinson (1992: 140).

46. Perhaps it is such public secrecy that we find in Kafka's "Before the Law." The door to the Law is open, indicating that it is "in force without significance," as Agamben (1998: 51), following Gershom Scholem, notes.

47. Public secrecy differs from the now-familiar concept within organization studies of tacit knowledge (Polyani, 1966). Knowledge of public secrets is indeed tacit, but, more than that, it has to remain tacit: it cannot be rendered explicit not just in principle—because by definition it is unarticulated—but in practice, because at the moment of becoming explicit it ceases to be secret. That is different from tacit knowledge, which may in practice be made explicit; and although doing so would mean it was no longer tacit, it would still be knowledge (Nonaka & Takeuchi, 1995). To put it another way, knowledge that is tacit is only contingently tacit; public secrecy is necessarily secret.

48. Žižek (2011). See also *Open Secrets*, the aptly named collection of *New York Times* articles on WikiLeaks and US diplomacy (Star, 2011).

49. On the significance of secrecy in diplomacy, more generally, see Roberts (2004).

50. Woods (1993: 175). See also Cowan (2014) on sharing and hearing stigmatizing secrets.

51. Woods picks up this term from Ponse (1976), and it recalls the term "sham secrecy" used by Wilson (2008), which as we suggested in chapter 1 is a misnomer: this is genuine secrecy but it is in the form of public secrecy.

52. Woods (1993: 158).

53. Grey (1994: 489–91).

54. Garsten & Grey (1997).

55. Zerubavel (2006: 4).

56. This recalls the example in chapter 1 of women showing an understanding of the sexual jokes they were not supposed to understand precisely by not reacting to them.

57. See also Alvesson & Kärreman (2004), Anderson-Gough et al. (2001).

58. Van Iterson & Clegg (2008: 1126–27; emphasis in original).

59. Zerubavel (2006: 41).

60. Taussig (1999: 268).

61. An example of what Nils Brunsson (1989) calls the "organization of hypocrisy."

62. See Grint (2005).

63. Slater (1998), Miles (2003). In this context it is interesting that Peters and Waterman's (1982) management bestseller *In Search of Excellence* was originally planned to be called *The Secrets of Excellence*, but the title was vetoed in case it implied the McKinsey's clients' secrets would be revealed (Butler & Spoelstra, 2012: 891). The implication perhaps is that it is fine for such books to reveal secrets, as long as they are not the "real" secrets.

64. See, e.g., Parker (2000).

65. Vaughan (1996).

CHAPTER 5: THE HIDDEN ARCHITECTURE
OF ORGANIZATIONAL LIFE

1. Dostoyevsky (1860/1985: 84).

2. This approach is line with many contemporary "post-dualist" approaches to social science, e.g., Giddens's (1979) structuration theory, Eliasian figurational sociology, or Foucauldian post-structuralism.

3. E.g., Paulsen & Hernes (2003). We do not explore the general topic of boundaries and boundary work in organizations here. Instead, our focus is purely on secrecy and boundaries.

4. This is not a unique case. For example, the very existence of MI6, the UK foreign intelligence service, was not officially acknowledged until 1994.

5. Gabriel (2005).

6. *Forbes* (2013).

7. Gusterson (1998).

8. Gusterson (1998: 70–71).

9. Hernes (2004:81–82) argues that organizational boundaries, in general, have three dimensions: physical, social, and mental.

10. See Berg (1991). The term has also been adopted by computer security specialists to denote the segmentation of access to information.

11. E.g., Schein (1990), Trice & Beyer (1993).

12. Gusterson (1998: 71).

13. Indeed, as we mentioned in chapter 2, following Argyris (1957: 212), secrecy may be a means by which the line between formal and informal is constructed.

14. Lanchester (2013: 16).

15. Gusterson (1998: 155).

16. Grey (2012: 163).

17. Della Porta & Vanucci (2012).

18. *New York Times* (2008).

19. Gusterson (1998: 75).

20. Gusterson (1998: 256 n.15).

21. For Enron, see Hirsch (2003). More generally, see Lehar & Randl (2006), Sullivan (2008).

22. Stiglitz (2002).

23. Grey (2003).

24. Lehar & Randl (2006).

25. See Behr (2006) for secrecy in groups in general (i.e.. not just in the workplace).

26. Franklin (1734: 12).

27. *The Star*, Canada (2014).

28. In the United Kingdom, e.g., see Open Rights Group: https://wiki.open rightsgroup.org/wiki/UK_Privacy_Debacles [Accessed March 27, 2015].

29. This is a variant of a wider issue, discussed by Perrow (2011), about how vulnerability comes with the concentration of assets in one place, e.g., power stations, airport hubs. In other words, it is not just about secrecy.

30. *Guardian* (2013b).
31. *Guardian* (2014).
32. Brown (2001).
33. Lampel (2001).
34. *PC World* (2013).
35. *Computerworld* (2014).
36. Brown (2001: 85–86).
37. Simmel (1906: 464–65).
38. Herman (1996).
39. Grey (2012: 160).
40. Ellsberg (2002: 46).
41. Ellsberg (2002: 307).
42. Hill (2004: 130), Grey (2012: 124).
43. Simmel (1906: 486).
44. Snow (1954).
45. Grey (1996).
46. Snow (1954: 250).
47. Parker (2000: 110).
48. Bok (1989).
49. Fenster (2008).
50. Liebeskind (1997: 640).
51. Wyndham (1963: 40). John Wyndham had extensive personal experience of organizational secrecy, having worked as a censor in the Ministry of Information and subsequently as a cipher operator during the Second World War.
52. Gusterson (1998: 99).
53. Ellsberg (2002: 329).
54. Mlinek & Pierce (1997).
55. Ubel et al. (1995).
56. As we pointed out in chapter 3, Everett Hughes (2009) identifies confidentiality as being at the heart of many occupations and professions.
57. Hoyt (1978).
58. Younggren & Harris (2008).
59. Luepker (2012).
60. Sharkin & Birky (1992).
61. Pearlman & Saakvitne (1995).
62. Keane (2008: 106).
63. Hirschhorn (1990).
64. Freud (1919).
65. We are talking here about accidental revelations of secrets. There is a whole other area where secrets are deliberately disclosed, e.g., by whistleblowers.
66. Gusterson (1998: 79). This is probably one reason why cultures of secrecy develop: it is easier to treat everything as secret than to try to recall in each and every situation what may and may not be said.
67. Gusterson (1998: 87).

68. In our references to various architectural styles, we have drawn on Kostof (1995).

69. Less obvious, although difficult to assess, are cases in which organizations may falsely claim to have secrets precisely in order to boost the perceived value of their products. This might well apply to much-vaunted claims about "secret ingredients" in some foods. It would be invidious to give examples and by definition one cannot know the truth of the matter. But it is an interesting possibility because it is at least a hypothetical illustration of how secrecy may bestow value upon otherwise worthless knowledge. It has repeatedly been noted by theorists of secrecy that this is possible. For example, Erving Goffman remarks that "often the real secret behind the mystery is that there really is no mystery; the real problem is to prevent the audience from learning this too" (1959/1990: 76). In the metaphor of architectural styles, these could be considered follies—buildings that, from a distance, look to be real and substantial but are in fact not.

70. Tefft (1980: 2).

71. Jackall (1988: 133).

72. Trice (1993).

73. Parker (2000).

74. Dalton (1959), Feldman (1988), Collinson (1992).

75. E.g., the Lloyd's insurance building in London, sometimes called the "inside-out" building, designed by Richard Rogers.

76. Gusterson (1998: 80).

77. Simmel (1906: 465).

CONCLUSION

1. E.g., Cerne et al. (2014).

2. In this way, our insights are in line with Eisenberg and Witten's (1987) critical discussion of the limits and illusion of the efficacy of open communication in organizations.

3. See also Roberts (2004), Arellano-Gault & Lepore (2011).

4. See also Tsoukas (1997).

5. E.g., Strathern (2000), Hood & Heald (2006), Neyland (2007), Horn (2011).

6. See also Brunsson (1989), Power (1997), Levay & Waks (2009).

7. Goldhagen (1996); see also Hughes (2009: 92).

8. Kennedy (1961).

9. Simon (1997: 18).

10. See also Ashcraft et al. (2009), Cooren et al. (2011), Brummans et al. (2014).

11. March & Simon (1993: 2). For a critical discussion of this definition, see Czarniawska (2013).

12. Building on March and Simon, among others, Ahrne and Brunsson (2011) define an organization as "a decided order, including one or more of the elements of membership, hierarchy, rules, monitoring and sanctions" (2011: 85). As we have seen, secrecy impinges on or is related to each of these.

13. See Weick (1979) and subsequent discussions of process perspectives on organizations by Hernes (2007) and Langley & Tsoukas (2010).

14. Zerubavel (2006: 13); see also Greve et al. (2010: 69).

15. Keane (2008).

16. E.g., Davies (2004).

17. Schein (2010: 100).

18. Taussig (1999: 50).

19. Parker (2000: 237).

20. For some detailed strategies in such situations, see Lee (1993).

21. Taussig (1999: 50).

22. Grey (2012).

23. Abraham & Torok (2008).

Works Cited

Abraham, N. & Torok, M. (2008) *Kryptonymie: Das Verbarium des Wolfsmanns*. Hamacher, W. (trans.) Basel, Switzerland: Urs Engeler.

Adler, P. (2001) Market, Hierarchy and Trust: The Knowledge Economy and the Future of Capitalism. *Organization Science*, 12 (2): 215–34.

Adweek (2014) http://www.adweek.com/news/advertising-branding/5-most-embarrassing-revelations-sonys-sprawling-hack-161937 [Accessed January 2015].

Ahrne, G. & Brunsson, N. (2011) Organization outside Organizations: The Significance of Partial Organization. *Organization*, 18 (1): 83–104.

Agamben, G. (1998) *Homo Sacer: Sovereign Power and Bare Life*. Heller-Roazen, D. (trans.). Stanford, CA: Stanford University Press.

Agamben, G. (2011) *Nudities*. Kishik, D. & Pedatella, S. (trans.). Stanford, CA: Stanford University Press.

Albu, O. B. & Flyverbom, M. (2013) Problematizing the Study of Sunlight: Categories and Dimensions of Organizational Transparency. Paper presented at the 3rd Global Conference on Transparency Research. Paris, France. October 24–26.

Alvesson, M. & Kärreman, D. (2004) Interfaces of Control: Technocratic and Socio-Ideological Control in a Global Management Consultancy Firm. *Accounting, Organizations and Society*, 29: 423–44.

Anand, V. & Rosen, C. (2008) The Ethics of Organizational Secrets. *Journal of Management Inquiry*, 17 (2): 97–101.

Anderson-Gough F., Grey C., & Robson, K. (1998) Work Hard, Play Hard: An Analysis of Cliché in Two Accounting Firms. *Organization*, 5 (4): 565–92.

Anderson-Gough F., Grey C. & Robson, K. (2000) In the Name of the Client: The Service Ethic in Two Professional Services Firms. *Human Relations*, 53 (9): 1151–74.

Anderson-Gough F., Grey C., & Robson, K. (2001) Tests of Time: Organizational Time-Reckoning and the Making of Accountants in Two Multi-national Accounting Firms. *Accounting, Organizations and Society*, 26 (2): 99–122.

Anderson-Gough F., Grey C., & Robson, K. (2002) Connecting Professional Power and Professional Socialization. *Accounting and Business Research*, 32 (1): 41–56.

Anderson-Gough F., Grey C., & Robson, K. (2005) Helping Them to Forget . . . The Organizational Embedding of Gender Relations in Public Audit Firms. *Accounting Organizations and Society*, 30 (5): 469–90.

Anderson-Gough F., Grey C., & Robson, K. (2006) Professionals, Networking and the Networked Professional. *Research in the Sociology of Organizations*, 24: 231–56.

Anton, J. & Yao, D. (2004) Little Patents and Big Secrets: Managing Intellectual Property. *RAND Journal of Economics*, 35 (1): 1–22.

Argyres, N. (1999) The Impact of Information Technology on Coordination: Evidence from the B-2 "Stealth" Bomber. *Organization Science*, 10 (2): 162–80.

Argyris, C. (1957) *Personality and Organization. The Conflict between System and the Individual*. New York: Harper & Row.

Arellano-Gault, D. & Lepore, W. (2011) Transparency Reforms in the Public Sector: Beyond the New Economics of Organization. *Organization Studies*, 32 (8): 1029–50.

Ashcraft, K. L., Kuhn, T. R., & Cooren, F. (2009) Constitutional Amendments: "Materializing" Organizational Communication. *Academy of Management Annals*, 3 (1): 1–64.

Ashforth, B. & Anand, V. (2003) The Normalization of Corruption in Organizations. *Research in Organizational Behavior*, 25 (Annual): 1–52.

Ashforth, B. E., Gioia, D. A., Robinson, S. L., & Trevino, L. K. (2008) Re-viewing Organizational Corruption. *Academy of Management Review*, 33 (3): 670–84.

Bachrach, P. & Baratz, M. S. (1962) Two Faces of Power. *American Political Science Review*, 56 (4): 947–52.

Baker, W. & Faulkner, R. (1993) The Social Organization of Conspiracy: Illegal Networks in the Heavy Electrical Equipment Industry. *American Sociological Review*, 58 (6): 837–60.

BBC (2013) http://www.bbc.co.uk/news/health-21483103 [Accessed March 2014].

Beamish, T. D. (2000) Accumulating Trouble: Complex Organization, a Culture of Silence, and a Secret Spill. *Social Problems*, 47 (4): 473–98.

Beare, M. E. (Ed.). (2003). *Critical Reflections on Transnational Organized Crime, Money Laundering and Corruption*. Toronto: University of Toronto Press.

Behr, H. (2006) *Special Section: Secrecy and Confidentiality in Groups. Group Analysis*, 39 (3): 356–65.

Bendix, R. (1966) *Max Weber*. London: Methuen (University Paperbacks).

Berg, A. (1991) Chinese Walls Come Tumbling Down. *International Financial Law Review*, 10 (1): 23.

Berger, P. L. & Luckmann, T. (1967) *The Social Construction of Reality: A Treatise in the Sociology of Knowledge*. New York: Anchor Books.

Bergström, O., Hasselbladh, H., & Kärreman, D. (2009) Organizing Disciplinary Power in a Knowledge Organization. *Scandinavian Journal of Management*, 25 (2): 178–90.

Birchall, C. (2011a) Introduction to Secrecy and Transparency—The Politics of Opacity and Openness. *Theory, Culture & Society*, 28 (7–8): 7–25.

Birchall, C. (2011b) Transparency, Interrupted: Secrets of the Left. *Theory, Culture & Society*, 28 (7–8): 60–84.

Birkinshaw, P. (2006) Transparency as a Human Right. In C. Hood & D. Heald (Eds.), *Transparency: The Key to Better Governance?* Oxford: Oxford University Press: 3–22.

Blackler, F. (1995) Knowledge, Knowledge Work and Organizations: An Overview and Interpretation. *Organization Studies*, 16 (6): 1021–46.

Blau, P. (1955) *The Dynamics of Bureaucracy*. Chicago: University of Chicago Press.

Bok, S. (1989) *Secrets: On the Ethics of Concealment and Revelation*. New York: Vantage Books.

Bone, R. G. (1998) A New Look at Trade Secret Law: Doctrine in Search of Justification. *California Law Review*, 85 (2): 241–76.

Boston Globe (2005) http://www.boston.com/business/technology/biotechnology/articles/2005/09/22/boston_scientific_medinol_settle_row/?page=full [Accessed February 2014].

Bourdieu, P. (1984) *Distinction: A Social Critique of the Judgement of Taste*. Cambridge, MA: Harvard University Press.

Boyle, A. (1979) *The Climate of Treason: Five Who Spied for Russia*. London: Hutchinson.

Brass, D. (1995) Men's and Women's Networks: A Study of Interaction Patterns and Influence in an Organization. *Academy of Management Journal*, 28 (2): 327–43.

Brewis, J. & Grey, C. (2008) The Regulation of Smoking at Work. *Human Relations* 61 (7): 965–87.

Brewis, J., Sanderson, C., & Wray-Bliss, E. (2006) The Normalisation of "Excessive" Workforce Drug Testing? *Tamara. The Journal of Critical Organisation Inquiry*, 5 (1): 39–53.

Brown, S. (2001) Torment Your Customers (They'll Love It). *Harvard Business Review*, October: 83–88.

Brummans, B., Cooren, F., Robichaud, D. & Taylor, J. R. (2014) Approaches in Research on the Communicative Constitution of Organizations. In: L. L. Putnam & D. Mumby (Eds.), *SAGE Handbook of Organizational Communication*. 3rd ed. Thousand Oaks, CA: Sage, 173–94.

Brunsson, N. (1989) *The Organization of Hypocrisy. Talk, Decision and Actions in Organizations*. Adler, N. (trans.). New York: Wiley.

Buchanan, D. & Badham, R. (1999) *Power, Politics and Organizational Change*. London: Sage.

Burawoy, M. (1979) *Manufacturing Consent: Changes in the Labor Process under Monopoly Capitalism*. Chicago: University of Chicago Press.

Butler, N. & Spoelstra, S. (2012) Your Excellency. *Organization* 19 (6): 891–903.

Calvocoressi, P. (2001) *Top Secret Ultra*, 2nd ed. Kidderminster, UK: Baldwin.

Canetti, E. (1981) *Crowds and Power*. Stewart, C. (trans.). New York: Continuum.

Cawelti, J. & Rosenberg, B. (1987) *The Spy Story*. Chicago: University of Chicago Press.

Cerne, M., Nerstad, C., Dysvik, A., & Skerlavaj, M. (2014) What Goes Around Comes Around: Knowledge Hiding, Perceived Motivational Climate, and Creativity. *Academy of Management Journal*, 57 (1): 172–92.

Cheung, S. N. S. (1982) Property Rights in Trade Secrets. *Economic Inquiry*, 20 (1): 40–53.

Claire, J. A., Beatty, J. E., & Maclean, T. L. (2005) Out of Sight but Not Out of Mind: Managing Invisible Social Identities in the Workplace. *Academy of Management Review*, 30 (1): 78–95.

CNN (2012) http://edition.cnn.com/2012/08/07/business/stealing-information -work/ [Accessed February 2014].

CNN (2014) http://edition.cnn.com/2014/02/02/opinion/greene-corporate-surveil lance/ [Accessed March 2014].

Coleman, E. G. (2013) Anonymous and the Politics of Leaking. In B. Brevini et.al. (Eds.), *Beyond WikiLeaks: Implications for the Future of Communications, Journalism and Society*. Basingstoke, UK: Palgrave Macmillan, 209–28.

Colella, A., Paetzold, R. L., Zardkoohi, A., & Wesson, M. (2007) Exposing Pay Secrecy. *Academy of Management Review*, 32 (1): 55–71.

Collinson, D. L. (1992) *Managing the Shopfloor: Subjectivity, Masculinity and Workplace Culture*. Berlin: De Gruyter.

Computerworld (2014) http://www.computerworld.com/s/article/9246281/Sam sung_hints_at_new_UI_for_upcoming_Galaxy_S5 [Accessed May 2014].

Connelly, C. E., Zweig, D., Webster, J., & Trougakos, J. P. (2012) Knowledge Hiding in Organizations. *Journal of Organizational Behavior*, 33 (1): 64–88.

Coombs, T. W., & Holladay, S. J., (2013) The Pseudo-Panopticon: The Illusion Created by CSR- Related Transparency and the Internet. *Corporate Communications: An International Journal*, 18 (2): 212–227.

Cooren, F., Kuhn, T., Cornelissen, J., & Clark, T. (2011) Communication, Organizing, and Organization: An Introduction to the Special Issue. *Organization Studies*, 32 (9): 1149–70.

Costas, J. (2012) "We Are All Friends Here": Reinforcing Paradoxes of Normative Control in a Culture of Friendship. Journal of Management Inquiry, 21 (4): 377–95.

Costas, J. (2013) Problematizing Mobility: A Metaphor of Stickiness, Non-places and the Kinetic Elite. Organization Studies, 34 (10): 1467–85.

Costas, J. & Fleming, P. (2009) Beyond Dis-identification: A Discursive Approach to Self-alienation in Contemporary Organizations. *Human Relations*, 62 (3): 353–78.

Costas, J. & Grey, C. (2014) The Temporality of Power and the Power of Temporality: Imaginary Future Selves in Professional Services Firms. *Organization Studies*, 35 (6): 909–37.

Costas, J. & Kärreman, D. (2013) Conscience as Control: Managing Employees through CSR. *Organization*, 20 (3): 394–415.

Costas, J. & D. Kärreman (2015) The Bored Self in Knowledge Work. *Human Relations*. DOI 10.1177/0018726715579736.

Covaleski, M. A., Dirsmith, M. W., Heian, J. B., & Samuel, S. (1998) The Calculated and the Avowed: Techniques of Discipline and Struggles over Identity in Big Six Public Accounting Firms. *Administrative Science Quarterly*, 43 (2): 293–327.

Cowan, S. K. (2014) Secrets and Misperceptions: The Creation of Self-Fulfilling Illusions. *Sociological Science*, 1: 466–92.

Cox, B. (1977) *The Fall of Scotland Yard*. London: Penguin.

Craft, N. (1994) Secrecy in the NHS. *British Medical Journal*, 309 (2): 1640.

Crozier, M. (1964) *The Bureaucratic Phenomenon*. Chicago: University of Chicago Press.

Czarniawska, B. (2008) *A Theory of Organizing*. Cheltenham, UK: Edward Elgar.

Czarniawska, B. (2013) Organizations as Obstacles to Organizing. In D. Robichaud, & F. Cooren, (Eds.), *Organizations and Organizing. Materiality, Agency, and Discourse*. New York: Routledge, 3–22.

Dalton, M. (1959) *Men Who Manage. Fusions of Feeling and Theory in Administration*. New York: Wiley.

Davies, P. (2004) *MI6 and The Machinery of Spying*. Abingdon, UK: Frank Cass.

Davis, J. (1998) Access to and Transmission of Information: Position of the Media. In V. Deckmyn & I. Thomson (Eds.) *Openness and Transparency in the European Union*. Maastricht, Netherlands: European Institute of Public Administration, 121–26.

Delarue, H. & Lejeune, A. (2011) Managerial Secrecy and Intellectual Asset Protection in SMEs: The Role of Institutional Environment. *Journal of International Management*, 17 (2): 130–42.

Della Porta, D. & Vannucci, A. (2012) *The Hidden Order of Corruption: An Institutional Approach*. London: Ashgate.

De Maria, W. (2006) Brother Secret, Sister Silence: Sibling Conspiracies against Managerial Integrity. *Journal of Business Ethics*, 65 (3): 219–34.

Dobusch, L. & Schoeneborn, D. (2015) Fluidity, Identity, and Organizationality: The Case of Anonymous. Working Paper. Freie Universität Berlin.

Dolar, M. (2006) Kafka's Voices. In S. Žižek (Ed.), Lacan: *The Silent Partners*. London: Verso: 312–35.

Donaldson, S. (1992) *Machiavelli and Mystery of State*. Cambridge: Cambridge University Press.

Dostoyevsky, F. (1860/1985) *The House of the Dead*. London: Penguin.

Dougherty, D. (2001) Reimagining the Differentiation and Integration of Work for Sustained Product Innovation. *Organization Science*, 12 (5): 612–31.

Dirsmith, M. W. & Covaleski, M. A. (1985) Informal Communications, Nonformal Communications and Mentoring in Public Accounting Firms. *Accounting, Organizations and Society*, 10 (1): 149–69.

Dufresne, R. & Offstein, E. (2008) On the Virtues of Secrecy in Organizations. *Journal of Management Inquiry*, 17 (2): 102–6.

Edwards, R. (1979) *Contested Terrain: The Transformation of the Workplace in the Twentieth Century*. New York: Basic Books.

Eisenberg, E. M. & Witten, M. G. (1987) Reconsidering Openness in Organizational Communication. *Academy of Management Review*, 12 (3): 418–26.

Ellsberg, D. (2002) *Secrets: A Memoir of Vietnam and the Pentagon Papers*. New York: Penguin.

Epstein, R. (2004) Trade Secrets as Private Property: Their Constitutional Protection. *University of Chicago Law Review*, 71: 57–75.

Erickson, B. H. (1981) Secret Societies and Social Structure. *Social Forces*, 60 (1): 188–210.

Erickson, P. E. (1979) The Role of Secrecy in Formal Organizations: From Norms of Rationality to Norms of Distrust. *Cornell Journal of Social Relations*, 14 (2): 121–38.

Feldman, M. & March, J. G. (1981) Information in Organizations as Signal and Symbol. *Administrative Science Quarterly*, 26 (2): 171–86.

Feldman, S. P. (1988) Secrecy, Information and Politics: An Essay in Organizational Decisionmaking. *Human Relations*, 41 (1): 73–90.

Feldman, S. P. (1996) The Ethics of Shifting Ties: Management Theory and the Breakdown of Culture in Modernity. *Journal of Management Studies*, 33 (3): 283–99.

Feldman, S. P. (2004) *Memory as a Moral Decision: The Role of Ethics in Organizational Culture*. New Brunswick, NJ: Transaction.

Fenster, M. (2006) The Opacity of Transparency. *Iowa Law Review*, 91: 885–949.

Fenster, M. (2008) *Conspiracy Theories: Secrecy and Power in American Culture*. Minneapolis: University of Minnesota Press.

Financial Times (2006) http://www.ft.com/cms/s/0/50aa3678-8dff-11db-aeoe -0000779e2340.html#axzz38MUi3eCZ [Paywalled: Accessed July 2014].

Financial Times (2011) http://www.ft.com/intl/cms/s/0/9d57f8da-f66d-11e0-86dc -00144feab49a.html#axzz38MUi3eCZ [Paywalled: Accessed July 2014].

Financial Times (2012) http://www.ft.com/cms/s/0/0e449b14-1dd9-11e2-8e1d -00144feabdco.html#axzz2uuwblofK [Paywalled: Accessed February 2014].

Financial Times (2014) http://www.ft.com/cms/s/0/b1504dba-9170-11e3-adde -00144feab7de.html#axzz2suS5DMjn [Paywalled: Accessed February 2014].

Fisher, M. (2012) *Wall Street Women*. Durham, NC: Duke University Press.

Fleming, P. & Zyglidopoulos, S.C. (2009) *Charting Corporate Corruption: Agency, Structure and Escalation*. Cheltenham, UK: Edward Elgar.

Florini, A. (2001) The End of Secrecy. In B. I. Finel & K. M. Lord (Eds.), *Power and Conflict in the Age of Transparency*. New York: Palgrave, 13–29.

Flyverbom, M., Thoger Christensen, L. & Krause Hanson, H. (2011) Disentangling the Power-Transparency Nexus. Paper presented at the First Global Conference on Transparency Research. New Brunswick, NJ: Rutgers University, May 19–20.

Forbes (2013) http://www.forbes.com/sites/alexknapp/2013/09/13/south-korea -will-soon-be-home-to-an-invisible-skyscraper/ [Accessed March 2015].

Forbes (2014) http://www.forbes.com/sites/martinzwilling/2014/11/11/gossip-at -work-undermines-every-business-leader/ [Accessed January 2015].

Foucault, M. (1980). *Power/Knowledge. Selected Interviews and Other Writings 1972–1977*. New York: Pantheon.

Franklin, B. (1734) *Poor Richard's Almanack*. http://internet.savannah.chatham
.k12.ga.us/schools/deRenne/staff/gelagay/Shared%20Documents/The%20
Hobbit%20Plans-Units%201-3/Poor_Richard's_Almanack_by_Franklin_Ben
jamin.pdf [Accessed May 2014].

French, J. & Raven, B. (1959) The Bases of Social Power. In D. Cartwright (Ed.),
Studies in Social Power. Ann Arbor, MI: Institute for Social Research, 150–67.

Freud, S. (1919/1955). The 'Uncanny'. In J. Strachey (ed. and trans.) *The Standard Edition of the Complete Psychological Works of Sigmund Freud*, Volume XVII (1917–1919): *An Infantile Neurosis and Other Works*. London:
Hogarth, 217–256.

Freudenberg, W. & Gramling, R. (2011) *Blowout in the Gulf. The BP Spill Disaster
and the Future of Energy in America*. Cambridge, MA: MIT Press.

Frois, C. (2009) *The Anonymous Society: Identity, Transformation and Anonymity in 12 Steps*. Cambridge: Cambridge Scholars Publishing.

Fung, A. (2013) Infotopia: Unleashing the Democratic Power of Transparency.
Politics & Society, 41 (2): 183–212.

Fung, A., Graham, M., & Weil, D. (2007) *Full Disclosure: The Perils and Promise
of Transparency*. Cambridge: Cambridge University Press.

Gabriel, Y. (2005) Glass Cages and Glass Palaces: Images of Organization in Im-
age-Conscious Times. *Organization*, 12 (1): 9–27.

Gabriel, Y. (2010) Organization Studies: A Space for Ideas, Identities and Agonies.
Organization Studies, 31 (6): 757–75.

Gaa, J. (2009) Corporate Governance and the Responsibility of the Board of
Directors for Strategic Financial Reporting. *Journal of Business Ethics*, 90
(Supplement 2): 179–97.

Garsten, C. & Grey, C. (1997) How to Become Oneself: Discourses of Subjectivity
in Post-bureaucratic Organizations. *Organization*, 4 (2): 211–28.

Garsten, C. & Lindh de Montaya, M. (Eds.) (2008) *Transparency in a Global
Order: Unveiling Organizations' Visions*. Cheltenham, UK: Edward Elgar.

Gatrell, C. (2011) Policy and the Pregnant Body at Work: Strategies of Secrecy,
Silence and Supra-Performance. *Gender, Work and Organization*, 18 (2):
158–81.

Giddens, A. (1979) *Central Problems in Social Theory: Action, Structure, and
Contradiction in Social Analysis*. Berkeley: University of California Press.

Goffman, E. (1959/1990) *The Presentation of Self in Everyday Life*. Edinburgh:
Bateman.

Goffman, E. (1962) *Asylums: Essays on the Social Situation of Mental Patients
and Other Inmates*. Chicago: Aldine.

Goffman, E. (1963/1990) *Stigma: Notes on the Management of Spoiled Identity*.
London: Penguin Books.

Goffman, E. (1969) *Strategic Interaction: An Analysis of Doubt and Calculation in
Face-to-Face, Day-to-Day Dealings with One Another*. New York: Ballantine.

Goldhagen, D. (1996) *Hitler's Willing Executioners*. London: Little, Brown.

Gouldner, A. W. (1954) *Wildcat Strike: A Study in Worker–Management Relation-ships*. New York: Harper & Row.

Gibson, D. R. (2014) Enduring Illusions: The Social Organization of Secrecy and Deception. *Sociology Theory*, 32 (4): 283–306.

Gioia, D. A. (1992) Pinto Fires and Personal Ethics: A Script Analysis of Missed Opportunities. *Journal of Business Ethics*, 11 (5): 379–89.

Greenwood, R. & Hinings, C.R. (2002) Disconnects and Consequences in Orga-nization Theory. *Administrative Science Quarterly*, 47 (3): 411–21.

Greve, H, Palmer, D., & Pozner, J-E. (2010) Organizations Gone Wild: The Causes, Processes and Conduct of Organizational Misconduct. *Annals of the Academy of Management*, 4 (1): 53–107.

Grey, C. (1994) Career as a Project of the Self and Labour Process Discipline. *Sociology*, 28 (2): 479–97.

Grey, C. (1996) CP Snow's Fictional Sociology of Management and Organizations. *Organization*, 3 (1): 61–83.

Grey, C. (1998) On Being a Professional in a Big Six Firm. *Accounting, Organiza-tions and Society*, 23 (5/6): 569–87.

Grey, C. (2003) The Real World of Enron's Auditors. *Organization*, 10 (3): 572–76.

Grey, C. (2010) Organizing Studies: Publications, Politics and Polemic. *Organiza-tion Studies*, 31 (6): 677–94.

Grey, C. (2012) *Decoding Organization. Bletchley Park, Codebreaking and Or-ganization Studies*. Cambridge: Cambridge University Press.

Grey, C. (2013) The Making of Bletchley Park and Signals Intelligence. *Intelligence and National Security*, 37 (6): 785–807.

Grey, C. (2014) An Organizational Culture of Secrecy: The Case of Bletchley Park. *Management and Organizational History*, 9 (1): 107–22.

Grey, C. & Garsten, C. (2001) Trust, Control and Post-bureaucracy. *Organiza-tion Studies*, 22 (2): 229–50.

Grey, C. & Sturdy, A. (2008) The 1942 Re-organization of GC & CS. *Cryptolo-gia*, 32 (4): 311–33.

Grey, C. & Sturdy A. (2009) Historicising Knowledge-Intensive Organizations: The Case of Bletchley Park. *Management and Organizational History*, 4 (2): 131–50.

Grey C. & Sturdy A. (2010) A Chaos That Worked: Organizing Bletchley Park. *Public Policy and Administration*, 25 (1): 47–66.

Grint, K. (2009) The Sacred in Leadership: Separation, Sacrifice and Silence. *Or-ganization Studies*, 31 (1): 89–107.

Guardian (2008) http://www.theguardian.com/world/2008/jun/22/india.human rights [Accessed July 2014].

Guardian (2012a) http://www.theguardian.com/commentisfree/2012/feb/19/syria -us-ally-human-rights [Accessed January 2014].

Guardian (2012b) http://www.theguardian.com/commentisfree/joris-luyendijk -banking-blog/2012/jul/13/former-investment-banker [Accessed February 2014].

Guardian (2013a) http://www.theguardian.com/books/2013/apr/12/john-le-carre -spy-anniversary [Accessed February 2014].

Guardian (2013b) http://www.theguardian.com/media/2013/feb/23/bbc-knew -jimmy-savile-tribute [Accessed May 2014].

Guardian (2014) http://www.theguardian.com/media/2014/jan/19/call-to-end-bbc -culture-of-secrecy [Accessed May 2014].

Gusterson, H. (1998) *Nuclear Rites: A Weapons Laboratory at the End of the Cold War*. Berkeley: University of California Press.

Halter, M. V., Continho de Arudda, M. C., & Halter R. B. (2009) Transparency to Reduce Corruption? Dropping Hints for Private Organizations in Brazil. *Journal of Business Ethics*, 84: 373–85.

Handy, C. (1985) *Understanding Organizations*, 3rd ed. London: Penguin.

Hannah, D. (2005) Should I Keep a Secret? The Effects of Trade Secret Protection Procedures on Employees' Obligation to Protect Trade Secrets. *Organization Science*, 16 (1): 71–84.

Hannah, D. (2007) An Examination of the Factors That Influence Whether Newcomers Protects or Share Secrets of Their Former Employers. *Journal of Management Studies*, 44 (4): 465–87.

Harrington, B. (Ed.) (2009) *Deception: From Ancient Empires to Internet Dating*. Stanford, CA: Stanford University Press.

den Hond, F. & de Bakker, F. (2007) Ideologically Motivated Activism: How Activist Groups Influence Corporate Social Change Activities. *Academy of Management Review*, 32 (3): 901–24.

Herman, M. (1996) *Intelligence Power in Peace and War*. Cambridge: Cambridge University Press.

Herman, M. (2001) *Intelligence Services in the Information Age*. New York: Frank Cass.

Hernes, T. (2004) *The Spatial Construction of Organization*. Amsterdam, Netherlands: John Benjamins.

Hernes, T. (2007) *Understanding Organization as Process*. London: Routledge.

Hettinger, E. C. (1989) Justifying intellectual property. *Philosophy & Public Affairs*, 18 (1): 31–52.

Hill, M. 2004. *Bletchley Park People*. Stroud, Gloucester, UK: Sutton.

Hirsch, P. M. (2003) The Dark Side of Alliances: The Enron Story. *Organization*, 10 (3): 565–67.

Hirschhorn, L. (1990) *The Workplace Within: Psychodynamics of Organizational Life*. Cambridge, MA: MIT Press.

Hood, C. & Heald, D. (Eds.) (2006) *Transparency: The Key to Better Governance?* Oxford: Oxford University Press.

Horn, E. (2011) Logics of Political Secrecy. *Theory, Culture & Society*, 28 (7–8): 103–22.

Hoyt, M. F. (1978) Secrets in Psychotherapy: Theoretical and Practical Considerations. *International Journal of Psychoanalysis*, 5 (2): 231–41.

Huffington Post (2011) http://www.huffingtonpost.com/2011/10/05/steve-jobs
-health-timeline_n_997313.html [Accessed February 2014].

Hughes, E. (2009) *The Sociological Eye: Selected Papers*. New Brunswick, NJ: Transaction.

Hurmelinna-Laukkannen, P. & Puumalainen, K. (2007) Nature and Dynamics of Appropriability: Strategies for Appropriating Returns on Innovation. *R&D Management*, 37 (2): 95–112.

Hurmelinna-Laukkannen, P., Sainio, L-M., & Jauhianen, T. (2008) Appropriability Regime for Radical and Incremental Innovations. *R&D Management*, 38 (3): 278–89.

Hutter, M. J. (1981) Drafting Enforceable Employee Non-competition Agreements to Protect Confidential Business Information: A Lawyer's Practical Approach to the Case Law. *Albany Law Review*, 45: 311–53.

Information Security (2009) *Securing Intellectual Property: Protecting Trade Secrets and Other Information Assets*. Burlington, MA: Butterworth-Heinemann.

Jackall, R. (1988) *Moral Mazes: The World of Corporate Managers*. New York: Oxford University Press.

Jones, C. (2008) Editor's Introduction [to a special essay section on secrecy]. *Journal of Management Inquiry*, 17 (2): 95–96.

Kafka, F. (1925/2000) *The Trial*. Parry, I. (trans.). London: Penguin.

Kanter, R. M. (1977) *Men and Women of the Corporation*. New York: Basic Books.

Kanter, R. M. & Khurana, R. (2009) Types and Positions: The Significance of Georg Simmel's Structural Theories for Organizational Behaviour. In P. Adler (Ed.) *The Oxford Handbook of Sociology and Organization Studies*. Oxford: Oxford University Press, 291–306.

Katila, R., Rosenberger, J. D., & Eisenhardt, K. M. (2008) Swimming with Sharks: Technology Ventures, Defense Mechanisms and Corporate Relationships. *Administrative Science Quarterly*, 53 (2): 295–332.

Keane, C. (2008) Don't Ask, Don't Tell: Secrets—Their Use and Abuse in Organizations. *Journal of Management Inquiry*, 17 (2): 107–10.

Kennedy, J. F. (1961) http://www.jfklibrary.org/Research/Research-Aids/JFK
-Speeches/American-Newspaper-Publishers-Association_19610427.aspx [Accessed March 2015].

Knott, A. M. & Posen, H. E. (2009) Firm R&D Behaviour and Evolving Technology in Established Industries. *Organization Science*, 20 (2): 352–67.

Knudsen, Morten (2011) Forms of Inattentiveness: The Production of Blindness in the Development of a Technology for the Observation of Quality in Health Services. *Organization*, 32 (7): 963–89.

Kostof, S. (1995) *A History of Architecture: Settings and Rituals*. 2nd ed. New York: Oxford University Press.

Kunda, G. (1992) *Engineering Culture*. Philadelphia: Temple University Press.

Kurland, N. B. & Pelled, L. H. (2000) Passing the Word: Towards a Model of Gossip and Power in the Workplace. *Academy of Management Review*, 25 (2): 428–38.

Lampel, J. (2001) Show and Tell: Product Demonstrations and Path Creation of Technological Change. In R. Garud & P. Karnøe (Eds.), *Path Dependence and Path Creation*. Mahwah, NJ: Lawrence Erlbaum, 303–28.

Lanchester, J. (2013) *Capital*. London: Faber & Faber.

Lange, D. (2008) A Multidimensional Conceptualization of Organizational Corruption Control. *Academy of Management Review*, 33 (3): 710–29.

Land, C. (2008) Organizational Taboos. In S. R. Clegg & J. R. Bailey (Eds.) *International Encyclopedia of Organization Studies*. London: Sage, 1195–97.

Langley, A. & Tsoukas, H. (2010) Introducing Perspectives on Process Organization Studies. In T. Hernes, & S. Maitlis (Eds.), *Process, Sensemaking, and Organizing 1*. Oxford: Oxford University Press, 1–26.

Leadership Review (2013) http://www.leadershipreview.net/gossip-can-undermine -leadership [Accessed January 2015].

Lee, R. (1993) *Doing Research on Sensitive Topics*. London: Sage.

Leeson, N. (1997) *Rogue Trade*. London: Time Warner.

Lehar, A. & Randl, O. (2006) Chinese Walls in German Banks. *Review of Finance*, 10 (2): 301–20.

Levay, C. & Waks, C. (2009) Professions and the Pursuit of Transparency in Healthcare: Two Cases of Soft Autonomy. *Organization Studies*, 30 (5): 509–27.

Lewicki, R. J., McAllistair, D. J., & Bies R. J. (1998) Trust and Distrust: New Relationships and Realities. *Academy of Management Review*, 23 (3): 438–58.

Liebeskind, J. (1997) Keeping Organizational Secrets: Protective Institutional Mechanisms and Their Costs. *Industrial and Corporate Change*, 6 (3): 623–64.

Liebeskind, J. P. & Oliver, A. L. (1998) From Handshake to Contract: Trust, Intellectual Property and the Social Structure of Academic Research. In C. Land & R. Bachmann, (Eds.), *Trust within and between Organizations*. Oxford: Oxford University Press, 118–45.

Luepker, E. T. (2012) *Record Keeping in Psychotherapy and Counselling: Protecting Confidentiality and the Professional Relationship*. New York: Routledge.

Luhrmann, T. M. (1989) The Magic of Secrecy. *Ethos*, 17 (2): 131–65.

Lukes, S. (2005) *Power: A Radical View*. 2nd ed. London: Macmillan.

Macpherson, C. B. (Ed.) (1978) *Property: Mainstream and Critical Approaches*. Toronto: University of Toronto Press.

Madsen, P. (2010) Dynamic Transparency, Prudential Justice, and Corporate Transformation: Becoming Socially Responsible in the Internet Age. *Journal of Business Ethics*, 90 (4): 639–48.

Manning, O. (1960) *The Great Fortune*. London: William Heinemann.

March, J. & Simon, H. (1993) *Organizations*. 2nd ed. Cambridge, MA: Blackwell.

Martin, J. (1990) Deconstructing Organizational Taboos: The Suppression of Gender Conflict in Organizations. *Organization Science*, 1 (4): 339–59.

Marx, G. T. (1999) What's in a Name? Some Reflections on the Sociology of Anonymity. *Information Society*, 15 (2): 99–112.

Marx, K. (1887/1978) *Capital*, Vol. 1. In R.C. Tucker (Ed.), *The Marx-Engels Reader*. London: Norton, 294–438.

Maurer, S. D. & Zugelder, M. T. (2000) Trade Secret Management in High Technology: A Legal Review and Research Agenda. *Journal of High Technology Management Research*, 11 (2): 155–74.

Miceli, M. P. & Near, J. P. (1992) *Blowing the Whistle: The Organizational and Legal Implications for Companies and Employees*. New York: Lexington.

Michels, R. (1911/1958) *Political Parties: A Sociological Study of the Oligarchical Tendencies of Modern Democracy*. Glencoe, IL: Free Press.

Michelson, G. & Mouly, S. (2000) Rumour and Gossip in Organisations: A Conceptual Study. *Management Decision*, 38 (5): 339–46.

Milberg, S., Smith, H. J., & Burke, S. (2000) Information Privacy: Corporate Management and National Regulation. *Organization Science*, 11 (1): 35–57.

Miles, R. P. (2003) *The Warren Buffett CEO: Secrets from the Berkshire Hathaway Managers*. New York: Wiley.

Milgrim, R. (1967) *Trade Secrets*. New York: Matthew Bender.

Millegan, K. (Ed.) (2004) *Fleshing Out Skulls and Bones. An Investigation into America's Most Powerful Secret Society*. Walterville, OR: TrineDay.

Miller, P. & Rose, N. (1994) On Therapeutic Authority. *History of the Human Sciences*, 7 (3): 29–64.

Mills, C. W. (1959) *The Power Elite*. New York: Oxford University Press.

Mintzberg, H. (1973) *Power in and around Organizations*. New York: Prentice-Hall.

Mitchell, A., Sikka, P., & Willmott, H. (1998) Sweeping It under the Carpet: The Role of Accountancy Firms in Moneylaundering. *Accounting, Organizations and Society*, 23 (5): 589–607.

Mlinek, E. J. & Pierce, J. (1997) Confidentiality and Privacy Breaches in a University Hospital Emergency Department. *Academic Emergency Medicine*, 4 (12): 1142–46.

Moore, W. E. (1962) *The Conduct of the Corporation*. New York: Random House.

Mone, M. & McKinlay, W. (1993) The Uniqueness Value and Its Consequences for Organization Studies. *Journal of Management Inquiry*, 2 (1): 284–96.

Morrison, E. W. & Milliken, F. J. (2000) Organizational Silence: A Barrier to Change and Development in a Pluralistic World. *Academy of Management Review*, 25 (4): 706–25.

Near, J. P. & Miceli, M. P. (1985) Organizational Dissidence: The Case of Whistle-Blowing. *Journal of Business Ethics*, 4 (1): 1–16.

New York Times (2005) http://www.nytimes.com/2005/09/22/business/22stent .html?_r=0 [Accessed May 2014].

New York Times (2008a) http://www.nytimes.com/2008/06/06/world/middleeast/06intel .html [Accessed July 2014].

New York Times (2008b) http://www.nytimes.com/2008/12/21/business/ worldbusiness/21siemens.html?pagewanted=all&_r=0 [Accessed March 2015].

New York Times (2012) http://www.nytimes.com/2012/02/15/world/asia/chinese -official-to-hear-trade-theft-tale.html?_r=0 [Accessed February 2014].

Neyland, D. (2007) Achieving Transparency: The Visible, Invisible and Divisible in Academic Accountability Networks. *Organization*, 14 (4): 499–516.

Nissenbaum, H. (1999) The Meaning of Anonymity in an Information Age. *Information Society*, 15 (2): 141–44.

Nonaka, I. & Takeuchi, H. (1995) *The Knowledge-Creating Company: How Japanese Firms Create the Dynamics of Innovation*. New York: Oxford University Press.

Noon, M. & Delbridge, R. (1993) News from Behind My Hand: Gossip in Organizations. *Organization Studies*, 14 (1): 23–36.

Page, G. (Ed.) (2002) *We Kept the Secret. Now It Can Be Told: Some Memories of Pembroke V Wrens*. Wymondham, Norfolk, UK: G R Reeve.

Paine, L. S. (1991) Trade Secrets and the Justification of Intellectual Property: A Comment on Hettinger. *Philosophy & Public Affairs*, 20 (3): 247–63.

Parker, M. (2000) *Organizational Culture and Identity*. London: Sage.

Parker, M. (2008) Eating with the Mafia: Belonging and Violence. *Human Relations*, 61 (7): 989–1006.

Patrick, K. (2012) Barriers to Whistleblowing in the NHS. *British Medical Journal*, 345: e6840.

Paulsen, N. & Hernes, T. (2003) *Managing Boundaries in Organizations: Multiple Perspectives*. Basingstoke, UK: Palgrave Macmillan.

PC World (2013) http://www.pcworld.com/article/2045077/apple-hints-at-new -products-this-year.html [Accessed May 2014].

Pearlman, L. A. & Saakvitne, K. W. (1995) *Trauma and the Therapist: Countertransference and Vicarious Traumatization in Psychotherapy with Incest Survivors*. New York: Norton.

Perrow, C. (2011) *The Next Catastrophe: Reducing Our Vulnerabilities to Natural, Industrial, and Terrorist Disasters*. Princeton, NJ: Princeton University Press.

Peters, T. & Waterman, B. (1982) *In Search of Excellence. Lessons from America's Best-Run Companies*. New York: Harper & Row.

Pettigrew, A. (1972) Information Control as a Power Resource. *Sociology*, 6 (2): 187–204.

Pfeffer, J. (1981) *Power in Organizations*. New York: Pitman.

Pilkington, J. (1998) "Don't Try and Make Out That I'm Nice!" The Difference Strategies Women and Men Use When Gossiping. In J. Coates (Ed.), *Language and Gender: A Reader*. Oxford: Blackwell, 254–69.

Piotrowski, S. J. (Ed.) (2010). *Transparency and Secrecy: A Reader Linking Literature and Contemporary Debate*. Lanham, MD: Lexington Books.

Polanyi, M. (1966) *The Tacit Dimension*. London: Routledge.

Pompa, V. (1992) Managerial Secrecy: An Ethical Examination. *Journal of Business Ethics*, 11 (2): 147–56.

Ponse, B. (1976) Secrecy in the Lesbian World. *Urban Life*, 5 (3): 313–338.

Power, M. (1997) *The Audit Society*. Oxford: Oxford University Press.

Rains, S. A. & Scott, C. R. (2007) To Identify or Not to Identify: A Theoretical Model of Receiver Responses to Anonymous Communication. *Communication Theory*, 17 (1): 61–91.

Ragins, B. R., Singh, R., & Cornwell, J. M. (2007) Making the Invisible Visible: Fear and Disclosure of Sexual Orientation at Work. *Journal of Applied Psychology*, 92 (4): 1103–18.

Rich, B. & Janos, L. (1994) *Skunk Works: A Personal Memoir of My Years at Lockheed*. Boston: Little Brown.

Rivkin, J. (2001) Reproducing Knowledge: Replication without Imitation at Moderate Complexity. *Organization Science*, 12 (3): 274–93.

Roberts, A. (2004) A Partial Revolution: The Diplomatic Ethos and Transparency in Intergovernmental Organizations. *Public Administration Review*, 64 (4): 410–24.

Roberts, A. (2006) *Blacked Out: Government Secrecy in the Information Age*. Cambridge: Cambridge University Press.

Rodriguez, N. & Ryave, A. (1992) The Structural Organization and Micropolitics of Everyday Secret Telling Interactions. *Qualitative Sociology*, 15 (3): 297–318.

Rousseau, D. M., Sitkin, S. B., Burt, R., & Camerer, C. (1998) Not So Different After All: A Crossdiscipline View of Trust. *Academy of Management Review*, 23 (3): 393–404.

Sagar, R. (2013) *Secrets and Leaks: The Dilemma of State Secrecy*. Princeton, NJ: Princeton University Press.

Schein, E. H. (1985/2010) *Organizational Culture and Leadership*. 4th ed. San Francisco: Jossey-Bass.

Scheppele, K. L. (1988) *Legal Secrets: Equality and Efficiency in the Common Law*. Chicago: University of Chicago Press.

Schoeneborn, D. & Scherer, A. G. (2012) Clandestine Organizations, al Qaeda, and the Paradox of (In)visibility: A Response to Stohl and Stohl. *Organization Studies*, 33 (7): 963–71.

Schuster, J & Colletti, J. (1973) Pay Secrecy: Who Is for and against It? *Academy of Management Journal*, 16 (1): 35–40.

Scott, A. (2009) Georg Simmel: The Individual and the Organization. In P. Adler (Ed.), *The Oxford Handbook of Sociology and Organization Studies*. Oxford: Oxford University Press, 268–90.

Scott, C. (2013) *Anonymous Agencies, Backstreet Businesses, and Covert Collectives: Rethinking Organizations in the 21st Century*. Stanford, CA: Stanford University Press.

Scott, C. R. & Rains, S. A. (2005) Anonymous Communication in Organizations: Assessing Use and Appropriateness. *Management Communication Quarterly*, 19: 157–97.

Scott, J. (1990) *The Sociology of Elites*. Aldershot, UK: Edward Elgar.

Scott, J. C. (1992) *Domination and the Arts of Resistance: Hidden Transcripts.* New Haven: Yale University Press.

Seibert, S., Kraimer, M., & Liden, R. (2001) A Social Capital Theory of Career Success. *Academy of Management Journal*, 44 (2): 219–37.

Sewell, G. & Wilkinson, B. (1992) Someone to Watch over Me: Surveillance, Discipline and the Just-in-Time Labour Process. *Sociology*, 26 (2): 271–89.

Sharkin, B. S. & Birky, I. (1992) Incidental Encounters between Therapists and Their Clients. *Professional Psychology: Research and Practice*, 23 (4): 326.

Shenhav, Y. (1999) *Manufacturing Rationality.* Oxford: Oxford University Press.

Sifry, M. L. (2011) *WikiLeaks and the Age of Transparency.* New Haven: Yale University Press.

Simmel, G. (1906) The Sociology of Secrecy and of Secret Societies. *American Journal of Sociology*, 11 (4): 441–98.

Simon, H. (1997) *Administrative Behavior: A Study of Decision-Making Processes in Administrative Organizations.* 4th ed. New York: Free Press.

Sinclair, A. (2005) Body Possibilities in Leadership. *Leadership*, 1 (4): 387–406.

Slater, R. (1998) *Jack Welch and the G.E. Way: Management Insights and Leadership Secrets of the Legendary CEO.* New York: McGraw-Hill.

Snow, C. P. (1954) *The New Men.* London: Macmillan.

Sotirin, P. & Gottfried, H. (1999) The Ambivalent Dynamics of Secretarial "Bitching": Control, Resistance and the Construction of Identity. *Organization*, 6 (1): 57–80.

Spiegel, Germany (2010) http://www.spiegel.de/international/europe/complicit-in-corruption-how-german-companies-bribed-their-way-to-greek-deals-a-693973.html [Accessed July 2014].

Star, A. (Ed.) (2011) *Open Secrets. WikiLeaks, War and American Diplomacy.* New York: New York Times Company.

The Star, Canada (2014): http://www.thestar.com/news/canada/2013/02/14/ottawa_sorry_for_losing_data_on_500000_canadians.html [Accessed May 2014].

Starbuck, W. H. (2003) Shouldn't Organization Theory Emerge from Adolescence? *Organization*, 10 (3): 439–52.

Stead, R. S. & Cross, A.R. (2009) The Management and Security of Trade Secrets: An Exploratory Study. *International Journal of Intellectual Property Management*, 3 (3): 256–77.

Steele, F. (1975) *The Open Organization: The Impact of Secrecy and Disclosure on People and Organizations.* Reading, MA: Addison-Wesley.

Stiglitz, J. (2002) The Roaring Nineties. *Atlantic Monthly*, 290 (3): 75–89.

Stohl, C. (1995) *Organizational Communication: Connectedness in Action.* Thousand Oaks CA: Sage.

Stohl, C. & Stohl, M. (2011) Secret Agencies: The Communicative Constitution of a Clandestine Organization. *Organization Studies*, 32 (9): 1197–1215.

Strathern, M. (2000) The Tyranny of Transparency. *British Educational Research Journal*, 26 (3): 309–21.

Suddaby, R., Hardy, C., & Huy, Q.N. (2011) Where Are the New Theories of Organization? *Academy of Management Review*, 36 (2): 236–46.

Sullivan, D. (2008) Big Boys and Chinese Walls. *University of Chicago Law Review*, 75 (1): 533–68.

Swasy, A. (1993) *Soap Opera. The Inside Story of Proctor and Gamble*. New York: Simon & Schuster.

Swedberg, R. (2003) The Case for an Economic Sociology of Law. *Theory and Society*, 32 (1): 1–37.

Taussig, M. (1999) *Defacement: Public Secrecy and the Labor of the Negative*. Stanford, CA: Stanford University Press.

Teece, D. J. (1986) Profiting from Technological Innovation: Implications for Integration, Collaboration, Licensing and Public Policy. *Research Policy*, 15(6): 285–305.

Teich, A., Frankel, M. S., Kling, R., & Lee, Y. (1999) Anonymous Communication Policies for the Internet: Results and Recommendations of the AAAS Conference. *Information Society*, 15 (1): 71–77.

Tefft, S. K. (1980) *Secrecy: A Cross-Cultural Perspective*. New York: Human Sciences Press.

Townley, B. (2008) *Reason's Neglect. Rationality and Organizing*. Oxford: Oxford University Press.

Treviño, L. K. & Nelson, K. A. (2007) *Managing Business Ethics: Straight Talk about How to Do It Right*. 4th ed. New York: Wiley.

Trice, H. M. (1993) *Occupational Subcultures in the Workplace*. Ithaca, NY: Cornell University Press.

Trice, H. M., & Beyer, J. M. (1993) *The Cultures of Work Organizations*. New York: Prentice-Hall.

Tsoukas, H. (1997) The Tyranny of Light: The Temptations and the Paradoxes of the Information Society. *Futures*, 29 (9): 827–43.

Tsoukas, H. & Vladimirou, E. (2001) What Is Organizational Knowledge? *Journal of Management Studies*, 38 (7): 973–93.

Ubel, P. A., Zell, M. M., Miller, D. J., Fischer, G. S., Peters-Stefani, D., & Arnold, R. M. (1995) Elevator Talk: Observational Study of Inappropriate Comments in a Public Space. *American Journal of Medicine*, 99 (2): 190–94.

Vaccaro, A. (2012) To Pay or Not to Pay? Dynamic Transparency and the Fight against the Mafia's Extortionists. *Journal of Business Ethics*, 106 (1): 23–35.

Vadera, A. K., Aguilera, R. V., & Caza, B. B. (2009) Making Sense of Whistle-Blowing's Antecedents: Learning from Research on Identity and Ethics Programs. *Business Ethics Quarterly*, 19 (4): 553–86.

Vaughan, D. (1996) *The Challenger Launch Decision*. Chicago: University of Chicago Press.

Van den Brink, M., Benschop, Y., & Jansen, W. (2010) Transparency in Academic Recruitment: A Problematic Tool for Gender Equality? *Organization Studies*, 31 (11): 1459–83.

Vandevoort, J. R. (1971) Trade Secrets: Protecting a Very Special "Property." *Business Lawyer*, January: 681–700.

Van Iterson, A. & Clegg, S. R. (2008) The Politics of Gossip and Denial in Interorganizational Relations. *Human Relations*, 61 (8): 1117–37.

Waddington, K. (2012) *Gossip and Organizations*. London: Routledge.

Weber, M. (1922/1978) *Economy and Society: Outline of Interpretive Sociology*, Vol. 2. Roth, G. & Wittich, C. (eds). Berkeley: University of California Press.

Weick, K. (1996) Drop Your Tools: An Allegory for Organizational Studies. *Administrative Science Quarterly*, 41 (3): 301–13.

Weick, K. E. (1979) *The Social Psychology of Organizing*. 2nd ed. New York: Random House.

Weisband, S. P. & Reinig, B. A. (1995) Managing User Perceptions of Email Privacy. *Communications of the ACM*, 38(12): 40–47.

Weiskopf, R. & Willmott, H. (2013). Ethics as Critical Practice: The "Pentagon Papers," Deciding Responsibly, Truth-Telling, and the Unsettling of Organizational Morality. *Organization Studies*, 34 (4), 469–93.

Wexler, M. N. (1987) Conjectures on the Dynamics of Secrecy and the Secrets Business. *Journal of Business Ethics*, 6 (6), 469–80.

Whitman, M. & Mattord, C. (2014) *Principles of Information Security*. 5th ed. Boston: Cengage Learning.

Wiener, D. & Cava, A. (1988) Stealing Trade Secrets Ethically. *Maryland Law Review* 47 (Summer): 1076–1128.

Wilson, E. (2008) *The Envoy*. London: Arcadia.

Woods, J. D. (1993) *The Corporate Closet: The Professional Lives of Gay Men in America*. New York: Free Press.

Wyndham, J. (1963) *Trouble with Lichen*. London: Penguin.

Younggren, J. N. & Harris, E. A. (2008) Can You Keep a Secret? Confidentiality in Psychotherapy. *Journal of Clinical Psychology*, 64 (5): 589–600.

Zald, M. N. & Lounsbury, M. (2010) The Wizards of OZ: Towards an Institutional Approach to Elites, Expertise and Command Posts. *Organization Studies* 31 (7): 963–96.

Zerubavel, E. (2006) *The Elephant in the Room: Silence and Denial in Everyday Life*. Oxford: Oxford University Press.

Žižek, S. (2011) Good Manners in the Age of WikiLeaks. *London Review of Books*, 33 (2): 9–10.

Index

Accountability, 146–47
Accounting firms, *see* Professional services firms
Aeneid, 34
Andersen, Hans Christian, *Emperor's New Clothes*, 36–37, 161n60
Anonymity: forms, 4; public secrecy and, 38–39; in public spaces, 117; relationship to secrecy, 4–5; in research, 154
Apple Computer, 8, 73, 126–27
Arcana imperii, 21, 24, 52, 111
Arcanum, logic of, 9–10, 26, 29, 86, 127
Architecture: form and function, 136–38; internal boundaries, 117–18; office buildings, 91–92, 117, 172n75; styles, 136, 137. *See also* Hidden architecture
Argyris, Chris, 59
Arthur Andersen, 124
Atomic weapons, *see* Nuclear weapons programs
Australian Wheat Board, 107
Authoritarian regimes, *see* Dictatorships

Backstage self, 31, 57, 96, 101–2
Bacon, Francis, 61
Bank secrecy, 46, 162n25. *See also* Financial services
Barings, 49
Barriers, *see* Boundaries; Walls
BBC (British Broadcasting Company), 125–26
Bendix, Reinhard, 84
Berger, Peter L., 63, 163n40
Betrayals of secrets, 10, 69–70. *See also* Revelation of secrets
Bletchley Park (BP): boundaries, 116–17; classified files in archives, 165n90; compartmentalized organization, 13, 73–74, 81–82; culture, 14; employees, 13–14, 73, 78–79, 88, 128, 129; hierarchies, 74, 122; insiders, 122, 128; knowledge sharing, 74, 81–82, 83; military use of intelligence, 86–87; neighbors, 79; secrecy, 73–74, 76, 78–79, 88; security regulations, 13–14, 73, 78–79, 83, 118; study of, 151, 165n90; work of, 13, 81–82, 83
Bok, Sissela, 3–4, 6, 42, 71, 102
Bosch, 72
Boston Scientific, 47
Boundaries: created by secrecy, 10, 11, 41, 55–56, 65–66, 70–71, 149; cultural, 119; in espionage fiction, 69–70; of groups, 55–56, 58–59; of organizations, 116–17, 119–20; within organizations, 12, 73–74, 75–76, 117–23, 124, 170n9; permeability, 123–27; physical, 116–18, 119; of professions, 139–40; between public and private spaces, 117; in public secrecy, 40; Simmel on, 25, 30; social, 118. *See also* Walls
BP, *see* Bletchley Park
Bribery, 48, 49, 107
Britain, *see* United Kingdom
British Broadcasting Company (BBC), 125–26
British Petroleum, 49
Bureaucracy: compartmentalization of knowledge, 57–58, secrecy in, 19, 20–21, 43, 57–58, 70, 84
Burgess, Guy, 159n12

Bush, George W., 27, 48
Businesses, *see* Firms

Canetti, Elias, 19, 21–23, 24, 41, 60,
  92, 99, 111
Capital (Lanchester), 120–21
Central Intelligence Agency (CIA), 98
Challenger space shuttle, 49, 111
Change management, 148
Chatham House Rule, 28, 160n32
Chinese walls, 118, 124
Chosroes II, 22
CIA, *see* Central Intelligence Agency
Ciba-Geigy, 55–56
Classified data: in archives, 165n90;
  leaks, 50–53, 72, 82, 103–4; of
  military, 77, 82, 128–29; in nuclear
  weapons laboratories, 119, 124; of
  state intelligence agencies, 77, 82,
  86. *See also* Security clearances
Cliques: secrets of, 56–57, 137, 143–44;
  social function, 56, 98–100; in
  total institutions, 32; vertical and
  horizontal, 57
Cold War, 117, 131. *See also* Lockheed
  Skunk Works; Nuclear weapons
  programs
Collinson, David L., 103
Communication: effects of secrecy,
  149; of informal secrets, 93–94, 95;
  managing, 99
Compartmentalization: of knowledge,
  57–58, 81–83, 88–89, 129–31; of
  organizations, 13, 73–74, 81–83,
  88–89, 123, 129–31, 136–37. *See
  also* Walls
Competitive advantage, 46–47. *See also*
  Strategic secrecy
Computer networks, 125. *See also*
  Technology
Concealment, 3, 10, 11–12, 37, 100.
  See also Secrecy
Concentric circles, 12, 74, 89, 123
Confessions, 64
Confidential gossip, 8, 93, 96, 97–98,
  112
Confidentiality: client, 15, 92, 95, 96,

169n63; ethics codes and norms,
  77–78; in health care, 132–33;
  in research, 152, 154. *See also*
  Strategic secrecy
Confidentiality agreements, 92, 95, 151,
  154
Conspiracy theories, 25, 87, 131, 144
Consulting firms, *see* Professional
  services firms
Corruption, 48, 49, 107, 123
Countertransference, 133
Covering and uncovering, 33, 42
Cover-ups, 39–40, 49, 162n18
Creativity, secrecy and, 144
Criminal activity, 5, 50. *See also*
  Corruption
Crozier, Michel, 59–60
Cuban missile crisis, 33
Cultures of secrecy, 84–88, 109–12,
  113, 119, 137, 145, 171n66.
  See also Hidden architecture of
  organizational life; Organizational
  culture
Cyber-espionage, 125

Dalton, Melville, 56–57, 60, 65, 98,
  152
Dark secrecy: consequences of
  revelations, 49; ethics of, 48–
  50; Goffman on, 34–35, 41; in
  governments, 24, 34, 50–52; leaks,
  50–53; in organizations, 45, 46,
  48–54, 145; power and, 24–25;
  preventing, 52
Data security, 77, 125. *See also*
  Classified data
Decision making, 61–63, 100
Democracies, 23–24, 52
Dictatorships, 21–23, 60, 159n13
Diplomacy, 103–4
Disclosure, *see* Revelation of secrets
Discrimination, 148
Doors: closed, 115; metaphor, 91,
  92–93, 103, 104, 112, 113; in office
  buildings, 91–92; open, 103
Dostoyevsky, Fyodor, *The House of the
  Dead*, 115, 140

Dramaturgical loyalty, discipline, and circumspection, 35
Drug testing of employees, 4
Dyson, 72

Elites, 23–24, 27, 74, 128, 144, 160n28. *See also* Insiders and outsiders; Leadership
Ellsberg, Daniel, 50–51, 86, 128–29, 131–32
Emails, 47, 94
Emotions: evoked by secrecy, 10, 28, 30, 42, 142; informal secrecy and, 134; self-control, 33–34
Emperor's New Clothes (Andersen), 36–37, 161n60
Employees: competition, 101; contracts, 47; drug testing, 4; effects of secrecy cultures, 131–32, 133; ethics codes, 77–78; ID badges, 80, 119, 124, 134; impression management, 59; informal secrecy among, 59–60, 100–103, 111–12; interviewing, 151, 152–53; layoffs, 47; loyalty, 59; pay secrecy, 48, 83–84, 103, 120–21; privacy, 4; protection of strategic secrets, 47; relations with managers, 59–60; searches of, 77; surveillance of, 78–80, 101, 102–3, 131–32, 146
Engineers, 72, 111. *See also* Lockheed Skunk Works
Enigma, *see* Bletchley Park
Enron, 48, 124
The Envoy (Wilson), 38–39
Epistemic architecture, 11, 115–16, 123, 138, 158n29. *See also* Hidden architecture of organizational life
Espionage, *see* State intelligence agencies
Espionage fiction, 69–70
Espionage films, 117
Ethics: business, 48–50; confidential information, 77–78; of dark secrecy, 48–50; norms, 77–78; professional codes, 77–78, 132–33; of secrecy, 5–6, 24–25, 40;

of transparency, 6. *See also* Dark secrecy
Experience Project, 4–5
Experts, 63, 64, 111
Expression games, 33–34
Extraordinary rendition, 34
Eyes Wide Shut, 29–30

Feldman, Martha, 62
Feldman, Steve P., 100
Financial secrecy index, 162n25
Financial services: bank secrecy, 46, 162n25; Chinese walls, 118, 124; scandals, 49, 50
Firms: misconduct, 48–50, 57–58, 162n11; partnerships, 47; pay secrecy, 48, 83–84, 103, 120–21; protection of secrets, 75–76; security regulations, 77. *See also* Employees; Managers; Organizations; Professional services firms; Trade secrecy
Fog of secrecy, 103, 130–31, 139
Formal organizations, 56, 59
Formal secrecy: boundaries created, 70–71, 73–74, 75–76; cultures, 84–88; definition of, 43; dilemmas, 76, 81–88, 89, 143; distinction from informal secrecy, 8, 90, 92–93, 94; informal disclosure, 83–84, 120; legal protection, 71–73, 80, 133; markers, 128, 134; organizational regulation, 73–78, 83, 89; physical records, 72, 76–77, 94, 125, 133; relationship to informal secrecy, 120–22, 143; research methods, 151; surveillance and, 78–80; transparency efforts and, 145; vulnerability, 72, 143; walls and corridors metaphor, 70, 74, 75, 77, 89; Weber on, 19, 20–21, 43. *See also* Strategic secrecy; Trade secrecy
Foucault, Michel, 39, 52, 63–64
Franklin, Benjamin, 124
Freemasons, 29
French language, 122
Freud, Sigmund, 134

Frontstage self, 31, 36, 58, 96

Gays, *see* Homosexuals
Germany, Holocaust, 146
Ghosting, 106, 109
Goffman, Erving: on expression games,
    33–34; on forms of secrecy, 34–36,
    41; on hinted communication,
    104–5; on impression management,
    31–32, 58, 59; on information,
    160n40; on secrecy, 2; on stigma,
    31–32, 161n53; on tact, 39; on
    total institutions, 32–33, 102; on
    value of secrets, 172n69
Google, 8, 46
Gossip: confidential, 8, 93, 96, 97–98,
    112; distinction from informal
    secrecy, 167n5; passing on, 97
Gouldner, Alvin W., 60
Governments: mistrust of, 52–53;
    political and administrative power,
    20–21, 38, 41; secrecy, 21–23,
    24–25, 33, 34, 50–52, 87. *See also*
    Bureaucracy; State intelligence
    agencies; Whistleblowing
The Great Fortune (Manning), 39
Greece, bribery, 49
Groups: boundaries, 55–56, 58–59;
    cliques, 32, 56–57, 98–100,
    137, 143–44; formation, 27, 43;
    Goffman on, 34–35; identity, 67,
    74, 75, 128, 139, 148; informal,
    124, 137; informal secrecy in, 93,
    94–97, 98–103, 112, 124, 134;
    inside secrecy in, 55–57; knowledge
    sharing in, 143–44; membership
    criteria, 94–95; secret, 29–31;
    sharing secrets in, 58–59; social
    cohesion, 28, 29, 30, 35, 65–66. *See
    also* Networks
Gusterson, Hugh, 118, 119, 122, 124,
    126, 131–32, 134, 135–36, 138,
    151

Harry Potter series (Rowling), 127
Health care, confidentiality in, 132–33
Herman, Michael, 85, 87, 128, 166n49

Hidden architecture of organizational
    life: cliques, 32, 56–57, 98–100,
    137, 143–44; fragility, 140;
    influence of secrecy, 1, 11–12, 141;
    living in, 127–35, 139; maintaining,
    115–16, 140; organizational
    characteristics and, 137–38;
    patterns, 138–39; study of, 148–50;
    temporal aspects, 122. *See also*
    Boundaries
Hitachi, 80
Holocaust, 146
Homosexuals: informal secrecy,
    168n22; in military, 8, 39; public
    secrecy, 8, 39, 105, 108, 109, 111
The House of the Dead (Dostoyevsky),
    115, 140
Hughes, Everett, 77

Identities: group, 67, 74, 75, 128,
    139, 148; secrecy and, 128, 139;
    of whistleblowers, 51. *See also*
    Anonymity
Impression management, 31–32, 33, 59,
    160n42
Informal networks, 15, 100, 126,
    143–44
Informal organizations, 56, 59. *See also*
    Cliques; Groups
Informal secrecy: among employees,
    59–60, 100–103, 111–12; barriers,
    101; casual, 93; definition, 43;
    distinction from formal secrecy,
    8, 90, 92–93, 94; distinction from
    gossip, 167n5; door metaphor,
    92–93, 112, 113; emotional charge,
    134; enforcing, 95–97; evolution
    into formal secrecy, 120; Goffman
    on, 36; in groups, 93, 94–97,
    98–103, 112, 124, 134; of leaders,
    110–11; in managerial circles,
    57–59, 60, 67; in organizations,
    53, 92–103, 109–10, 112–13,
    119–22, 134–35; processes, 93–97;
    relationship to formal secrecy, 120–
    22, 143; research methods, 151–52;
    as resistance, 60, 102–3; sharing

secrets, 93–94, 95, 102, 134–35; significance of secrets, 97–98, 143; social function, 102, 112–13; transparency efforts and, 145–46; trust and, 94–96, 100, 123. *See also* Public secrecy

Information: confidential, 77–78; in decision making, 62–63, 100; Goffman on, 160n40; transparency, 53–54, 147. *See also* Knowledge

Initiations, 10, 29, 38, 94

Innovation, 46–47, 148. *See also* Lockheed Skunk Works

Insiders and outsiders: creating, 28–29, 55, 121–22, 131, 148, 149; evolution of, 122; informal secrecy and, 134, 152; trust between, 144, 152. *See also* Boundaries; Elites; Initiations

Inside secrecy: Goffman on, 35, 41, 54; in organizations, 55–59; social function, 35, 41, 55–57, 58–59

Intellectual property rights, 71, 73. *See also* Strategic secrecy

Intelligence agencies, *see* Bletchley Park; State intelligence agencies

Investment banks, *see* Financial services

Jackall, Robert, 2, 57–59, 60, 67, 152

Jobs, Steve, 8

Kafka, Franz, *The Trial*, 19, 21, 43, 91, 130

Kanter, Rosabeth Moss, 84

Kennedy, John F., 33, 146

Keys and locks, 60, 91–92, 115, 140, 155

Kissinger, Henry, 86

Knowing, French verbs for, 122

Knowledge: in bureaucracies, 20–21, 57–58; compartmentalized, 57–58, 81–83, 88–89, 129–31; of experts, 63, 64, 111; relationship to power, 61–65, 100, 135–36; sharing, 15, 74, 81–82, 83, 115, 143; tacit, 169n47. *See also* Trade secrecy

Kubrick, Stanley, 29–30

Labor, *see* Employees; Wildcat strikes

Laboratories, 118. *See also* Lawrence Livermore nuclear weapons laboratory

Lanchester, John, *Capital*, 120–21

Law: exemptions, 24–25; formal secrecy, 71–73, 80, 133; hidden, 91; intellectual property, 71, 73; property rights, 71–72; trade secrecy, 47, 70, 71

Lawrence Livermore nuclear weapons laboratory, 118, 119, 122, 124, 126, 131–32, 134, 138

Leadership: effects of secrecy, 144; informal secrecy, 110–11; mystique, 22, 23, 24, 61, 110, 134, 148; of political parties, 23; public secrecy and, 107; trust in, 144. *See also* Managers

Le Carré, John, 69, 165n2

Leeson, Nick, 49

Liebeskind, Julia, 75–76, 80, 82, 131–32

Lockheed Skunk Works, 46–47, 74–75, 76, 78, 85–86, 88, 118

Loyalty, 35, 59

Luckmann, Thomas, 63, 163n40

Lukes, Steven, 62, 63

Managers: cliques, 56–57; informal secrecy in groups, 57–59, 60, 67; offices, 92; performance ranking of employees, 99; power, 60; relations with employees, 59–60; scientific management, 64. *See also* Leadership

Manning, Chelsea, 51–52, 72, 82, 103–4

Manning, Olivia, *The Great Fortune*, 39

March, James, 62, 149

Marketing, secrecy and, 126–27

Marx, Karl, 60

Medical confidentiality, 132–33

Medinol, 47

Meta-secrecy, 37, 106

Michels, Robert, 23, 41, 100

Military: classified data, 77, 82,
128–29; intelligence, 86–87;
punishments for betraying secrets,
73; remote locations of secret
operations, 166n34
Military, US: homosexuals in, 8, 39;
Vietnam War, 50–51. *See also*
Lockheed Skunk Works
Mills, C. Wright, 23–24, 41
Moore, Wilbert E., 60–61, 62
Morality, 59, 129. *See also* Ethics
Mysteriousness: auras of, 127; of
formal secrecy, 90; in groups, 56;
of leaders, 22, 23, 24, 61, 110, 134,
148; public secrecy and, 38–39; of
secrecy, 9–10, 29, 66, 144; social
organization and, 27

NASA, *see* Challenger space shuttle
National Health Service, UK, 87
National Security Agency (NSA), 24,
51–52
Need-to-know paradox, 81–84, 89
Need-not-to-know paradox, 107–8
Networks: electronic, 125; informal, 15,
100, 126, 143–44; informal secrecy
and, 100. *See also* Cliques
The New Men (Snow), 130, 131
Nixon administration, 50–51
Noncompete agreements, 47, 71, 76
Nondisclosure agreements, 71, 72, 76,
154
Norms: ethical, 77–78; of
heterosexuality, 109, 111; of
informal secrecy, 96, 109–10;
professional, 96; regulation of, 96,
97. *See also* Organizational culture
Northern Rock, 50
NSA, *see* National Security Agency
Nuclear weapons programs: British,
123, 130; Lawrence Livermore
laboratory, 118, 119, 122, 124,
126, 131–32, 134, 138

Office buildings, 91–92, 117, 172n75.
See also Architecture
Office secrets, 20–21, 69

Official secrets, *see* Formal secrecy
Oil-for-Food program, 107
Open secrets, *see* Public secrecy
Organizational culture: boundaries,
55–59, 119; of compartmentalized
organizations, 137; enforcement
of secrecy, 50–51, 119, 131–32;
formal secrecy and, 84–88, 133;
informal and public secrecy, 109–
12, 113, 125–26, 145; norms, 15,
109–10; of professional services
firms, 14–15; promoting, 59
Organizational secrecy, *see* Secrecy at
work
Organizational structure: complexity,
136–37, 140; hierarchical, 14–
15, 54, 66, 74, 98–99, 122–23;
interaction with secrecy, 50, 54,
66, 123
Organizational studies: methods, 150–
54; past research on secrecy, 1–2,
55–62; scientific management, 64;
secrecy incorporated in, 142–50
Organizations: boundaries of, 116–17,
119–20; boundaries within, 12,
73–74, 75–76, 117–23, 124, 170n9;
compartmentalized, 13, 73–74, 81–
83, 88–89, 123, 129–31, 136–37;
conflicts in, 137, 138; definitions,
148–49, 172n12; formal and
informal, 56, 59; secret, 5, 29–30,
34, 69. *See also* Firms
Organizing secrecy, 45–46

Parker, Martin, 98, 131
Patents, 71, 73
Pay secrecy, 48, 83–84, 103, 120–21
Pentagon Papers, 50–51
Petraeus, David, 98
Pettigrew, Andrew, 100
Political parties, 23, 100
Politics, organizational, 100, 111, 148
Power: disciplinary, 52, 64; of elites,
23–24, 160n28
Power and secrecy: Canetti
on, 19, 21–23, 24; dark
secrets, 24–25; Foucault on,

63–64; in governments, 20–21, 38, 41; informal secrecy, 100; key metaphor, 92; knowledge and, 61–65, 100, 135–36; Michels on, 23; mysteriousness and, 23, 24; in organizations, 60–65, 66, 100, 137; public secrecy, 38–39, 107–8; in research, 152; social inclusion and exclusion, 100; undermining, 131; Weber on, 20–21

Primark, 48

Privacy: distinction from secrecy, 3–4; of employees, 4

Private spaces, 117. *See also* Walls

Procter & Gamble, 79–80, 85

Professionalism, 96, 139–40. *See also* Professions

Professional services firms (PSFs): applicant ranking, 121; Chinese walls, 118, 124; client confidentiality, 15, 92, 95, 96, 169n63; cultures, 14–15; employees, 14–15, 84, 96, 99, 101, 105, 106, 108–9; ethics codes, 78; formal secrecy, 92; informal networks, 15, 100, 126; informal secrecy, 15–16, 92, 93–94, 96, 98–100, 101–2, 103, 135; initiation rituals, 94; knowledge sharing, 15; leadership, 98–99, 134, 167n3; offices, 91–92, 101; pay secrecy, 84, 103; public secrecy, 105, 106, 108–9, 121; security regulations, 77; social events, 101; studies of, 14–16; unspoken rules, 15, 105, 106; working hours, 15, 106, 108–9

Professions: boundaries of, 139–40; confidentiality, 132–33; ethics codes, 77–78, 132–33; norms, 96. *See also* Professionalism

Property rights, 71–72. *See also* Intellectual property rights

PSFs, *see* Professional services firms

Psychotherapy, patient confidentiality, 133

Public secrecy: communicating through, 149; distinction from

tacit knowledge, 169n47; door metaphor, 103, 104, 113; examples, 8, 54, 103–4, 121, 125–26; leadership role, 107; in organizations, 105–10, 112–13, 119–20; power and, 38–39, 107–8; processes, 104–7; purposes, 5, 108; research methods, 152; social relations and, 107–9; taboos and, 5, 39; tact and, 39–40, 104; tensions, 37–38, 43, 103–4, 107, 108, 146; theoretical foundations, 36–40; violations, 106–7. *See also* Informal secrecy

Regimes of appropriability, 71

Research methods, 150–54

Resistance: informal secrecy as, 60, 102–3; organizations, 130; secrecy and, 36, 146–47; in total institutions, 33

Revelation of secrets: as betrayal, 10; confessions, 64; of dark secrets, 49; of formal secrets, 72, 90; hints, 11, 29, 72, 126–27, 134, 144; inevitability, 123–25; of informal secrets, 96–97; initiation rituals, 94; intentional, 36, 90; motivations, 42, 124, 129, 144; punishments, 10, 73; as release of tension, 140; temptations, 11, 28–29, 42, 129; unintentional, 96–97, 125; vulnerability, 28–29, 42, 72, 75, 76, 90. *See also* Whistleblowing

Rich, Ben R., 47

Rituals, 29–30, 38, 55–56, 94

Rowling, J. K., 127

Rumors, 99, 107

Rumsfeld, Donald, 160n36

Sacredness, 24, 110

Samsung, 73, 127

Saville, Jimmy, 125–26

Scandals, 48, 49, 50, 124, 125–26

Schein, Edgar H., 2, 55–56, 57, 67, 152

Schmitt, Carl, 24

Scientific management, 64

Secrecy: allure, 10–11, 66, 145; anonymity and, 4–5; concealment and sharing, 10, 11–12; definitions, 3, 159n22; distinction from privacy, 3–4; distinction from secrets, 7, 8–9; emotional charge, 10, 28, 30, 42, 142; ethics of, 5–6, 24–25, 40; etymology of, 9; forms, 141; legitimate uses, 147; as organizing, 65–67, 149; richness, 9–11, 40; social functions, 26–31; universality, 6–7, 26, 40, 146. *See also* Formal secrecy; Informal secrecy; Public secrecy

Secrecy at work: endemic nature of, 1; functions, 1, 136; future research on, 142–50; language of, 45; patterns, 138–39; as process, 7, 149, 151; related concepts, 2; ubiquity, 153–54. *See also* Hidden architecture of organizational life

Secretaries, original meaning, 24

Secret organizations, 5, 29–30, 34, 69

Secrets: distinction from secrecy, 7, 8–9; etymology of, 9; fetish character, 37, 109; as informational assets, 9, 71–72; shared, 43; symbolic value, 61, 62, 144; value, 9, 26–27, 41, 86, 88, 89–90, 135–36, 172n69. *See also* Revelation of secrets

Security checks, 14, 118, 119

Security clearances, 50–51, 82, 86, 118, 123, 128. *See also* Classified data

September 11 terrorist attacks, 82

Sexuality, 39. *See also* Homosexuals

Siemens, 48, 49, 123

Signals intelligence, *see* Bletchley Park

Silence: practice of, 42; public secrecy and, 106; stone-faced, 58–59; in surveilled spaces, 101; on taboo subjects, 5

Simmel, Georg: on revelation of secrets, 42, 75, 129; on secrecy, 2, 25–30, 54, 128, 140, 159n22, 159–60n25; on secrecy enforcement, 59, 96; on social cohesion, 28, 29, 35; on trust, 95; on universality of secrecy, 6, 40, 146

Simon, Herbert, 148–49

Skull and Bones Society, Yale University, 27, 29, 38, 160n28

Skunk Works, *see* Lockheed Skunk Works

Snow, C. P., *The New Men*, 130, 131

Snowden, Edward, 51–52

Social cohesion, 28, 29, 30, 35, 65–66

Social construction of reality, 63, 138

Social differentiation, 26–27, 28–29, 30

Socialization processes, 28, 29–30, 93

Social organization: effects of secrecy, 1, 25–31, 41–42, 65–66, 116, 141–42; hierarchies, 22, 66, 74; informal secrecy and, 98–103, 112–13; public secrecy and, 107–9. *See also* Groups; Hidden architecture of organizational life

Social relations: impression management, 31–32, 33, 59, 160n42; ratio of secrecy, 26

Sony Pictures, 94

The Sopranos, 97–98

South Korea, invisible tower, 117

Space shuttle program, *see* Challenger space shuttle

Spatial metaphors, *see* Architecture; Doors; Walls

Specialness, sense of, 67, 74, 85, 109, 126–27, 128–29, 134–35, 139

Spy novels, *see* Espionage fiction

State intelligence agencies: British, 166n49, 170n4; classified data, 77, 82, 86; cultures, 85; double agents, 69, 159n12; hints of secrets, 127; information sharing, 82; leaks from, 51–52, 72, 82; need-to-know culture, 82; in novels, 69; personalities of recruits, 129; secrecy, 24, 85, 86–87, 170n4; study of, 151; US, 24, 51–52, 98. *See also* Bletchley Park

Stealth aircraft, *see* Lockheed Skunk Works

Stiglitz, Joseph, 124
Stigma, 31–32, 95, 102, 161n53. *See also* Homosexuals
Strategic secrecy: Goffman on, 34–35, 41; leaks, 47; in organizations, 45, 46–48, 54, 70, 144
Strikes, wildcat, 60, 103
Structural isolation, 75–76
Structural secrecy, 50
Sullivan, Louis, 136
Surveillance: in organizations, 78–80, 101, 102–3, 131–32, 146; technological, 80; transparency and, 52, 146
Switzerland, bank secrecy, 46

Taboos, 5, 39, 161n73
Tacit knowledge, 169n47
Tacitus, 21
Tact, 39–40, 104
Taussig, Michael, 2, 37–38, 39, 54, 108, 109, 152
Tax evasion, 50, 162n25
Teams, 34–35
Technology: computer networks, 125; data security, 77, 125; digital ID badges, 80; surveillance, 80; user agreements, 53, 147
Teece, David J., 71, 80
Terrorism: organizations, 130; September 11 attacks, 82. *See also* War on Terror
Theoretical foundations, 19–20, 40–43; Goffman on, 31–36, 41; power and secrecy, 20–25, 41; public secrecy, 36–40; Simmel on, 25–30, 40; social functions of secrecy, 26–31
Total institutions, 32–33, 53, 102, 146
Totalitarian regimes, 22
Trade secrecy: competitive advantage, 46–47; examples, 8, 46–47; false, 172n69; legal protection, 47, 70, 71; violations, 47, 72, 73. *See also* Strategic secrecy
Transparency: advocates, 24, 52, 87, 131, 147; age of, 52–53; ethics of, 6; of glass, 117; information

obscured by, 53–54, 147; limits, 53, 163n40; negative effects, 52; organizational, 145; of public spaces, 117; relationship to secrecy, 145–47; surveillance and, 52, 146
The Trial (Kafka), 19, 21, 43, 91, 130
Trojan horse, 34
Trouble with Lichen (Wyndham), 132
Trust: of governments, 52–53; in groups, 58, 59; informal secrecy and, 94–96, 100, 123; in insiders, 144, 152; sharing secrets, 116

Ultra, *see* Bletchley Park
Uncanny, 134
United Kingdom: atomic weapons program, 123, 130; cabinet, 28, 87, 167n60; Cambridge spy ring, 159n12; Chatham House Rule, 28, 160n32; intelligence agencies, 166n49, 170n4; National Health Service, 87; Official Secrets Act, 73; permanent secretaries, 24; scandals, 125–26. *See also* Bletchley Park
United Nations, Oil-for-Food program, 107
US Commission on Protecting and Reducing Government Secrecy, 86
US military, *see* Military, US
US State Department, 103–4

Vaughan, Diane, 49, 50
Vietnam War, 50–51
Virgil, Aeneid, 34

Walls: Chinese, 118, 124; corridors and, 11, 70, 74, 77, 89, 124–25; cracks in, 124; metaphorical, 70, 74, 75, 77, 89, 118–20; removing, 131; windows in, 125–26. *See also* Boundaries; Compartmentalization
War on Terror: dark secrets, 52; extraordinary rendition, 34; intelligence sharing, 82
Web-based services, user agreements, 53, 147

Weber, Max, 19, 20–21, 41, 43, 54, 67, 85

Whistleblowing: definition, 163n28; motivations, 42, 51, 90, 129; reactions to, 51, 72; social and organizational factors, 50–52

Wikileaks, 51–52, 72, 82, 103–4

Wildcat strikes, 60, 103

Wilson, Edward, *The Envoy*, 38–39

Woods, James D., 105, 108, 109, 111

Workers, *see* Employees; Wildcat strikes

World War II, *see* Bletchley Park; Holocaust

Wyndham, John: career, 171n51; *Trouble with Lichen*, 132

Yale University, Skull and Bones Society, 27, 29, 38, 160n28

Zerubavel, Eviator, 36–37, 38, 106

Žižek, Slavoj, 104

Lightning Source UK Ltd.
Milton Keynes UK
UKOW04f0617310717
306362UK00001B/251/P